THE AGING ADULT
IN CHILDREN'S BOOKS & NONPRINT MEDIA

An Annotated Bibliography

Catherine
Townsend
Horner

 The Scarecrow Press, Inc.
Metuchen, N.J., & London
1982

Library of Congress Cataloging in Publication Data

Horner, Catherine Townsend, 1937-
    The aging adult in children's books and nonprint media.

    Includes indexes.
    1.   Children's books--Bibliography.   2.   Old age in literature
--Bibliography.   I.   Title.
Z1037. H779   [PN1009. A1]   011'. 62   81-14446
ISBN 0-8108-1475-7   AACR2

This one is for my mother, Catherine Hill Townsend, who started the stone rolling and saw to it that it gathered no moss; for Great-aunt Alice Wittich Sanders, 1876-1981, who was an incredible inspiration to all who knew her; for Laurella Sanders Clark who has kept pace admirably with her remarkable mother; and for my father, William Stewart Townsend, 1909-1966, who did not live to age.

TABLE OF CONTENTS

INTRODUCTION

On Ageism

The aging are one of the latest minorities to organize and lobby for belated recognition and, as a result, there has been a spate of activity in recent years in definition and defense of the rights and changing images of senior adults. This trend is being closely observed by those who are concerned with children and books, several of whom conclude that older people are stereotyped in children's literature.

Phyllis Barnum,[1] an educational psychologist, in a random sampling of fifty preschool and primary books published in the years 1950 to 1959 and fifty more appearing from 1965 to 1974, found that the aged represent a smaller proportion of characters in books than their actual occurrence in the population; that they engage in little social activity or interaction; that they are employed in prosaic activities requiring no mental or physical dexterity, and that they demonstrate not only more infirmity than other adults, which was to be expected, but also greater passivity and reduced self-reliance. Grandmothers are almost invariably behind aprons in the kitchen, preoccupied with food preparation, and grandparents as a whole are portrayed as gray-haired individuals in rocking chairs, although in reality many persons become grandparents in their forties. Barnum also objected to the portrayal of old people as "almost unfailingly pleasant," a false image that implies a "lack of humanness" and impaired range of realistic emotions. While she found that children participate in agreeable activities with their own grandparents, they rarely have enjoyable encounters with the unrelated aging.

Edward Ansello,[2] a social scientist, directed an exhaustive study of 656 juvenile titles, classified as easy or picture books, with aging characters depicted, including humans, animals, magical and even mechanical ones, but only in one-sixth of these are the old people major characters. The study contained contemporary and classic stories, but the majority were published from 1967 to 1976. Those appearing more recently demonstrated slightly less evidence of the ageism that seems to pervade children's first literature.

Ansello revealed that there is heavy underrepresentation of females and non-whites in relationship to their demographic distribution. The most frequent physical descriptions of elders are "old," followed by "little," while the most common personality descriptions are "poor" and "sad." Most recurrent behavioral manifestations are routine-repetitive (eating, rocking); nurturant (praising, serving); and directive (directing, demonstrating). Like Barnum, Ansello discovered passive and peripheral characters who are denied full range of behavior and roles, whether intentionally or unintentionally. Ansello, because of the breadth of his study, encountered both more negative and more positive images than did Barnum.

Gladys F. Blue,[3] an educator, in a study of 125 realistic fiction trade books, including picture, easy, and juvenile fiction-- a random sampling culled from 173 titles in active public library circulation in 1978--found, conversely, no evidence to uphold Ansello's contentions. She reported that "portrayals were not disparaging, derogatory, or otherwise negative, nor were they stereotypic." She noted many diverse lifestyles and varying types of behavior, and indicated, moreover, a "general humanistic concern for understanding the elderly as individuals."

Blue conjectured that one reason her findings were inconsistent with Ansello's was the latter's inclusion of so many books (five-sixths) in which aging figures are absent or very marginally present, although, she admitted, "omission is in itself a subtle form of stereotyping." Another divergent variable was her examination of titles that included a higher readership level than Ansello's, leading her to the conclusion that there is greater stereotyping at earlier developmental levels, possibly because of the necessity for authors to employ a more limited vocabulary for young readers.

Gerontologist David A. Peterson and curriculum enrichment specialist Elizabeth L. Karnes[4] analyzed fifty-three books which were awarded the John Newbery Medal from 1922 through 1975, considered to be the outstanding literature for adolescents, and found them to reflect the reality of the world as perceived by the authors. While aging adults are generally depicted with a positive image; are not necessarily grandparents in three-generation households; are not usually discriminated against; and are not underrepresented, they were nonetheless judged to be victims of subtle, traditional bias. While declining to be as hypercritical as either Barnum or Ansello, Peterson and Karnes still deplored the facts that older characters are generally given supporting roles that are underdeveloped; that women are bound to home and neighborhood; that there is a preponderance of men; and that death, disability, and infirmity are conveniently ignored. Senior adults in Newbery books, they confirmed, are "useful only for their relationship with important people. In short, they are there, but no one seems to notice them."

Carol Katz,[5] a librarian who is also co-author of Past Sixty: The Older Woman in Print and Film, disputed Peterson and Karnes' conclusions by contending that research in aging should not be directed at literature which is not concerned with aging, and that such studies should approach children's fiction from the standpoint of the literature that it is, not from the viewpoint of the social science that it is not. She argued, moreover, that contem-

porary American judgments on ageism should not be imposed on
books which reflect other cultures and other times.   As for current
fiction, she averred that today's authors, observers of a society in
which old people are often victimized by forces beyond their control, are creating characters that vent their sense of despair, out-
rage, and injustice, challenging their readers to think and to act.
Problems such as poverty, idleness, isolation, and loss of dignity
are usually seen from the position of children who have great sympathy for the older person who has the difficulty, partly because
both are relatively powerless against the intervening generation.
In addition to discharging their social responsibilities, Katz declared that contemporary novelists are depicting with wit, imagination, and individuality senior adults who are in control of their
lives and who enjoy unique bonds with the young.   She cited several
books that are exemplary and meritorious in their treatment of the
aging.

In an examination of the changing attitudes toward death in
children's books, Maxine Walker[6] noted that folklore from the preliterate past realistically reflected life, but deaths were invariably
violent.   The Puritans treated death with "threats and thunderings."
The Victorians emasculated it with "sentimental sureties," while
the early twentieth century authors relegated it to obscurity with
"bland disregard."   Death retreated to the grandparents' generation
where it was treated lightly.   Death was often used as a device to
free fictional children in mystery and adventure books from close
supervision.   In the form of accidents it removed adults from the
scene so that children could "undertake daring deeds unhampered."
It has only been very recently, she asserted, that the important
role played by grandparents in the child's early years has been reflected in the literature.   This return to reality and the acceptance
of death as a fact of life has parallels to the preliterate folklore
but with a difference--the concern for the individual.   Christian
morality has disappeared and the rites of passage have been balanced.

The new realism can be seen to provide emotional inocula-
tion against future trauma, according to Joan Fassler,[7] a child
psychologist whose children's book My Grandpa Died Today appears
in the Bibliography.   She also declared that fictional accounts of
troubling events and situations are often sounder therapy than in-
formational books, because children need distance from experiences
in which they have emotional stakes.   They can choose whether or
not to identify with a fictional character, and by returning to the
same book can gradually come to accept or handle the traumatic
occurrence, but she also stated that the most important function of
a story is its enjoyment quotient, not its literary merit.

The controversy surrounding ageism in children's books depends upon viewpoint and bias, with librarians and educators seem-
ing to square off against psychologists and sociologists.   It is not
the purpose of this book to support either faction, lacking a definition of the problem that would be acceptable to both, but some

expatiation is merited upon some of the views expressed elsewhere by others.

Ansello and Peterson/Karnes are arguing apples and oranges when they scrutinize so many titles that exclude or have only incidental appearances of older adults. Sins of commission are so overtly more damaging to the image of any subculture than are sins of omission that it seems wasteful to concentrate time and energy on condemning existing stories that would probably not benefit by the interjection of fully developed aging people. Nor should authors feel compelled by charges of discrimination to interpolate an obligatory token senior into a story line in which none is needed just to placate a vested-interest group. There is room for all kinds of books with all kinds of characters, but they should not all be judged by the same standards. The distortion created by the Ansello and Peterson/Karnes investigations with their application of a single yardstick to a dichotomous body of literature, therefore, seems unfair, unreasonable, and unjustified. They are carrying objectivity too far.

Much of children's fiction is historical and biographical in nature, reflects the author's own experiences and observations from the past, or was simply written in an era when alternatives for the elderly either in behavior or lifestyle did not exist or were not condoned. These anachronistic manifestations actually occurred, cannot be expunged from history, and therefore are unwarrantedly castigated as stereotypic or discriminatory, e. g. , the grandmother in the kitchen, the widower living with his married son or daughter, the indigent elderly committed to the County Farm, the retiree walking his grandchildren to the park. (Ironically, the latter may no longer be stereotypic. If he walked in the park today he might be mugged, and only the most intrepid or foolhardy would risk it.)

A stereotype may be hackneyed but it need not be dismissed as spurious if there is a suitable balance of incisive new material also available that conveys innovations in lifestyle and developments in behavior. Modern grandparents and great-grandparents in books deserve the option of rocking small boys (or girls) with skinned knees on comforting laps, and modern children are entitled to choose books depicting grandparental cosseting for their mental salubrity. Many senior adults would simply not be comfortable in the lotus position or picketing city hall behind Gray Panther placards. Many feel they have earned the right to retire and rest from their labors and are content without some of the frenetic new activities that are now open to them. These persons' rights to traditional representation should not be denied. Change is inevitable, but not all of it is viewed as progress by some who have had little opportunity or inclination to adapt.

Eccentricity is usually vilified as being stereotypic. Ansello denoted the adjectives "angry" and "crazy" as frequently occurring negative descriptors, but these terms may be misleading. The authors may have been portraying individuality in their aging characters,

but to the child through whom the action is perceived, who is often
a slave to conformity and whose vocabulary does not ordinarily include either "individuality" or "unconventionality," it is interpreted
as being abnormal. This initial interpretation, moreover, is often
reversed as the story evolves, when the child, through closer acquaintance with the older character, develops a better understanding,
appreciation, and even respect for his actions. This is equally true
of many characters described initially as old witches or even less
adulatory appellations. The author's purpose in writing the story
should be considered before judgment is passed.

Walker's citation of death as an agent for removing children
from their parents' jurisdiction seems to work to the advantage of
the genre of the aging in children's books because of the many instances in which a grandparent or other aging individual becomes
sole guardian. In most cases, this results in a fully developed role
which otherwise might have been lacking or peripheral.

Of course there is more realism and greater character development for older readers, just as there is more humor and fantasy for younger ones. As with sex education, children are not
given more than they can handle at each developmental level. A
book about the death of an aging person, for instance, even though
it is neither bland nor pat, must end on a note of reassurance for
the very young child. With increasing attention span, reading comprehension, and emotional and social awareness, children can be
led into more sensitive probings and broader perspectives on such
subjects as senility, suicide, loss of independence, and segregation
of the elderly.

There is little agreement on what constitutes ageism, nor can
accord be expected when Ansello reports that there is not even con-
sensus on terminology for the aging. Most prefer the term "senior"
or "senior citizen," citing that "old" and "aged" are opprobrious
and hopelessly negative. The Gray Panthers, however, decry this
practice as being patronizing and euphemistic attempts to avoid confronting the reality of old age. No one, presumably, has asked the
42-year-old grandmother or the single career woman who can no
longer be called a spinster how she wishes to be alluded to.

The purpose of this bibliography, with its lengthy annotations
of books from preschool through high school reading levels, is to
allow every interested individual to decide from one's own particular
perspective or bias what is constructive or relevant to any given
situation, be it librarian, educator, psychologist, gerontologist, parent helping children adjust to the death or physical or mental im-
pairment of an aging loved one, or grandparent concerned with how
his or her generation and foregoing ones are represented in the literature available to grandchildren through school and public libraries
and bookstores. Because it is a survey of books in which one or
more aging human adults, past or nearing the midcentury mark, play
significant roles, no attempt was made to be selective, and no literary criticism was implied. Because of this comprehensiveness

and the lack of screening, there will be some books that are negative, some that are specious, some that are pedestrian, and some that are sterling. With such an eclectic representation, let the stories speak for themselves.

Survey of the Genre

Books for children addressing the issues of the aging realistically and candidly are legion. Elderly victims of stroke or heart attack who survive appear in Two That Were Tough (Burch), Queen of Hearts (Cleaver), The Winds of Time (Corcoran), and Oma (Hartling).

Those who don't survive or who are left totally incapacitated appear in Foster Child (Bauer), Thank You, Jackie Robinson (Cohen), The Green of Me (Gauch), A Girl Called Al (Greene), Hotheads (LeRoy), Cinnamon Cane (Pollowitz), The Dream Watcher (Wersba), and The Pigman (Zindel), all for intermediate or older readers.

Senility strikes aging principals to greater or lesser degree in Grandma Didn't Wave Back (Blue), The Faraway Island (Corcoran), The Swallow's Song and If You Love Me, Let Me Go (Johnston), Grandpa and Frank (Majerus), A Figure of Speech (Mazer), The Minnow Leads to Treasure (Pearce), Evy-Ivy-Over (Rodowsky), Grandpa--And Me (Tolan), and Ludell and Willie (Wilkinson). Two of these exert control over their own lives by committing suicide in A Figure of Speech and Grandpa--And Me; one dies a natural death in Ludell and Willie; one is institutionalized in Grandma Didn't Wave Back; and one comes to live with her daughter's family against her will and eventually dies in If You Love Me, Let Me Go. Two remain independent in The Faraway Island and Grandpa and Frank.

Illnesses and causes of death in books for younger readers are usually not identified. This is true of Nonna (Bartoli), Never Is a Long, Long Time (Cate), Nana Upstairs and Nana Downstairs (dePaola), A Private Matter (Ewing), My Grandpa Died Today (Fassler), Why Did He Die? (Harris), and Annie and the Old One (Miles), all of which treat of death, and My Aunt Rosie (Hoff), The Yellow Pom-Pom Hat (Kaye), and Benjie on His Own (Lexau) which deal with undisclosed illness. One story, The Violin (Allen) portrays a poignant leavetaking that symbolizes death. The redoubtable protagonist of the subtly allegorical Come Again in the Spring (Kennedy) cheats the Grim Reaper because he is simply too busy to die. All instances of death or illness are the cause of distress and concern to the young protagonists on all the reading levels and are handled with great sensitivity by the authors.

Natural death of undisclosed cause or probable heart failure for older readers is treated variously in The Education of Little Tree (Carter), Transport 7-41-R (Degens), Duffy's Rocks (Fenton), Figgs and Phantoms (Raskin), The Thanksgiving Treasure (Rock), and Walking Away (Winthrop).

Other afflictions often associated with aging include hip or leg
fractures in The Eyes of the Amaryllis (Babbitt), A Home With Aunt
Florry (Talbot), Mary Jo's Grandmother (Udry), and Mad Martin
(Windsor) and cataracts or glaucoma in The Long Journey (Corcoran),
Reubella and the Old Focus Home (Newton), and The Gray Ghosts
of Taylor Ridge (Shura).   Cancer occurs in Then Again, Maybe I
Won't (Blume), alcoholism in Up a Road Slowly (Hunt) and Hotheads
(LeRoy), and pneumonia in A Boy of Tâché (Blades).   A melange of
blindness, lameness, and deafness appear in Cunningham's symbolic
Come to the Edge.   Debilitating injuries are common to Mr. McFad-
den's Hallowe'en (Godden), The Hammerhead Light and The Shadow
on the Hills (Thiele).

Loss of independence is an emotionally charged subject
plumbed by numerous books in which there is typically an alliance
of weakness between youth and old age against the omnipotent adult
for the control, often reluctantly and sometimes unsuccessfully
sought, of the aging one's life and liberty, a conflict which frequently results in loss of dignity and even the death of spirit.

Committed to nursing and retirement homes with varying de-
grees of resistance are seniors in Grandma Didn't Wave Back (Blue),
The Rocking Chair Rebellion (Clifford), The Amazing Miss Laura
(Colman), The Stones (Hickman), Matt's Grandfather (Lundgren),
The Hammerhead Light and The Shadow on the Hills (Thiele).   Those
who escape placement in homes include the two suicides of A Figure
of Speech (Mazer) and Grandpa--And Me (Tolan).   Two drive themselves out of town in obsolete conveyances to reach safety in The Get-
Away Car (Clymer) and The Glad Man (Gonzalez).   One is "kidnapped" for his own protection by heroic children also driving a
derelict vehicle in Grandpa and Frank (Majerus).   One is saved
from being declared incompetent by the intervention of a young doctor in The Faraway Island (Corcoran).   Three others evade institutionalization with the connivance of children in Mildred Murphy, How
Does Your Garden Grow? (Green), The Clearance (Lingard), and
Keep Stompin' Till the Music Stops (Pevsner).   One nonagenarian,
long immured in a nursing home, is "sprung" for a one night stand
by teenagers in Kidnapping Mr. Tubbs (Schellie).   The title character of Matt's Grandfather (Lundgren) has to feign senility and docility
to please the nurses and Matt's parents but confides to Matt the
elaborate and clever ruses he employs to maintain a modicum of individuality and independence and occasionally to "split" the irksome
scene.   Nursing and retirement homes are almost universally treated
as abhorrent--fates literally worse than death.

Two books are notable for their common theme of exploring
alternative answers to conventional retirement homes which segregate
the aging.   The Rocking Chair Rebellion (Clifford) probes an experi-
ment in the communal sharing of a private home by a group of active
aging, pooling their assorted contributions which range from financing
the purchase of the house to tilling a garden for the group's produce.
Reubella and the Old Focus Home (Newton) is similar but involves a
company of semi-retired female professionals, a composer, an artist,

and an athletic coach who incorporate, lease a house, hire a manager, and screen future applicants while pursuing their diverse interests and abilities.

Bringing aging grandparents into the family home can engender as much conflict as placing them in institutions, though it may be of a different nature. Compromise or capitulation occur in Then Again, Maybe I Won't (Blume), Two That Were Tough (Burch), The Cartoonist (Byars), Our Snowman Had Olive Eyes (Herman), If You Love Me, Let Me Go (Johnston), Emma's Dilemma (LeRoy), The Hundred Penny Box (Mathis), A Figure of Speech (Mazer), and Cinnamon Cane (Pollowitz).

One unique character deserves special mention, not as a figure for emulation but to indicate the range of realism existing in the genre of the aging in children's books. The grandmother of the Cleavers' Queen of Hearts, following a disabling stroke, perversely refuses to abandon her home and so alienates two housekeeper/companions with her rudeness and malediction that both leave. She chooses her granddaughter, whom she belabors incessantly, to be her live-in lackey. The girl, with the patience of Job, rises to the challenge. Another resident companion situation involving a teen and an octogenarian in The Amazing Miss Laura (Colman) evolves far more amicably.

Friction and confrontation are also observed when families live under a grandparent's roof, as in Julia and the Hand of God (Cameron), The Amazing Miss Laura (Colman), Hotheads (LeRoy), and Grandpa and Frank (Majerus).

Instances in which an aging person is sole guardian of an orphan raise the inherent question of the fate of the child if the guardian is disabled or dies. While thirty-eight books evince aging guardians, only eight address this specific problem, including Foster Child (Bauer), The Education of Little Tree (Carter), Duffy's Rocks (Fenton), Oma (Hartling), Benjie on His Own (Lexau), Philomena (Seredy), A Home With Aunt Florry (Talbot), and The Miller's Boy (Willard).

There is some support for both the contention that the elderly are portrayed as "unfailingly pleasant" and the paradoxical finding of "angry," "crazy" and other negative depictions. Of ten elderly witches and wizards (defined here as ones who observably change the form or substance of an entity by supernatural means), only three are malevolent, appearing in The Stolen Telesm (Baxter); Mrs. Beggs and the Wizard (Mayer), a whimsical vehicle for the author's comical monsters; and Naylor's trilogy, Witch's Sister, Witch Water, and The Witch Herself. All others are benevolent, and some characters that are described as witches prove to be wise elders (usually in non-Western cultures) or benign herbalists. There are other odious witches, but because they are of indeterminate ages are not considered detrimental to the image of the aging.

More amorphous as an identifiable body than necromancers
are the misanthropes. The assortment includes a sour old woman
who trades places with a miscast young witch in The Jolly Witch
(Burch), an angry man who puts a curse on a small town before
dying in The Deadly Mandrake (Callen), an obnoxious Scot in Mr.
McFadden's Hallowe'en (Godden), the disaffected alcoholic Italian-
American in Hotheads (LeRoy), the immutably mean black woman of
No Trespassing (Prather), the usurious Japanese landlord of Once
Under the Cherry Blossom Tree (Say), and the ornery and can-
tankerous mountaineer of The Old Man and the Mule (Snyder).

Not all grandparents and guardians prove to be paragons.
Among the worst are the cruel and nefarious grandfather of Tough
Chauncey (Smith), the scurrilous and scathing grandmother of Marra's
World (Coatsworth), and the peevish and disparaging grandmother of
Queen of Hearts (Cleaver). Others who nettle their grandchildren or
charges include the fulminant and deprecatory grandmother of My
Brother Stevie (Clymer) and the taciturn and intransigent great-uncle
of Big Blue Island (Gage). Two grandmothers and their grand-
daughters are temperamentally opposed. In Mandy's Grandmother
(Skorpen) they compromise and are reconciled at the end, but in
Julia and the Hand of God (Cameron), resentment is harbored throughout. The protagonist of The Amazing Miss Laura (Colman) also resents her grandfather for his obstinate selfishness and other annoying attributes but eventually makes peace with him.

Recluses can be construed as having negative characteristics,
but in every case within this collection, the younger persons who be-
come well acquainted with the reclusive characters develop an appreciation and understanding of their independent lifestyles. This is
true of Shelter from the Wind (Bauer), After the Goat Man (Byars),
Grandmother Cat and the Hermit (Coatsworth), The Long Journey and
The Winds of Time (Corcoran), Gone-Away Lake and Return to Gone-
Away (Enright), The Glad Man (Gonzalez), Heidi (Spyri), and The
Shadow on the Hills (Thiele). Two recluses are accused of being
Nazis, the one falsely so in The Stones (Hickman) by youthful tor-
mentors. The other, an urbane grandfather, is exposed as a heinous
war criminal in Gentlehands (Kerr) to the jarring disillusionment of
his teenaged grandson.

Another descriptor that has dubious connotations is that of the
eccentric or, more accurately, the nonconformist, embracing as it
does some highly original individuals, among them characters in
Billy Bedamned, Long Gone By (Beatty), The House of Wings (Byars),
Remove Protective Coating a Little at a Time (Donovan), From the
Mixed-Up Files of Mrs. Basil E. Frankweiler (Konigsburg), Onion
John (Krumgold), Mrs. Piggle-Wiggle (MacDonald), Reubella and the
Old Focus Home (Newton), Evy-Ivy-Over (Rodowsky), Magdalena
(Shotwell), A Home with Aunt Florry (Talbot), and Kevin's Grandma
(Williams). The latter is the embodiment of both the liberated wom-
an and the emancipated elder who pursues her own pleasures without
guilt, even to celebrating her grandson's birthday by going sky diving
while the birthday boy watches impassively from the airplane. Three

seniors share a proclivity for roller skating in Miss Tessie Tate
(Berg), Grandmother Oma and Traveling with Oma (Kleberger), and
The Pigman (Zindel).

Perhaps the most damaging stereotype is that of the "little
old man/woman" syndrome. Some of the most vaunted modern
classics suffer its symptoms. Such characters are identified by the
use of all three words in succession, by the appearance of two or
more of the words in the text having initial capitals, i. e., "Old
Man, " "Little Woman, " and by the physical description, either in
illustration or text, ascribing them to be short and plump, destitute
and doddering, or foolish and ludicrous. They range from the most
reprehensible, The Little Old Woman Who Used Her Head (Sewell)
and the equally execrable Adshead Brownies series to the more positive Old Man Up a Tree (Adamson) and Old Man Riddle (Memling).
The shame is that this image is still being perpetuated in books of
the late 1970's, including It's So Nice to Have a Wolf Around the
House (Allard, 1977), Old Man Whickutt's Donkey (Calhoun, 1975),
and A Bucket Full of Moon (Talbot, 1976). Others that fit this cate-
gory are Nine Hundred Buckets of Paint (Becker, 1949), The Little
Old Man Who Cooked and Cleaned (Black, 1970), Mr. Penny (Ets,
1935), Millions of Cats (Ga'g, 1928), Halfway Up the Mountain (Gilchrist, 1978), The Old Woman Who Lived in a Vinegar Bottle (Godden, 1972), The Old Woman Who Lived in Holland (Howells, 1973),
Little Old Mrs. Pepperpot (Proysen, 1959), The Old Woman and the
Pedlar (Taylor, 1969), The Little Woman Wanted Noise (Teal, 1943),
and Babushka and the Pig (Trofimuk, 1969). Given the benefit of
the doubt and exempted from this list are certain traditional folk
tales retold for American audiences, such as The Old Woman and the
Red Pumpkin and The Old Woman and the Rice Thief (Bang), The
Funny Little Woman (Mosel), Baboushka and the Three Kings (Robbins), Befana (Rockwell), and The Old Man and the Tiger (Tresselt).

An equally invidious type of story, and one which is closely
related to the "little old man/woman" syndrome, is that in which
aging characters are portrayed fatuously and stultifyingly to milk
cheap laughs. Culpable are Charlie and the Chocolate Factory and
Charlie and the Great Glass Elevator (Dahl) and The House That
Sailed Away (Hutchins). Ludicrous and embarrassing illustrations
spoil another otherwise commendable book, Ultra-Violet Catastrophe
(Mahy).

There is certainly a lack of discernible employment among
senior adults except for women, of course, who are almost always
found in the role of homemaker. In one case, however, a grandmother who has found fulfillment in the important post of family
cook loses her sense of self-esteem when the crass family hires a
housekeeper/cook in Then Again, Maybe I Won't (Blume). Instances
of arbitrary retirement that are reversed by the intervention of children occur to the cabinetmaker of Dream Dancer (Bolton) and the
shoemaker of A Likely Place (Fox). Retirement mandated by their
families occurs to the miller of Two That Were Tough (Burch) and
the farmer of Cinnamon Cane (Pollowitz). Some other occupations

represented are piano tuner, nanny, knight, vicar, medicine man, baker, tailor, chef, cobbler, rug hooker, herdsman, handyman, composer, artist, actress, musician, corporate executive, entomologist, librarian, teacher, book seller, shopkeeper, housekeeper, clerk, building superintendent, factory worker, fish packer, domestic, scavenger, panhandler, farmer, fisherman, sea captain, horse trainer, moonshiner, and jill-of-all-trades, including karate instructor. One working grandmother is also a part time student in Grandma Is Somebody Special (Goldman), and there is one work force re-entry woman in the fantasy, The Downtown Fairy Godmother (Pomerantz), who acknowledges that she hates housework, as does the title character of Kevin's Grandma (Williams) and one of the grandmothers of A Mitzvah Is Something Special (Eisenberg).

Among those who are not visibly employed, poverty is not common except to certain minorities and the "little old man/woman" characters, although financial concerns do touch every walk of life in retirement years in a number of books. Hartling's Oma expresses the anxiety of inflation on a fixed income.

Sexuality of the aging is discussed candidly in I Met a Traveler (Hoban), alluded to in A Certain Magic (Orgel), and inferred from A Mitzvah Is Something Special (Eisenberg), all outside of marriage. Sexuality is rather coyly skirted in The Rocking Chair Rebellion (Clifford) in which an elderly couple marries to allay the suspicion of illicit cohabitation, as if such a thing were possible "at their age." One widower shies away when marriage is mentioned in Our Snowman Had Olive Eyes (Herman), and a lonely old bachelor finds love and matrimony in later years in The Duck of Billingsgate Market (Ziner).

A number of deceased characters exert a posthumous influence in the books in which they appear, among them The Treasure of Alpheus Winterborn (Bellairs), The Deadly Mandrake (Callen), Philomena (Seredy), The House on Pendleton Block (Waldron), Unleaving (Walsh), and My Grandson Lew (Zolotow). In three others, elderly apparitions materialize to accomplish posthumous missions before passing on, including A Question of Time (Anastasio), The Ghosts (Barber), and A Christmas Card (Theroux).

Stories from England account for twenty-seven titles, while five take place in Germany. Other locations represented more than once are India, Japan, Sweden, France, Italy, Canada, Scotland, China, Southeast Asia, Africa, Australia, Russia, and Eastern Europe. Appearing only once are Mexico, Austria, Israel, Spain, New Guinea, Peru, Holland, Switzerland, and the West Indies. The agonizing plight of Displaced Persons of World War II is explored in Transport 7-41-R (Degens), In Search of Coffee Mountains (Gottschalk), and A Certain Magic (Orgel).

Ethnic minorities appear in proportionately few numbers. Blacks are the most recurrent minority in stories taking place in the United States, appearing in Trouble on Treat Street (Alexander),

The Story Grandmother Told (Alexander), Raccoons Are for Loving (Bourne), Thank You, Jackie Robinson (Cohen), Grandmother's Pictures (Cornish), The House of Dies Drear (Hamilton), Benjie and Benjie on His Own (Lexau). Elderly blacks are also principals in The Hundred Penny Box (Mathis), Shuttered Windows (Means), Lavender-Green Magic (Norton), No Trespassing (Prather), Song of the Trees (Taylor), The Cay (Taylor), Ludell and Ludell and Willie (Wilkinson).

Jews are identified in The House on the Roof (Adler), The Bagel Baker of Mulliner Lane (Blau), Grandma Didn't Wave Back (Blue), Stories My Grandfather Should Have Told Me (Brodie), Hey, That's My Soul You're Stomping On (Corcoran), A Mitzvah Is Something Special (Eisenberg), Two Piano Tuners (Goffstein), I Met a Traveler (Hoban), and A Certain Magic (Orgel). American Indians are seen in The Shaman's Last Raid (Baker), The Education of Little Tree (Carter), The Shy Stegosaurus of Indian Springs and Navaho Sister (Lampman), Annie and the Old One (Miles), and Walks Far Woman (Stuart).

Italian-Americans follow with aging characters in Then Again, Maybe I Won't (Blume), Watch Out for the Chicken Feet in Your Soup (dePaola), Hotheads (LeRoy), Nonna (Bartoli), and Dark Dreams (Rinaldo). Hispanics appear in Trouble on Treat Street (Alexander), A Likely Place (Fox), Three Stalks of Corn (Politi), and Magdalena (Shotwell). Eastern Europeans are represented in After the Goat Man (Byars) and Onion John (Krumgold). Irish-American and Chinese-American grandmothers are principals, respectively, in Duffy's Rocks (Fenton) and Child of the Owl (Yep).

Aging characters appear in five books that were awarded the Caldecott Medal, including The Big Snow (Hader), They Were Strong and Good (Lawson), The Egg Tree (Milhous), The Funny Little Woman (Mosel), and Baboushka and the Three Kings (Robbins). Caldecott Honor Books include Strega Nona (dePaola) and Hildilid's Night (Ryan).

Newbery Medal recipients appearing herein are Secret of the Andes (Clark), Up a Road Slowly (Hunt), From the Mixed-Up Files of Mrs. Basil E. Frankweiler (Konigsburg), Onion John (Krumgold), Roller Skates (Sawyer), and Dobry (Shannon). Prominent aging roles in Newbery Honor Books are found in Gone-Away Lake (Enright), The Middle Moffat (Estes), Millions of Cats (Ga'g), The Hundred Penny Box (Mathis), Annie and the Old One (Miles), Figgs and Phantoms (Raskin), and The Egypt Game (Snyder).

Some Recent Findings

In the plethora of titles published since 1978, some unique ones merit highlighting. The theme of incipient reversible senility is shared by two. In A Piano for Mrs. Cimino (Oliphant), the counteraction is effected by a strict regimen of physical and mental therapy im-

posed by the enlightened and unequivocating staff of a rehabilitative
convalescent home.   In the other, I Don't Belong Here (French),
symptoms of senility are precipitated by the trauma of recent widowhood, compounded by the haphazard ingestion of medications.   When
the drug dosages are administered judiciously and the missing emotional support is supplied, the symptoms disappear and the patient
regains her acuity.   One advanced case of senility is found in
Anastasia Krupnik (Lowry), but it is treated with unusual insight.

Another shared theme is that of role reversal between young
and old as their capabilities change.   In both A Special Trade (Wittman) and The Two of Them (Aliki), the nurturing role is played by
aging men while their charges are babies.   In both cases the roles
are eventually reversed with the passage of time, the maturation of
the young girls, and the declining proficiency of the elderly men.
The Two of Them carries the theme to its ultimate conclusion with
the poignant death of the grandfather.

One unusual and compelling character is the elderly protagonist of The 79 Squares (Bosse), a convicted wife-murderer who
is released from prison into his daughter's custody only because
he is dying of cancer.   An even less laudable and sympathetic character is the grandmother of The Shared Room (Potter) whose be-
nighted attitude toward mental illness almost ruins her daughter's
life and causes her granddaughter great anguish.

Two books that equably combine fantasy with reality are The
Silver Coach (Adler), in which the offspring of divorced parents mature under the influence of their grandmother, and The Lightning
Time (Maguire), wherein grandmother and grandson collaborate to
circumvent the commercial development of a wilderness area.   A
picture book that blends fantasy with reality, How I Hunted the Little Fellows (Zhitkov), may be disquieting to the more sensitive of
the younger set and is recommended instead for intermediate readers.
It deals with heavy doses of guilt and remorse when a boy heedless-
ly destroys his grandmother's most prized possession.

Misunderstanding between youth and age that is resolved
amicably is explored in The Lilith Summer (Irwin), in which an
elderly lady and an adolescent girl, unbeknownst to one another,
are both paid to babysit the other, and in Carrie Hepple's Garden
(Craft), in which British children discover that their apprehension
of an old neighbor woman lies mainly in their imaginations.   The
antithesis occurs in Summer of the Stallion (Hanson), wherein another pre-teen perceives her adored grandfather in a less rosy light
after an unsettling incident with a horse.

Among pre- and post-retirement occupations identified in
books since 1978 are that of lumber yard owner in All Together Now
(Bridgers), scavenger in The Amazing Memory of Harvey Bean
(Cone), authors in The Boy Who Wanted a Family (Gordon) and A
Morgan for Melinda (Gates), migrant laborers in Foster Mary (Strang),
shepherd in Grandfather's Cake (McPhail), piano teacher and saxo-

phonist in A Piano for Mrs. Cimino (Oliphant), stonemason in Granny Reardun (Garner), nurse in Horowitz and Mrs. Washington (Denker), and blacksmith in Tom Fobble's Day (Garner). One resident of a custodial care home finds an avocation in recording oral history in Throwing Shadows (Konigsburg), and one septuagenarian becomes a champion equestrienne in A Morgan for Melinda.

While numerous characters suffer from the effects of cataracts, only two are permanently blind, the active old musician of Through Grandpa's Eyes (MacLachlan), and the former race car driver of Dirt Bike Racer (Christopher). One instance of false teeth is denoted in I Hate Red Rover (Lexau). Arthritis is a reasonably common complaint, but hip fractures are conspicuously absent. Specific cardiovascular afflictions are fatal to elderly protagonists in The Two of Them (Aliki), A Morgan for Melinda (Gates), and Someone Slightly Different (Mearian), which also deals with cremation. Related maladies spare but weaken characters in Grandpa, Me and Our House in the Tree (Kirk) and Misty and Me (Girion), while in Horowitz and Mrs. Washington (Denker), the Jewish stroke victim is rehabilitated by a black nurse in a story that contains an ethnic conflict as well as a medical and social one.

Other ethnic minorities that add robust and piquant demographic flavor include Eastern Europeans in Carnival and Kopeck and More About Hannah (Skolsky), Freddy My Grandfather (Langner), and Odd Girl Out (Lingard); an Alaskan Eskimo in A Hunter Comes Home (Turner); Latin-American in I Love My Grandma (Palay); an American Indian in When Grandfather Journeys into Winter (Strete); and blacks in Tough Tiffany (Hurmence) and The Lucky Stone (Clifton). Hi, Mrs. Mallory! (Thomas) concerns the friendship of a middle-class black girl and an aged poor white woman that concludes in the death, of undisclosed cause, of the old woman.

A Grandmother for the Orphelines (Carlson) takes place in France, while several transpire in England. Among them are the sublime picture books, Grandmother (Baker) and Timothy and Gramps (Brooks); two adventure stories for older readers, Mrs. Flannagan's Trumpet (Cookson) and The Robbers (Bawden); and two of an arcanely idiomatic tetralogy that would benefit immeasurably from glossaries, Granny Reardun and Tom Fobble's Day (both by Garner). An unfortunate offering from England is Mr. Simkin's Grandma (Allen), a dubious comedy.

The occult is common to The Magic Grandfather (Williams) and The River Witches (Shecter). The misanthropic recluse of Carrie's Gift (Holmes) responds eventually to the young girl's friendly overtures.

Other notable picture books published since 1978 portraying memorable older people and their warm personal relationships with young people include Grandpa and Me Together (Goldman), a companion piece to the author's earlier Grandma Is Somebody Special, and My Island Grandma (Lasky), which also has its counterpart in

Lasky's previous <u>I Have Four Names for My Grandfather.</u> <u>In the</u>
<u>Morning Mist</u> (Lapp) chronicles an intimate fishing expedition shared
by grandfather and grandson, and the photo story <u>Special Friends</u>
(Berger) depicts the special bond between a girl and her elderly
neighbor.

Two additional stories for intermediate readers with strong
sociological and psychological themes are <u>Now Is Not Too Late</u> (Holland), which also has an island setting, and <u>Tread Softly</u> (Gerson).

Conclusion

"Old is not dead," as the vibrant characters of <u>Reubella and the Old</u>
<u>Focus Home</u> (Newton) so convincingly proclaim and prove. While it
appears from this discussion that most of the children's books in the
Bibliography dwell morbidly on the depressing aspects of aging,
namely death, infirmity, irascibility, and the triple losses of employment, independence, and even dignity, such a conclusion is in-
accurate. It is simply that the buoyant, reassuring, and even in-
spiring situations are too manifold to mention individually, and it
would be unfair to single out a few to laud. Illustrative of what
Barnum calls "unfailingly pleasant" are <u>Jumping Jackdaws! Here</u>
<u>Comes Simon</u> (Roberts), in which a small English boy enjoys a
warm and salubrious relationship with his energetic and original
grandmother, and <u>Burt Dow, Deep-Water Man</u> (McCloskey) who sails
intrepidly into a colorful adventure of his own creation. Many other
books occupy a middle ground between problem exploration and pure
entertainment. Exemplifying these is <u>The Faraway Island</u> (Corcoran)
in which Grandmother Linley is charming and intelligent, independent
enough to live alone and drive a car, active enough to go clamming,
experienced enough to be patient and tolerant, and traditional enough
to enjoy gardening and cooking, but what makes her plausible is
that she suffers an occasional migraine headache and infrequent and
fleeting memory lapses. In short, this gem is slightly flawed and
fallible and therefore endowed with a unique and refreshing wearing
quality.

The purpose of this commentary has been to communicate the
responsiveness of contemporary authors to the inherent problems of
aging, to introduce some of the books they are promulgating to help
sensitize children to these difficulties as they meet them, and to
demonstrate their increasing practice of portraying senior adults
realistically and positively. It is suggested that the reader peruse
the Ready Reference Profile which also serves as the title index to
the Bibliography as a guide to locating stories to fit specific situations and to get a perspective on the genre, the aging in children's
books. Grade level divisions in the Bibliography are purely arbitrary, and individual titles often overlap boundaries. Non-fiction
books on and about aging will be found in the Multimedia Section
(Part III).

It is appropriate to conclude this discourse with the words

of Elizabeth Gray Vining whose children's book <u>Adam of the Road</u> received the 1943 Newbery Medal and whose <u>Jane Hope</u> appears in the Bibliography. Both books were written under her maiden name, Elizabeth Janet Gray. Mrs. Vining's diary chronicling her seventieth year, <u>Being Seventy, The Measure of a Year</u>, [8] is written with charm and verve, and is especially useful for sensitizing young adults to the psyche of old adults. It was a vintage year of extensive travel to Japan (where she was appointed in 1946 as tutor to Crown Prince Akihito) and other stimulating locales to renew old friendships and participate in writers' conferences; of writing a biography of John Greenleaf Whittier; of serving as Trustee Emerita at Bryn Mawr, her alma mater; and of active membership in the Society of Friends. It was, moreover, a reflective and decisive year in which she frequently pondered her impending move to a retirement home. She admitted, in her youth, to stereotyping the elderly:

> When we were in our thirties, my friend Marjorie and I used to classify old ladies in four categories. We said there were the Whiny Old Ladies, the Bossy Old Ladies, the Fussy Old Ladies, and the Batty Old Ladies. I decided that if I lived so long--which I did not intend to do-- I would be a Batty Old Lady. Well, I am. (She had just misplaced her plane ticket to Japan.)

On her fiftieth class reunion:

> Thirty-three old women, all asserting how young they feel, ... old friends who are still friends in spite of the strange disguise we all wear.... There were several canes and post-cataract spectacles, much fuzzy white hair, some deafness, but all of us were mentally vigorous.... I will not attend any more.... It was a good reunion, perhaps the best we had, and for that reason it is well to end on it. Later we shall be putting a brave face on age; now we are enjoying its rewards.

On recourses in living arrangements for the aging:

> There are two basically different ways of approaching what is so mincingly called the Later Years: the stick-it-out-in-the-world policy, and the duck-into-safety policy. The first one sounds so much more gallant, the second slightly craven. If you have a family ... to step in and take responsibility if you fall in the bathroom and break your hip, then you can afford to live dangerously.

She, being entirely alone, had to examine the second alternative:

> The depressing part of a retirement community, even the best of them: the segregation of the aged. That and the finality of it. Once in, will one feel trapped?

On visiting a friend in a nursing home:

> But before I ever got to her I was caught in the reception
> room by a smartly dressed old lady who sat there like a
> spider waiting for someone to come by. She told me all
> about her arthritis and the treatments she was getting. . . .
> This is the real loneliness of old age--to be surrounded
> by people and yet not to have anyone to hear and respond
> . . . .   Should I be surrounded at Kendal by people like that
> well-dressed, well-groomed old bird who buttonholes
> strangers to talk about her ailments?

On her final commitment to the retirement community:

> As I look forward to Kendal--and I do--I sometimes catch
> myself thinking of all the nice things I am going to do for
> those old people there, and then I remember that I am
> one of those old people myself. I don't think I want any-
> body doing kindly things for me!... As to everybody's
> being old there, they will, most of them, be young old,
> enjoying the first exhilaration of retirement. There is a
> difference between young old and old old. But that stage,
> too, will come, of course.

And finally, in haunting imagery, Elizabeth Gray Vining's vision of
old age:

> A door shuts. It is shut not in one's face but behind one.
> In front is a new landscape, bleak perhaps at times, lit
> no doubt at others with mysterious beauty, but cut off in
> the distance by a wall, which for the first time is close
> enough to be visible. One stands in a limited space, with
> the door behind and the wall somewhere in front.

References

1. Barnum, Phyllis. "Aging in Children's Books, " Human Nature,
    1:13, September 1978.
2. Ansello, Edward. "Ageism in Children's Books, " Interracial
    Books for Children Bulletin, 7:6, 8, 1976.
3. Blue, Gladys F. "The Aging as Portrayed in Realistic Fiction
    for Children 1945-1975, " The Gerontologist, 18:187-192,
    April 1978.
4. Peterson, David A. and Elizabeth L. Karnes. "Older People in Ad-
    olescent Literature, " The Gerontologist, 16:225-230, June 1976.
5. Katz, Carol. "Outcasts and Renegades: Elderly People in Cur-
    rent Children's Fiction, " Horn Book, 54:316-321, June 1978.
6. Walker, Maxine. "Last Rites for Young Readers, " Children's
    Literature in Education, 9:188-197, 1978.
7. Fassler, Joan. Helping Children Cope. New York: Macmillan,
    1978.
8. Vining, Elizabeth Gray. Being Seventy; The Measure of a Year.
    New York: Viking, 1978.

I. ANNOTATED BIBLIOGRAPHY

Preschool and Primary Grades

1.   Adamson, Gareth. OLD MAN UP A TREE. London:
Abelard-Schuman, 1963. Illus. by the author. Unpaged.
Grades 1-3.

     An Old Man climbs a tree to catch the view, while below
a baker, a peddler, a soldier, a sailor, a rich man and a tramp
gather to speculate why he climbs. Overhearing him mumble, "It's
cold up here," they erroneously conclude that he has gold stashed
in a hole in the tree. As the Old Man climbs higher, the greedy
gathering decides to climb up, ostensibly to protect the Old Man's
interests from one another, but in reality to help themselves to the
purported treasure. A thief comes along and appropriates the par-
cels the others have left below and makes off with them in the rich
man's car. The branch breaks beneath the combined weight of the
opportunists, plunging them into a pond, while the Old Man climbs
obliviously to the top of the tree where he is rewarded by a pano-
rama of the sea. He congratulates himself upon such a feat at his age.

2.   Adler, David. THE HOUSE ON THE ROOF: A SUKKOT
STORY. New York: Bonim, 1976. Illus. by Marilyn
Hirsh. Unpaged. Grades K-3.

     When an old man begins collecting crates, magazines, dis-
carded clothing, and autumn leaves in his modest, aging apartment,
his critical and inquisitive landlady becomes suspicious. After a
week of hammering, he brings his grandchildren to the building one
day, and the landlady follows them to the roof where he has con-
structed a traditional Jewish Sukkah in celebration of Sukkoth, walled
with crates, latticed with branches, and decorated with colorful
swatches and magazine pictures. She shrewishly shoos them off
the roof and brings suit against the old man for building on her
roof. After hearing the man's explanation of the four-day holiday,
the sympathetic judge, a virtual Solomon, gives the pleasantly surprised defendent ten leisurely days in which to dismantle the offending temporary symbolic shelter.

3.   Adler, David A. A LITTLE AT A TIME. New York:
Random, 1976. Illus. by N. M. Bodecker. Unpaged.
Grades K-1.

     On a walk through the winter city to the museum, a very
inquisitive boy asks his mustached grandfather a barrage of questions:

how does a tree get so tall, a hole so deep, a building so high, a
street so dirty, and Grandpa explains that these things occur by degree.   When the boy wants to see all the museum exhibits in one
day, Grandpa advises patience, and at the soda fountain afterward,
the boy eats his ice cream quickly, while Grandpa enjoys his slowly.
The boy asks, "How did you get so smart, Grandpa? How did you
learn so much?"   "I'm just like you! I ask many questions, and
little by little I learn a lot.   As long as I keep asking, I'll keep
learning a little at a time."

4.   Adshead, Gladys L.   BROWNIES--HUSH!   New York:
          Walck, 1938.   Illus. by Elizabeth Orton Jones.   Unpaged.
          Grades K-2.

          An elderly couple so decrepit they cannot sweep the floor
or make the fire take their tired old bones to bed, while a troupe
of merry but bashful brownies steals into the cottage and quietly
does the chores by firefly light.   One night the old people watch
for them silently and, noticing that the elven clothes are threadbare,
they fashion new suits and pointed shoes for them.   When the startled brownies, having donned their fine new apparel, spot their
benefactors, they flee back into the woods, never to be seen again.

5.   Adshead, Gladys L.   BROWNIES--IT'S CHRISTMAS!   New
          York: Walck, 1955.   Illus. by Velma Ilsley.   Unpaged.
          Grades K-2.

          The brownies know it is Christmas, for they see Old Grand-
father dodder out with snowshoes, cane, and axe to chop down a
fir.   They follow him home and hide until the exertion of cutting
the tree and crafting the ornaments exhaust Old Grandfather and
Old Grandmother who snooze in their chairs.   The engaging gnomes
creep out, trim the tree, and melt away into the night.   When the
delighted couple discover the brownies' handiwork, they return the
favor by decorating a miniature tree outdoors.

6.   Adshead, Gladys L.   BROWNIES--THEY'RE MOVING!
          New York: Walck, 1970.   Illus. by Richard Lebenson.
          Unpaged.   Grades K-2.

          Finding their old home to be too much work for their tired
old bones, Old Grandfather and Old Grandmother decide to move to
a new "laborsaving" house.   Of course the brownies help them pack
and stow away in the moving van to help them get settled.   They
solve the dilemma of how to return by deciding to move, too, and
take up residence among the apple tree roots in the orchard.   In
gratitude the old couple fashion delicate furnishings, utensils, and
culinary treats for them so they, too, will have labor saving homes.

7.   Aichinger, Helga. THE SHEPHERD. New York: Crowell,
        1967. Illus. by the author. Unpaged. Grades K-1.

        A picture book of reverent simplicity about the Nativity in
which an angel appears in a dream to a poor and lonely old shepherd to tell of the birth of the Christ Child. He follows the star,
as directed, past a beautiful town and a magnificent castle to an
old hut like his own. He thinks he has lost his way, but when the
Babe smiles at him as he covers it with his coat, he knows the
child is not poor. "Heaven and earth belong to you," he says.

8.   Aldridge, Josephine Haskell.   FISHERMAN'S LUCK.
        Berkeley: Parnassus, 1966. Illus. by Ruth Robbins.
        Unpaged.   Grades 1-2.

        "Some storms thrash and blow and pound around," thinks
Sy, the old fisherman, "and some storms come quietly like this
one." Nonetheless he battens down his shack on the jetty, makes
his cat comfortable, and walks to the store to wait it out with his
cronies. Laconically they watch the rolling black seas flood
Fletcher's Ledge and sweep Sy's fish house with it. "Fisherman's
luck," he mutters tersely, mourning his cat in private. The salvage crew finds the cabin of his boat intact, though the hull is
hopelessly smashed, and in it he rejoices to find his charmed feline. The others help him rebuild his wharf, and for an abode,
they secure the cabin of the boat to it.

9.   Alexander, Martha. THE STORY GRANDMOTHER TOLD.
        New York: Dial, 1967. Illus. by the author. Unpaged.
        Grades K-1.

        Lisa asks her black grandmother for a story of Lisa and
her cat Ivan, and relates it herself so Gramma will remember:
Lisa decides to buy a big green cat balloon instead of an ice cream
cone, and she and Ivan are entranced with it until friends glorify
the balloon cat, and the real tabby grows more and more jealous.
He rectifies the problem with a sharp claw, and Lisa, unaware of
how the balloon burst, sees Ivan's remorse and mistakes it for
sorrow at the balloon cat's demise. She comforts him and all is
well. Gramma interrupts her cooking to tell the twice-told tale.

9a.   Aliki. THE TWO OF THEM. New York: Greenwillow,
        1979. Illus. by the author. Unpaged. Grades 3-4.

        An intensely warm and personal story of the nurturing bond
between a girl and her grandfather from the moment of her birth
until his death--and beyond, in memory. The attachment develops
as he tenderly tucks her into a hand-crafted cradle, cushions her
first pratfalls, takes her to the beach, the mountains, and to his
small grocery store. He sings to her and tells her stories of his

love.   The relationship begins to change subtly after he retires and she realizes that she loves the man more than the material things he creates for her.   Passage of time and a paralyzing stroke shift the nurturing role from him to her.   She knows he will die "But when he did, she was not ready, and she hurt inside and out. " She carries on the way he would wish her to--and remembers.

10.   Allard, Harry.   IT'S SO NICE TO HAVE A WOLF AROUND THE HOUSE. Garden City: Doubleday, 1977. Illus. by James Marshall. Unpaged. Grades K-2.

Cuthbert Q. Devine, wolf, answers the Old Man's ad for a charming companion for himself and his three equally decrepit pets, a dog, a cat, and a tropical fish that can only float.   He quickly makes himself indispensible to the four and introduces them to comforts and divertissements that rejuvenate them.   His sordid past catches up with him, however, when the Old Man learns he is wanted for bank robbery.   Confronted with his past misdeeds, Cuthbert faints dead away in an attack of nerves that requires a long convalescence through which the four cosset him.   After his recovery, he takes the Old Man's advice and throws himself on the mercy of the judge who is lenient with the chastened wolf, and they all move to Arizona for Cuthbert's health.

10a.   Allen, Linda. MR. SIMKIN'S GRANDMA. New York: Morrow, 1979. Illus. by Loretta Lustig. Unpaged. Grades 2-3.

A lumpy old lady purporting to be Mr. Simkin's Grandma appears at the door of the menagerie the Simkin's call home, appropriates his easy chair, and refuses to budge.   By the time she turns dusty and sprouts cobwebs, Mr. Simkin is desperate to reclaim his chair and advertises in the Lost and Found and on the telly in hopes someone will claim the sedentary simpleton.   The response is amazing, but she rejects all offers.   Eventually a bearded, myopic dotard knocks, claiming to be Mr. Simkin's Grandpa, and promptly usurps Mrs. Simkin's easy chair.   "Grandma" stalks out peevishly, Mr. Simkin recovers his chair, and it is Mrs. Simkin's turn to be punctiliously perturbed in this offensive game of musical armchairs.

11.   Anderson, Lonzo and Adrienne Adams.   TWO HUNDRED RABBITS.   New York: Viking, 1968. Illus. by Adrienne Adams. 32pp. Grades K-3.

A comely Medieval boy desires to entertain the king, but his efforts at singing, fiddling, and juggling earn the derision of the forest denizens.   He shares his lunch and woes with a starving crone who bids him to whittle a slippery-elm slide whistle and blow it.   All the rabbits in the forest come flocking, and at another toot they martial themselves into twenty rows of ten each, the last line

lacking one hare. Marching to the boy's tune, they troop to the
castle where they are reviewed by the king. The asymmetry of the
last line annoys the monarch who is about to dismiss them when the
narrator, a vagabond and a rabbit himself, scampers from his observation post beneath the throne and completes the ranks. "Oh,
well. I was tired of traveling anyway."

12.   Ardizzone, Edward. LITTLE TIM AND THE BRAVE SEA
        CAPTAIN. New York: Walck, 1955. Illus. by the author.
        Unpaged. Grades 1-3.

        Little Tim lives by the sea and longs to be a sailor, but
his parents are merely amused at the idea. One day he stows away
on a big steamer, but when he is discovered he is made to swab
the decks. Gradually he becomes useful to the crew, but when a
storm blows up he feels queasy. Suddenly the ship begins to founder
and everyone abandons ship but the staunch, gray-bearded captain
and poor Tim who is forgotten in the shuffle. The two stoically
prepare to meet Davy Jones when Tim spots a lifeboat. They and
their rescuers are received as heroes following the ordeal, and the
captain asks Tim's parents if he can join him on his next voyage
because he has the makings of a fine seaman.

12a.   Baker, Jeannie. GRANDMOTHER. London: Andre Deutsch,
        1978. Illus. by the author. Unpaged. Grades K-1.

        Beautifully textured, three-dimensional collages tell the
simple story of a visit to the Victorian house peeping through the
verdure behind a high board fence where Grandmother lives with
her many cats. While Grandmother finishes her sewing, the girl
wanders through the treasure-filled rooms and plays at the old up-
right piano. Together they stroll through the overgrown garden with
its lichened statuary that Grandmother sculpted long ago, feed the
birds, dabble toes in the pond, and examine toadstools. The girl
helps Grandmother take the laundry off the line before going in for
tea. With scraps of yarn, Grandmother helps the girl start a rainbow scarf, and they share an affectionate hug.

13.   Bang, Betsy. THE OLD WOMAN AND THE RED PUMPKIN.
        New York: Macmillan, 1975. Trans. by the author. Illus.
        by Molly Garrett Bang. Unpaged. Grades 2-3.

        In this Bengali folk tale, a palsied and emaciated but spir-
ited old lady sets out on her walking stick to visit her granddaughter.
On the way she encounters, in turn, a jackal, a tiger, and a bear,
all of whom declare their intention of eating her. She cannily begs
them to wait for her return when she will be sleek and plump. Sure
enough, her granddaughter fattens her on curry and curds until she
cannot even waddle. The younger woman packs her in an empty
pumpkin shell and rolls her in the direction of home. The bear and

tiger are fooled by this disguise but follow along out of curiosity. The jackal is shrewder and cracks open the marrow squash, but with more quick-witted cunning, the old woman provokes a fight among them, and while they are quarreling slips away to safety, "tok, tok."

14.   Bang, Betsy. THE OLD WOMAN AND THE RICE THIEF. New York: Greenwillow, 1978. Illus. by Molly Garrett Bang. Unpaged. Grades K-2.

A wizened old woman of India is content until thieving vermin invade her rice pots in the night, and she sets out to seek redress from the Raja. Along the way she meets a scorpion-fish, a wood-apple, a razor, a cowpat, and an alligator to all of which she repeats her complaints. Each one tells her to take it along with her on her way home. Disappointed at the Raja's absence, she is forced to return but remembers to take her anthropomorphic acquaintances of the road with her. When the little rodent returns to pillage her larder, the old woman's companions mete out their unique retribution and she is left to enjoy her rice in peace, "achchha."

15.   Bartoli, Jennifer. NONNA. New York: Harvey House, 1975. Illus. by Joan E. Drescher. Unpaged. Grades K-3.

When Nonna dies, the family is initially very quiet, hasn't much appetite, and feels relieved to cry. Big brother Anthony comes home from the army, and the telephone rings constantly. They begin reminiscing about the good times with Nonna and, before his death, with Nonno. They go to church to pray for Nonna and then to the cemetery to bury her body. On Saturday morning the extended family gathers at Nonna's house as they did when she was living, and little sister Amy wanders from room to room looking for her, not believing she is gone. Anthony gravely accepts Nonno's old mandolin and Amy the quilt Nonna was making. During the summer, family and neighbors harvest the vegetable legacy from Nonna's garden, but in the autumn the house is sold. When the family gathers again at Christmas, Amy crowns the feast with cookies she baked from Nonna's recipe. Boy narrator says, "Amy, these cookies are almost as good as Nonna's."

16.   Becker, Edna. NINE HUNDRED BUCKETS OF PAINT. Nashville: Abingdon, 1949. Illus. by Margaret Bradfield. Unpaged. Grades 2-3.

An Old Woman who lives alone with her two cats, her donkey, and her cow decides that her house is too shabby and packs up her belongings to move. She settles into the next three vacant houses she passes, but each one proves to be displeasing to one or other of the animals. They try one more house that appears eminently satisfactory to all, but she fears it may already be occupied because a man is painting it. He reassures her that he is only refurbishing the neighborhood because he has had a windfall of paint. Because she has made only right turns in her peregrinations, she has returned to her own house but doesn't recognize it until she spots the alarm clock she left behind.

17.   Berg, Jean Horton. MISS TESSIE TATE. Philadelphia:
        Westminster, 1967. Illus. by Lee deGroot. Unpaged.
        Grades K-2.

Miss Tate earns the derision and disapprobation of her pedestrian Medieval neighbors when she anachronistically straps on roller skates and frolics about town in rollicking rhyme. Her anomalous mode of locomotion proves useful, however, when the king and queen develop domestic difficulties, and the legions of enthusiastic but unimaginative dust-hustlers they recruit as scab labor rattle the royal nerves. The intrepid, individualistic heroine rolls to the rescue, cleans the castle in five minutes flat, and collects the gold. Now all the housewives in the kingdom are trading in their brooms for roller skates.

17a.   Berger, Terry. SPECIAL FRIENDS. New York: Messner,
        1979. Illus. by David Hechtlinger. 64pp. Grades 1-4.

"Sometimes when there's no one to talk to or listen to me, " the girl next door goes to visit the elderly widow she respectfully calls "Aunt Rose, " who lives alone and cares for herself but whose family lives nearby in case she needs someone. Candid photos and simple text chronicle their activities. Because she remembers so much history and watches the TV news, Aunt Rose is very useful for helping with homework. She also bandages knees, bakes cookies, teaches her friend the foxtrot, helps with her great-grandson, and tends her garden, but, because of failing eyesight and weak knees, she does little sewing anymore and needs a bar to help her in and out of the tub. Together they reminisce over pictures of Aunt Rose's childhood and her late husband, and sometimes Aunt Rose gets a faraway look in her eyes. While resting, Aunt Rose swaps old songs for the girl's new "elephant" jokes and laughs till the tears come. When it's time to go home, the girl expresses her fondness in a heartfelt hug.

18.   Beskow, Elsa. PELLE'S NEW SUIT. New York: Harper
        and Row, 1929. Trans. by Marion Letcher Woodburn.
        Illus. by the author. Unpaged Grades K-1.

Swedish Pelle's new lamb grows bigger, but his old suit seems to grow smaller. He shears the lamb's wool and asks his babushka-coifed granny to card it in exchange for weeding her carrot patch. He asks his other shawled grandmother to spin it for him

in return for tending her cows. He acquires dye by doing an er-
rand for the painter and dyes the yarn himself. Mother weaves
the cloth while Pelle cares for his baby sister. He barters farm
chores with the tailor to have the new suit cut and sewn, and
proudly models it on Sunday morning.

19.   Black, Irma Simonton. THE LITTLE OLD MAN WHO
        COOKED AND CLEANED. Chicago: Whitman, 1970. Illus.
        by Seymour Fleishman. Unpaged. Grades 2-3.

This nameless and rotund old man normally prefers making
wooden toys for children, but when his wife is called away, he volunteers to do the housework and discovers it is not as easy as he be-
lieved. He begins by losing the cat in the sock drawer, shaking the
dirty dust cloth on the rug, and misconnecting the vacuum cleaner so
that it spews dirt all over the room to the tune of some interesting
expletives. In preparing dinner, the spaghetti boils over, the sauce
overturns on the floor, and the rolls burn. With a little luck he
salvages the meal just as his wife returns. She is none the wiser,
but he is happy to return to toymaking.

20.   Blades, Ann. A BOY OF TACHE. Plattsburgh: Tundra,
        1973. Illus. by the author. Unpaged. Grades 2-3.

Charlie, a British Columbian Indian boy, feels fortunate to
have been chosen from among his eleven brothers and sisters to
live with his grandfather Za and grandmother Virginia. He helps
with the chores but also gets special privileges, such as being taken
beaver trapping on the Taché River when the ice breaks up in the
spring. While they are camping in the snowy woods, Za, 74, takes
cold. Virginia directs Charlie to gather medicinal bark for tea to
try to prevent pneumonia, but Za worsens and Virginia sends Charlie alone in the motorboat for help. Za is airlifted out of the wilderness and will recover but will never return to hunt. That will be
Charlie's job now.

21.   Blau, Judith Hope. THE BAGEL BAKER OF MULLINER
        LANE. New York: McGraw-Hill, 1976. Illus. by the au-
        thor. Unpaged. Grades 2-4.

Grandpa Izzy not only bakes and sells bagels but brings
home the stale ones to sleep, eat, and bathe with. To Grandma
Sonny they seem oddly animate, and Grandpa Izzy assures her that
his bagels are magic. Just before Hanukah, snow buries Mulliner
Lane and traps Grandpa Izzy in his bakery. Everyone abandons
holiday plans to dig him out, and when they burst through the door,
they find Grandpa Izzy frolicking with hundreds of gaily decorated
bagels. There are bagel crafts for everyone on the block, and at
last Grandma Sonny believes in magic.

22.   Borack, Barbara. GRANDPA. New York: Harper and
          Row, 1967. Illus. by Ben Shecter. 32pp. Grades K-1.

          When Marilyn stays with her grandparents, Grandpa makes
mundane things more fun by saying boo from behind a door, lather-
ing her chin with shaving cream, letting her try on his shirts,
snipping off her nose between his fingers, bouncing her on his leg,
making chicken noises and paper hats, and letting her "help" at his
mom-and-pop hardware store. When she slurps her soup in emulation of him, Grandma clucks, but when she accidentally breaks
Grandma's best vase and is reproved, Grandpa comforts her. She
writes him a letter when he is sick in the hospital and composes a
song for him. And when it is time for her to leave, Grandma and
Grandpa give her a sandwich kiss between them.

23.   Bourne, Miriam Anne. RACCOONS ARE FOR LOVING.
          New York: Random House, 1968. Illus. by Marian Morton.
          44pp. Grades 2-3.

          When Josephine visits her grandmother's tidy tenement, the
old South Carolina woman tells her stories of her childhood on the
farm. Josie's favorite tale is of the raccoon that came out of the
woods, let her grandmother fondle it, and whispered, "Annie, you
got any loving for me?" One day Josephine's inner city third grade
teacher announces a field trip to the country to see some animals.
They are met by a lady who introduces them to a rabbit, a snake,
a squirrel, and best of all, a raccoon. Josephine is selected to
hold the soft, warm, nice-smelling, inquisitive creature. In her
ear he whispers, "Josie, you got any loving for me?"

23a.   Brooks, Ron. TIMOTHY AND GRAMPA. Scarsdale, N.Y.:
          Bradbury, 1978. Illus. by the author. Unpaged. Grades
          K-2.

          Timothy lives alone with his grandfather in a quaint old
English cottage, but, while he and Gramps are inseparable, fishing,
tramping the countryside, and telling stories to one another, Timothy
is ambivalent about school because of his difficulty in making friends.
One day he brings his grandfather for Show and Tell, but the occasion is awkward and strained. The next time Gramps comes prepared and regales the class with a cracking good story. Timothy's
appreciative classmates beg him for more details about his grandfather's fascinating life of adventure, and in obliging them he
emerges from his shell. The pictures, full of homely detail and
subtle color, are eloquent.

24.   Brown, Fern and Andree Vilas Grabe. WHEN GRANDPA
          WORE KNICKERS. Chicago: Whitman, 1966. Illus. by
          Joe Lasker. Unpaged. Grades 2-4.

Recaptures with droll candor the nostalgic nuances of dress, school and homelife, entertainment, and transportation of the Great Depression from voluminous woolen bathing suits to pullman cars on the train sans plastic and chrome, thermostats and ubiquitous electrical appliances, zippers and miracle fabrics, frozen foods or inflation, antibiotics or novocaine, ballpoint pens or pushbutton telephones, tubeless tires or jet aircraft. "But our world seemed very new and up-to-date to us when we were young. Doesn't your world seem that way to you? Yet your children will probably think how old-fashioned it was when you were little."

25.   Bryan, Ashley. THE DANCING GRANNY. New York: Atheneum, 1977. Illus. by the author. Unpaged. Grades K-3.

West Indian Granny Anika beats a rhythm and swings to it all day long as she industriously tends her vegetable garden. Lazy Spider Ananse knows Granny's penchant for dancing and sees a way to feed his family without lifting a finger. He sings a siren song that Granny can't resist, and as she whirls off to the north, south, east and west, he methodically plunders her plot. When she sees what her gyrations have cost her, she quickly harvests what remains, and when Spider returns to seduce her with song, she draws him into her dance until he is as spellbound as she.

26.   Buckley, Helen E. GRANDFATHER AND I. New York: Lothrop, Lee and Shepard, 1959. Illus. by Paul Galdone. Unpaged. Grades K-1.

Mothers, fathers, brothers and sisters hurry, and so do cars, trains and boats. But "Grandfather and I never hurry. We walk along and walk along and stop ... and look ... just as long as we like." Boy in short pants and his cane-carrying, overcoat-clad grandfather enjoy the intricacies of nature, rain or shine, at leisure. Last page shows that they are capable of hurrying when induced!

27.   Buckley, Helen E. GRANDMOTHER AND I. New York: Lothrop, Lee and Shepard, 1961. Illus. by Paul Galdone. Unpaged. Grades K-1.

While grandfathers walk slowly (see 26), grandmothers rock slowly. Other laps are good for other purposes, but to this small girl, her grandmother's lap is perfect for contemplating things, taking comfort through measles and lightning, and mourning the missing cat. "We sit in the big chair and rock, back and forth, and back and forth. And Grandmother hums little tunes. And her shoes make a soft sound on the floor."

28.   Bunting, Eve. MAGIC AND THE NIGHT RIVER. New York:
         Harper and Row, 1978. Illus. by Allen Say. 44pp.
         Grades 2-4.

         Yoshi and his grandfather catch fish in the traditional
Chinese manner, using domesticated cormorants with rings about
their necks to prevent their swallowing any but small fry. Kano,
who exacts half their catch for rental of his boat, taunts them that
Grandfather is losing his skill, but Yoshi defends him. One night
in the dim torch-light, all the fishing boats collide, and the cords
by which the cormorants are controlled become entangled. Grandfather, who does not want his birds to strangle, releases his, knowing that his livelihood will be over. Miraculously, one bird and
then another returns to the boat because Grandfather has treated
them kindly, but Kano believes it is magic and becomes more respectful. The real magic, thinks Yoshi, is that he and Grandfather
will have many more nights of fishing together.

29.   Burch, Robert. THE JOLLY WITCH. New York: Dutton,
         1975. Illus. by Leigh Grant. 31pp.   Grades 2-3.

         Kind young Cluny is drummed out of her coven and is de-
livered by mistake to a cross old woman who wanted a holly
switch, not a jolly witch, to use on her son, Harmon, in case he
ever acted cheerful. Obviously this is no place for sunny Cluny,
but the old woman grudgingly keeps her to teach her to ride a
broomstick and cook in a caldron. In the meantime, the oppressed
Harmon teaches Cluny to cook on a stove and use her broom for
sweeping, human attributes she has a natural affinity for. When
the woman becomes so proficient on her own broomstick that she
no longer needs Cluny, Cluny lends her her own broom without betraying that it is very headstrong and always makes a beeline for
its home stable. As the old woman disappears over the treetops,
Cluny and Harmon rejoice.

30.   Calhoun, Mary. EUPHONIA AND THE FLOOD. New York:
         Parents, 1976. Illus. by Simms Taback. Unpaged.   Grades
         K-2.

         Gregarious old Euphonia (who does well by every living
thing) believes that anything worth doing is worth doing well, so
when a flood comes up her doorpath, she doesn't stay home hollering for help but goes out to meet it, with her pig Fatly and her
broom Briskly, and to find out where it is rushing to. Along the
way they take in tow a shy skunk, a flock of clucking hens, and a
bashful bear. Before the floodwaters plunge over the falls beyond
Farmer Stump's millpond, they pull for shore where the good farmer
has hospitably spread a feast for man and beast on high ground.

31.   Calhoun, Mary. OLD MAN WHICKUTT'S DONKEY. New

York: Parents, 1975. Illus. by Tomie dePaola. Unpaged.
Grades K-2.

Everyone along the road has gratuitous advice on how Old
Man Whickutt and his boy should load their donkey with a sack of
corn for the trip to the mill, so they wind up by carrying the donkey
and his load between them and succeed only in amusing a wagonload
of revelers. But when they reach the river, they are stymied until
Old Man Whickutt devises the plan of heaving over first the corn,
then the boy and the donkey, and finally himself, and no one gets
wet. "Derned if they did!"

32.   Careme, Maurice. MOTHER RASPBERRY. New York:
Crowell, 1969. Illus. by Marie Wabbes. Unpaged. Grades
K-2.

In the remote house in the woods, old French Mother Raspberry and the village children make raspberry jam all summer long
to last through the winter. One icy morning, the children notice
that Mother Raspberry's chimney is not smoking. Hearing the
bloodcurdling ulalation of Crooked Tail the wolf, they know that
something is terribly amiss. They slog through the darkling forest
and shovel a path to her door, all the while hearing ominous growls
from within. In the bedroom they find the frail woman literally
swathed in fur. Having used the last of her firewood, she has invited her forest friends to share jam and bed. Crooked Tail is at
the foot, snoring from a surfeit of raspberry jam.

33.   Clymer, Eleanor. TAKE TARTS AS TARTS IS PASSING.
New York: Dutton, 1974. Illus. by Roy Doty. Unpaged.
Grades 2-3.

Jeremiah, industrious but unimaginative, and Obadiah, an
artistic dreamer, are sent out into the world to make their fortunes.
Aunt Hattie, the wise old woman of the village, advises them cryp-
tically and enigmatically to "Take tarts as tarts is passing, " as she
puffs at her pipe. Jeremiah passes up opportunities which he feels
are beneath him and, taking Aunt Hattie literally, snatches tarts
from a peddler's cart and lands in jail. Obadiah, following fortune,
succeeds felicitously in painting, music, and matrimony. The
happy-go-lucky brother finds a fortune in fulfillment, while the hapless one blames all his misfortunes on Aunt Hattie.

34.   Cornish, Sam. GRANDMOTHER'S PICTURES. Scarsdale:
Bradbury, 1974. Illus. by Jeanne Johns. Unpaged. Grades
2-3.

Small black boy visits his grandmother in her tenement
rooms, festooned with fly paper, clotheslines, and spider webs, and
observes that "getting older seemed to mean needing more heat. "

He chops wood for her stove, and she chips ice from her icebox
for him.   She loves to sit by the window, and he loves to listen to
her reminiscences.   Endlessly, she clips pictures from the Sunday
paper, and one day she shares her scrapbook with him, explaining
the people and events, often violent or tragic, that are depicted.
The history of his family fascinates him.

34a.   Craft, Ruth. CARRIE HEPPLE'S GARDEN.   New York:
          Atheneum, 1979. Illus. by Irene Haas.   Unpaged.   Grades
          1-3.

          On Midsummer Eve when the westering sun casts long,
eerie shadows across the lawn, a ball belonging to three English
urchins sails over the wall into the garden next door.   "We can't
go in there! Carrie Hepple has a glittering glare and whiskery
hair."   Their active imaginations conjure up fearsome amorphous
wraiths of their elderly neighbor until the smallest conquers her
trepidations, finds a loose board, and crawls through into the somber, murky shade of the rankly overgrown garden.   The ball has
landed at the feet of the intimidating old woman, but she invites
them to have a look at her "curiosities," and they tremulously com-
ply.   She introduces them to her cat and offers them "hermits" to
munch on.   Again, disquieting images titillate their minds until they
discover that hermits are buns.   Safely back on their side of the
gate, the children realize they have left the ball behind, when suddenly, out of the starry darkness, Carrie Hepple lofts it back to
them.

34b.   Cressey, James. FOURTEEN RATS AND A RAT-CATCHER.
          Englewood Cliffs, N. J.: Prentice-Hall, 1976.   Illus. by
          Tamasin Cole.   Unpaged.   Grades K-2.

          In this once-upon-a-time tale, a nice old lady's placid ex-
istence is disrupted by the presence of a droll rat family in her
cellar.   The rodents, in turn, are annoyed at having to share their
accommodations with an obnoxious human and rejoice when the old
lady vacates the premises to go shopping.   She returns with a cat
who soon proves so inept at curbing the rat population that he is
banished in disgrace.   Once again the rats are elated until the old
lady solicits the aid of the town's aging rat-catcher.   The old man
and woman take a shine to one another, but the rats are morose
and hold a council of war to rid themselves of their nemesis.
Rat-catcher and chief rat stalk out to the barn in the dead of night
to negotiate a truce while the old lady sleeps peacefully.   The elderly couple marry, and the rats agree to be quiet as mice.

34c.   DeLage, Ida. THE OLD WITCH'S PARTY.   Champaign,
          Ill.: Garrard, 1976. Illus. by Mimi Korach.   48pp.
          Grades 1-3.

On her way to procure poison ivy for her magic brew, a warty old witch sees school children having a Halloween party and considers it too tame, so she invites them to a party of her own. Mistaking her for Grandma Petticoat in a witch's costume, the children repair to her cave for a display of creepy creatures and games of toadstool on a string, ducking for rotten eggs, and pin the tail on the rattlesnake. When the children perceive that it is a real rattlesnake, they bound in horror from the cave and require a dose of tonic from old Dr. Pinkpill to cure their jitters. Later, while trick-or-treating, they pull malicious mischief on old Mr. Crabtree, and when Grandma Petticoat, dressed as a witch, invites them in to her party, they recoil in terror. Several other "Old Witch" stories perpetuate this insensitive attempt at humor.

34d.   dePaola, Tomie. BIG ANTHONY AND THE MAGIC RING. New York: Harcourt, Brace, Jovanovich, 1979. Illus. by the author. Unpaged. Grades 2-3.

Because Big Anthony is moping about with spring fever, Strega Nona (see 37) prescribes a little Night Life. The suggestion gives her an idea, and she rummages for her magic ring, intones her incantation, and is transformed into a beautiful and elegant lady who trips off to dance the night away. Big Anthony, observing with awe, snatches the first opportunity to change himself into a handsome swain. It works like a charm, and soon he is surrounded by adoring damsels. When he grows tired of dancing, he tries to reverse the spell but finds that the ring is stuck on his finger. Panicky, he is relentlessly pursued by his bevy of inamorate until Strega Nona delivers him. To his dismay, only the baker's homely daughter still finds oafish Big Anthony attractive.

35.   dePaola, Tomie. NANA UPSTAIRS AND NANA DOWNSTAIRS. New York: Putnam, 1973. Illus. by the author. Unpaged. Grades K-2.

Every Sunday, Tommy, 4, visits his grandmother, who is usually busy in the kitchen, and his 94-year-old great-grandmother, who is bedridden upstairs, but he spends most of his time with Nana Upstairs. She shares mints with him, tells him allegorical stories, and when she is tied into a chair by Nana Downstairs so she won't fall out, Tommy asks to be tied into a chair also. One day his mother tells him that Nana Upstairs has died, and he runs up to find her bed empty. A few nights later the grieving boy sees a falling star, and his mother suggests it is a kiss from Nana Upstairs. Many years later when he is grown and his other grandmother has died, Tommy sees another falling star and thinks, "Now you are both Nana Upstairs."

36.   dePaola, Tomie. PANCAKES FOR BREAKFAST. New York: Harcourt, Brace, Jovanovich, 1978. Unpaged. Grades K-2.

An old woman arises at the break of dawn with appetizing thoughts of pancakes for breakfast. She reads the recipe, collects eggs, milks the cows, and laboriously churns the butter. She trudges through snow to buy maple syrup, occupying her thoughts with visions of mixing, baking, and eating the steaming cakes. Her gustatory dreams go aglimmering when she returns to find that the cat and dog have demolished the assembled ingredients. As she contemplates the disaster, an aroma wafts through the door. She follows it across the way where startled neighbors accept their unexpected breakfast guest at a pancake feast. The only words in this picture story are the recipe and a sampler admonishing, "If at first you don't succeed, try, try again."

37.   dePaola, Tomie. STREGA NONA. Englewood Cliffs: Prentice-Hall, 1975. Illus. by the author. Unpaged. Grades K-1.

Strega Nona or "Grandma Witch" is a fixture in her Calabrian town where even the priest and nuns consult her. When she advertises for help, Big Anthony applies for the job. One day he sees her singing incantations over the cooking pot and witnesses the astonishing materialization of pasta. Seeing his chance to impress the villagers, Big Anthony ignores Strega Nona's instructions not to touch the pot when she goes out of town. The townspeople's admiration turns to alarm when Big Anthony cannot discourage the pot from engulfing the village in pasta. Strega Nona returns to save the day, but Big Anthony's punishment is to clear the town of surplus pasta--by eating every strand. (In BIG ANTHONY AND THE MAGIC RING, he again tampers with Strega Nona's magic and lives to regret it.)

38.   dePaola, Tomie. WATCH OUT FOR THE CHICKEN FEET IN YOUR SOUP. Englewood Cliffs: Prentice-Hall, 1974. Illus. by the author. Unpaged. Recipe. Grades K-2.

Raven-haired Joey takes his blond, bespectacled friend to visit his plump Italian grandmother, warning him that she cooks a lot and talks oddly. Eugene is disconcerted when she mispronounces his name and serves him soup with chicken anatomy in it, but when she brings on the spaghetti, his favorite, his attitude alters. His appreciation is ingratiating, and she invites him to help her make braided bread dolls, while a disgruntled Joey is left stewing over his pasta. Joey is placated when she gives him the fanciest doll, and they both depart declaring their love for Joey's grandma.

39.   Dillon, Eilis. THE WISE OLD MAN ON THE MOUNTAIN. New York: Atheneum, 1969. Illus. by Gaynor Chapman. Unpaged. Grades 3-4.

A poor farmer with wife and ten children is unhappy with

his hand-to-mouth subsistence and consults the wise man on the
mountain for relief.   The old guru demonstrates graphically that
nothing is so bad it can't be worse by directing the farmer to bring
his three beasts, a donkey, a cow, and a goat, into the already
overcrowded house for a month.   When the animals are removed
one by one, the house seems larger, cleaner, and more restful by
comparison.   The family discovers satisfaction and even contentment.

40.   Eisenberg, Phyllis Rose.   A MITZVAH IS SOMETHING
         SPECIAL.   New York: Harper, 1978.   Illus. by Susan
         Jeschke.   30pp.   Grades 2-3.

         Lisa's Grandma Esther is ample of hip and bosom, calls
Lisa Bubeleh or "little grandmother, " loves to cook and quilt, had
a model husband, now deceased, and has four gold fillings, one of
which she acquired when Lisa's father was a baby.   A neighbor
volunteered to keep the infant so that she could go to the dentist,
a good deed and great blessing that Grandma Esther calls a mitzvah.
Lisa's maternal grandmother, Dorrie, calls her Cookie Pie, although she hates to cook; wears tinted contacts, slacks and platform
shoes; has two wigs; plays the flute; had an unstable husband, whereabouts unknown; and now has a male companion.   One evening when
her parents go out, Lisa invites her divergent grandmothers to spend
the night, and a memorable mitzvah is had by all.

41.   Ets, Marie Hall.   MISTER PENNY.   New York: Viking,
         1935.   Illus. by the author.   46pp.   Grades 2-3.

         Patient Mr. Penny works day in, day out at the safety pin
factory in the village of Wuddle to support his menage of lazy barn-
yard animals.   One day in his absence, they wriggle through a
broken gate and gorge on the neighbor's garden.   The irate and vindictive neighbor demands usurious reparation from Mr. Penny or
the confiscation of his beloved beasts.   Limpy the horse overhears
his master's despair and marshalls his fellow sluggards to perform
clandestinely the tasks demanded of Mr. Penny.   The humble old
man at first believes it is the work of fairies, and is incredulous
and overjoyed when he learns otherwise.   The animals, meanwhile,
discover that the virtue of the work ethic is its own reward and continue toiling for Mr. Penny alone, who is finally able to retire with
pride and build a fine new house to replace their sagging shack.

42.   Ets, Marie Hall.   MISTER PENNY'S RACE HORSE.   New
         York: Viking, 1956.   Illus. by the author.   63pp.   Grades
         2-3.

         With his "family's" help, Mr. Penny's garden prospers (see
41), and he decides to enter his produce and animals at the fair.
The goat and rooster, curious about the competition, leave their pens
during the night, wreaking havoc among the pavilions, bringing dis-

grace to Mr. Penny, and dashing their own hopes for a ferris wheel ride. Mr. Penny loads them into the two-wheeled cart for the ride home, but Limpy the horse thinks the cart resembles a sulky and, with a flair for comedy, decides to enter the harness races to the amusement of the crowds. The fair director signs Limpy to a contract on the spot, vindicates Mr. Penny, and treats them all to a ferris wheel ride to generate additional publicity.

43.   Ets, Marie Hall. MISTER PENNY'S CIRCUS. New York: Viking, 1961. Illus. by the author. 64pp. Grades 1-3.

Two runaway circus animals seek asylum from benevolent Mr. Penny who vows to return to work in the safety pin factory (see 41) so he can buy them on installment. The circus owner demurs but agrees to let Mr. Penny board them for the winter. Susie, the chimp, and Olaf, the bear, quickly teach Mr. Penny's barnyard pets all their tricks, enabling Mr. Penny to open a two-penny backyard circus of his own. When the county fair director (see 42) gets wind of it, he buys the act outright to make his the biggest little fair in the country, and Mr. Penny adds two permanent members to his family.

44.   Farber, Norma. WHERE'S GOMER? New York: Dutton, 1974. Illus. by William Pene duBois. Unpaged. Grades K-2.

Mischievous, insouciant Gomer, Noah's favorite grandson, Japheth's boy, misses the boat, and the family, dressed in nineteenth century nautical attire for the outing, grieves for the hapless chap. But waiting to greet them as they disembark at Ararat is none other than Gomer, who has ridden out the Flood on the back of a dolphin. Grandpa Noah and Gomer dance a hornpipe.

45.   Fassler, Joan. MY GRANDPA DIED TODAY. New York: Human Sciences, 1971. Illus. by Stuart Kranz. Unpaged. Grades K-3.

A boy's grandfather teaches him to play checkers, build models, and bat a ball, but one day they take a long, slow walk, and Grandpa explains that he is growing very old and cannot live forever. Enigmatically he says that he is not afraid to die, because he knows his grandson is not afraid to live. Two days later, the old gentleman passes away peacefully in his rocking chair, and the house becomes one of mourning. The boy discovers a "funny, empty, scary, rumbly kind of feeling" at the bottom of his stomach and sheds some tears. To escape the grieving adults, he plays quiet games in his room, and when a friend asks him to play ball, he goes out and hits a grand slam homerun. Suddenly he understands what Grandpa meant. He knew that the boy would have many more hits and plenty of growing and living ahead of him. The rumbles in his stomach disappear.

46.   Flora, James. GRANDPA'S FARM. New York: Harcourt, Brace and World, 1964. Illus. by the author. Unpaged. Grades 1-3.

The Big Wind of '34 that blew Grandpa's bushy eyebrows down to his chin also wafted in the big blue barn that broke off the cow's tail, but Grandma's growing salve grew the cow a new tail and raised a new cow on the stump of the old tail. It also husbanded a colossal pig who didn't fare too well the Terrible Winter of '36 when even the flames of the Christmas tree candles froze. Luckily, they kept Hatchy Hen indoors that winter, for she went on to hatch out new clothes from buttons and thread and an automobile and tractor from a spark plug and steering wheel. She even saved the farm from fire by hatching firehose from spaghetti.

47.   Flora, James. GRANDPA'S GHOST STORIES. New York: Atheneum, 1978. Illus. by the author. Unpaged. Grades 1-3.

When the thunder roars and the lightning blazes and Grandpa's house creaks and groans, grandson allows himself to be titillated by Grandpa's tales of how, in his youth, he obligingly assembled a bag of bones, only to have the skeleton chase him for dinner. Taking refuge in a witch's cave, he was shocked to be turned into a loathsome spider. He was rescued, unfortunately, by a disembodied hand belonging to a sanguinary witch who watched ghoul TV. And when he was devoured whole by her pet werewolf, he luckily found the first witch's magic wishbone in his pocket and used it to return home where he found his grandson on his knee. He proffers the wishbone to the boy who steels himself to try it one day.

48.   Flory, Jane. THE UNEXPECTED GRANDCHILDREN. Boston: Houghton Mifflin, 1977. Illus. by Carolyn Croll. 31pp. Grades K-3.

A meticulous and stolid childless old couple are puzzled to receive a letter announcing the imminent arrival of their "unexpected grandchildren," but they make preparations nonetheless. When no one arrives, they realize that the letter was delivered to the wrong address, but instead of feeling relieved, they are curiously disappointed. They advertise for borrowed grandchildren, and Mr. Newton goes outside to find out why no one comes. A boy on a trike gets the surprise of his life when Mr. Newton says "Hi" instead of "Get off my grass." He spreads the word of the metamorphosis and soon the house is teeming with boisterous tots who promise to return the following week. The house is a mess, but "we've got until next Saturday to get it straightened up." They are bursting with love.

49.   Ga'g, Wanda. MILLIONS OF CATS. New York: Coward-
        McCann, 1928. Illus. by the author. Unpaged. Grades
        K-1.

        The very old couple live comfortably in their small, neat
cottage, but they are lonely and want a cat.   The old man searches
over hill and dale till he comes upon a hill that is virtually covered
with cats.   It is impossible to select just one, so he adopts the lot
who follow him home, draining a pond and denuding a hill of grass
in their collective hunger and thirst.   Realizing they cannot keep
them all, the old couple ask the cats to determine among themselves which is prettiest, and in the ensuing donnybrook the cats
literally eat each other up.   The dismayed couple peep out to find
only one lean, scraggly kitten left whose homeliness saved it from
the fate of the others.   With doting care, the kitten turns into the
world's most beautiful cat.   They should know; they have seen
"hundreds of cats, thousands of cats, millions and billions and tril-
lions of cats."

50.   Gauch, Patricia Lee. GRANDPA AND ME. New York:
        Coward, McCann and Geoghegan, 1972. Illus. by Symeon
        Shimin. Unpaged. Grades K-2.

        The boy and his grandfather like summertime best, for
every year they spend the idyllic months in solitude at their cottage
on the Great Lakes. Alone with the freighters and gulls, they explore
the beach, skip stones, and build castles in the morning calm.   In
the heat of the afternoon they play quiet games or roam the wooded
trails, then watch from the porch as summer thunderstorms march
across the lake.   At dusk they drift in their rowboat, fishing and
watching the stars come out.   At the end of the day they swap
stories in the dark to the lulling serenade of crickets, lapping waves,
and haunting freighter horns.

51.   Gilbert, Helen Earle. MR. PLUM AND THE LITTLE
        GREEN TREE. New York: Abingdon, 1946. Illus. by
        Margaret Bradfield. Unpaged. Grades 2-3.

        Mr. Plum looks up from his cobbling to rest his eyes on
the little green tree in its tiny oasis at the confluence of bustling
city streets.   He crosses in winter to shake heavy snow from its
limbs; in summer to water its roots.   When men from the public
works department arrive to cut it down, Mr. Plum's dander is up.
He takes a taxi to city hall and with mounting trepidation confronts
the mayor.   Hizzoner is out of sorts because of an ill-fitting shoe
which plucky Mr. Plum fixes on the spot because he forgot to remove his conveniently equipped cobbler's apron when he left home
in haste.   Humor restored, the mayor rescinds the tree-felling
order and sends another crew to cultivate the burgeoning sapling.

52.   Gilchrist, Theo E.   HALFWAY UP THE MOUNTAIN.   Philadelphia: Lippincott, 1978.   Illus. by Glen Rounds.   47pp.
Grades 1-3.

The old woman doesn't mind that her husband is halt, and
the old man is not disturbed by his wife's blindness except that she
never varies their menu of strongly seasoned beef.   One night a
notorious bandit blunders down their mountain, evicts them from
their hovel, and falls into a drunken stupor on top of the still-warm
stove.   Wakening in the cowshed in the morning, the old woman
absent-mindedly begins her morning routine, reaching by touch and
smell for the seasonings to treat the mound of "beef" on the stove.
The startled bandit believes the devil himself is after him and exits
rapidly, leaving his gold behind.   The old woman invites her husband to buy some chicken or pork with it, but the thankful old man
embraces his wife and tells her "there are worse things then beef."

53.   Godden, Rumer.   THE OLD WOMAN WHO LIVED IN A
VINEGAR BOTTLE.   New York: Viking, 1972.   Illus. by
Mairi Hedderwick.   Unpaged.   Grades 2-3.

Subsisting cozily with her cat, Malt, in her tall, round,
conical-roofed cottage by the lake, the little old woman is nevertheless frequently hungry.   Finding a silver sixpence, she decides to
treat them to a bit of fish.   The tiny fish she buys is still alive;
she cannot bear to eat it and throws it back into the lake.   The
grateful fish rises from the water to reveal that he is prince of
the lake and will grant any wish she desires.   She can think of
nothing but a good hot meal which she requests humbly and apolo-
getically.   During the night a storm buffets the odd abode, and in
the morning she asks for a new one.   Of course, her old furnishings
are too shabby for the fine new house, and one request leads to another until she has a grand wardrobe, a smart maid, and a fancy
conveyance.   With each request she grows more imperious and de-
manding, and Malt grows more bewildered and alienated.   The little
fish finally loses patience on her churlish command for a chauffeur
and instantly withdraws his largesse.   The contrite old woman begs
his forgiveness, and he graciously grants her timid petition for a
good hot meal once in a while.

54.   Goffstein, M. B.   FISH FOR SUPPER.   New York: Dial,
1976.   Illus. by the author.   Unpaged.   Grades K-1.

This grandmother sports slacks and lives for fishing, rising
at 5:00 a.m. and whisking through the breakfast dishes to do so.
Armed with all the tools of the trade, she spends all day on the
lake, coming home to clean and fry the fish and prepare for the
next day's angling--in complete solitude.

55.   Goffstein, M. B.   MY NOAH'S ARK.   New York: Harper

and Row, 1978. Illus. by the author. Unpaged. Grades
K-2.

A nonagenarian reminisces over a hand-carved ark her
father made for her, "his voice ... booming like God's: 'Make it
three hundred cubits long.'" She removes each piece, two by two,
Noah carrying a hammer and mop, Mrs. Noah brandishing a saw,
and the small gray horse looking so sad that she strokes the paint
off it as a child but for its two "grateful"-looking eyes. She recalls how her husband teased her about preserving the toy but how
tenderly he carried it to their new home. When her children were
born she used the ark to teach them Noah's story, and now that
they are grown, the ark holds a rainbow of memories that warm
her like sunshine.

56.   Goldman, Susan. GRANDMA IS SOMEBODY SPECIAL.
        Chicago: Whitman, 1976. Illus. by the author. Unpaged.
        Grades K-2.

A cute, bespectacled redhead visits her working grandmother's apartment and gets to sleep on a rollaway cot in Grandma's
room, peruse old photo albums, order her favorite meal, take
Grandma at cards, and be babied a little bit. Grandma, a widow,
even shows her where she takes classes and tells the story of when
she dumped noodles on Grandpa's head during an argument.

56a.   Goldman, Susan. GRANDPA AND ME TOGETHER. Chi-
        cago: Whitman, 1980. Illus. by the author. Unpaged.
        Grades K-2.

This retired grandfather is always the first one up in the
morning, and when his preschool granddaughter Katherine comes to
visit, he sings her a good morning song and together they squeeze
orange juice for breakfast. While Grandma attends an art show,
Grandpa and Katherine drive downtown to his old appliance store
where the new management asks his advice while Katherine types
him a love letter. After they root their home team to victory at
the ball park, Grandpa shows her a picture of himself in the uniform of his college baseball team and teaches her its fight song.
When Grandpa comments that she is growing, Katherine asks if she
can attend his alma mater; after all, she already knows the song!

57.   Hader, Berta and Elmer Hader. THE BIG SNOW. New
        York: Macmillan, 1948. Illus. by the authors. Unpaged.
        Grades 1-3.

The furred and feathered folk of field and forest observe
the wild geese winging south and instinctively forage food for weather-
ing the winter. On the night after Christmas, a silent snowfall
buries meadow and wood so deeply that when its denizens burrow

free, they search in vain for their food caches.   As the sun rises,
the elderly couple in the stone house shovel a path from their snow-
banked door and scatter seed, nuts, and grain for their hungry wild
neighbors.   The weather remains severe, and the groundhog wakes
in February to see his shadow, prognosticating another six weeks of
winter, but the old couple sustain them all, small and large, winged
and earthbound, throughout the Big Snow.

58.   Harris, Audrey.   WHY DID HE DIE?   Minneapolis: Lerner,
        1965.   Illus. by Susan Sallade Dalke.   Unpaged.   Grades
        K-3.

        Jim's grandfather has just passed away.   There is lots of
sad company at his house, and he cannot come out to play.   His
friend Scott asks his own mom if that means that Jim's granddad
died.   In a quiet, pastoral setting, mother and son hold a simple
dialogue in verse to plumb the complexities of death and rebirth.
"All things, machines, plants, animals/And human beings, too, /
Rust, or decay, or die and pass away. /These changes happen all
the time, /All life flows on, it cannot stay. "   Spring leaves replace autumn leaves, and like leaves, old, old people must die
someday, but new babies are born instead.   Mother explains that
the worn out body cannot be repaired but rests peacefully in a
cemetery park with flowers and trees.   She reassures Scott that
she and father will not die soon.   Jim is sad because he misses
his grandfather, but his happy memories of him will never die.
And then one day, "Jim just called and asked if he/Could come
and spend the day. /He won't forget his Granddad, /But now it's
time to play!"

59.   Hirsh, Marilyn.   THE RABBI AND THE TWENTY-NINE
        WITCHES, A TALMUDIC LEGEND.   New York: Holiday
        House, 1976.   Illus. by the author.   Unpaged.   Grades
        K-2.

        When an old woman expresses the desire to see the full
moon once in her life before she dies, the wise rabbi devises a
plan for ridding the village of the cave full of witches that bedevils
them in monthly sorties carried out when the weather is dry.   Em-
ploying the bravest men of the village, he sets out in the rain for
the witch cave.   There he tricks the malevolent crones into coming
out into the drizzle where they melt clean away.   The old woman
and the villagers feast their eyes on the full moon at long last.

60.   Hoff, Syd.   MY AUNT ROSIE.   New York: Harper and
        Row, 1972.   Illus. by the author.   32pp.   Grades K-2.

        Sherman hates to visit his old Aunt Rosie because she
makes such an unwarranted fuss over his modest achievements.
Even her cakes and cookies and presents when it's not his birthday

do not curry favor with him.   He is anxious to leave and loath to
return.   One day his parents go to visit Aunt Rosie without him.
At first he revels in his freedom, but then he realizes he is missing
something.   No one else makes him feel so special.   When he asks
why his parents don't take him along any longer, he discovers that
she has been ill and doesn't want to worry him.   He suddenly knows
that if he ever lost Aunt Rosie, things just wouldn't be the same.
"Well, what are we waiting for?" says Sherman.   "Let's go see
Aunt Rosie. "

61.   Holl, Adelaide.   THE WONDERFUL TREE, A STORY OF
           THE SEASONS.   New York: Golden, 1974.   Illus. by
           Gyorgy Lehoczky.   Unpaged.   Grades 2-4.

           On a chill autumn's day, Grandfather gives Christopher a
fragrant roasted apple and tells him that its seed will grow only
apple trees, not pears like their own.   They wake the following
morning to a mantle of snow on the ground, and Grandfather reminisces of sleigh rides and boyhood Christmases.   He explains why
spring is the most celebrated of all the seasons.   When Christopher
opines that summer is not long enough, Grandfather tells him that
it is just long enough to carry out nature's plan.   Christopher observes that autumn always follows summer.   He glances out the
window and envisions the pear tree as it appears in each season.

61a.   Holmes, Efner Tudor.   CARRIE'S GIFT.   New York: Col-
           lins and World, 1978.   Illus. by Tasha Tudor.   Unpaged.
           Grades 2-4.

           Old Duncan, the recluse who communes with the woodland
creatures, has always lived in the overgrown house across the field
from Carrie's family's farm, and she and her brother sometimes
try to spy on him unsuccessfully from behind the low wall.   One
day Carrie catches him unawares near the stream and is stricken
by his look of loneliness, but he takes umbrage at her friendly
overtures.   The following day, however, he diffidently directs her
to a wild strawberry patch, and she gratefully makes him a plate
of strawberry shortcake.   Before she can deliver it, though, her
dog Heidi steps into a hunter's cruel trap and becomes frenzied
with pain.   Old Duncan deftly releases Heidi and ministers to her
hurts.   Impulsively, Carrie kisses him and runs home.   It is only
then that Duncan discovers the culinary tribute and partakes of it,
lost in thought.

62.   Howells, Mildred.   THE OLD WOMAN WHO LIVED IN
           HOLLAND.   New York: Farrar, Straus and Giroux, 1973.
           Illus. by William Curtis Holdsworth.   Unpaged.   Grades
           K-1.

           An old Dutch woman with wooden shoes and winged cap has

a mania for scrubbing everything in sight, but when she polishes
the features off the children's faces and the weather vane off the
church steeple, the townsfolk grow alarmed.   One night a wild wind
whisks her from her gleaming doorstep into the sky where she is
busy to this day making the stars sparkle, but the neighbors still
"fear she may rub so hard they will disappear. "

63.   Hutchins, Pat. HAPPY BIRTHDAY SAM.   New York:
         Greenwillow, 1978. Illus. by the author.   Unpaged.
         Grades K-1.

         On the morning of Sam's birthday, he tries but fails to
reach the light switch in his room, the hooks in his closet, and
the taps in the bathroom basin.   His parents give him a toy sail-
boat, but he is still too short to sail it in the kitchen sink.   Then
a package arrives from Grandpa containing a toddler-sized chair.
Climbing on it, Sam turns on his bedroom light, dresses himself,
brushes his teeth, sails his new boat, and when Grandpa arrives
for his party, Sam uses his gift to reach the doorknob and admit
him--all by himself.

64.   Jackson, Louise A.   GRANDPA HAD A WINDMILL, GRAND-
         MA HAD A CHURN.   New York: Parents, 1977.   Illus.
         by George Ancona.   Unpaged.   Grades K-2.

         To a little Texas girl of the 1940's, the fascinations of
farm life include Grandpa's windmill, whetstone, corn crib, goldfish pond, chopping block and gold watch.   Grandma's domain includes her silver thimble, clear glass churn, cold cellar, guinea
fowl, quilting frame and friendship ring.   At night when work is
done, Grandpa plays his fiddle and Grandma plays her piano while
the girl sings.   Nostalgically photographed.

65.   Jarrell, Mary. THE KNEE-BABY.   New York: Farrar,
         Straus and Giroux, 1973. Illus. by Symeon Shimin.   Un-
         paged.   Grades K-2.

         Alan has his own small rocking chair, but, on the verge
of tears, longs for a lap to sit on.   His mother's is occupied with
the new baby, daddy's is at work, and Mam-mommy's is way down
South.   While Mama tends Baby Bee, she and Alan, at her knee,
imagine what Mam-mommy must be doing just then: making her
deep knee bends, dabbing scent behind her ears, feeding the cat and
the wild birds, even writing a letter to a little boy.   One day she
will come and hold him on her lap, but right now, after nap time,
it is Alan's turn to sit on Mama's lap and rock on and on.

66.   Jeschke, Susan. THE DEVIL DID IT.   New York: Holt,
         Rinehart and Winston, 1975. Illus. by the author.   Un-
         paged.   Grades K-2.

When told by her mother that the snarls in her hair are caused by the devil, preschool Nana wakes in the middle of the night to find a real and very frightening pointed-eared, long-nailed, long-tailed, horned and hirsute devil sharing her room. A stubborn and nettlesome creature, all his diabolical pranks are blamed on Nana. Only her grandmother believes the imp is real, though, alas, the devil-catching bottle she gives Nana proves ineffective. Eventually Nana grows used to him and learns to ignore his satanic tricks. When she finally turns the tables on the demon and begins to out-devil him, her tormentor leaves in high dudgeon over the roof tops. As she explains on Grandma's lap that he is gone, Grandma replies, "... that's how they are. They come and go, come and go. "

67.   Jeschke, Susan. MIA, GRANDMA AND THE GENIE. New York: Holt, Rinehart and Winston, 1978. Illus. by the author. Unpaged. Grades K-2.

Grandma is respectful of all nature and every inanimate object in her peasant cottage, but Mia thinks it is silly to apologize to the table for spilling tea on it. Grandma also talks to her genie friend, though Mia has never seen him. One day her grandmother is hospitalized, and Mia, lonely, sets off to visit her, taking the genie jar along to cheer Grandma. Alone in the woods that night, she lifts the lid of the jar and the genie materializes to keep her company. The following night she encounters two ruffians who have just stolen her grandmother's meager furnishings. When they try to wrest the genie jar from her, the kitchen chair trips one of them and the genie looms threateningly to frighten the other. Mia reaches the hospital just as her grandmother is being discharged, and to-gether they bless the sun and thank their inanimate possessions.

68.   Jewell, Nancy. BUS RIDE. New York: Harper and Row, 1978. Illus. by Ronald Himler. 32pp. Grades K-3.

Janie's parents put her on the bus in the city for the night ride to Grandpa's home in the country, ensuring that she has a mel-low elderly seat companion to look after her. Mrs. Rivers eases the qualms of departure by sharing her handkerchief and orange. Together they admire the city lights mirrored in the shimmering river. Janie shares her dinner and then investigates the tiny, bouncing bathroom. They nap together, but Mrs. Rivers wakes her in time to see the moonlit countryside. When the bus reaches Grandpa's stop, Janie is almost torn between going with him and staying with Mrs. Rivers. They promise to meet again on the bus.

69.   Kaye, Geraldine. THE YELLOW POM-POM HAT. Chicago: Childrens, 1976. Illus. by Margaret Palmer. 24pp. Grades K-1.

Gran, who hasn't been well but who likes to be useful,

comes for Easter, bringing her knitting.   It turns out to be a large, floppy yellow hat for Jane.   Jane hates it, and her playmates think she looks like a chicken.   She throws it into a tree, but a boy re-trieves it.   She buries it in the garden, but the dog digs it up. In desperation she snips off the tassel and cuts three holes in the hat.   Now her recuperating grandmother is upset.   Dad saves the day by slipping it over the teapot and calling it a cozy.   Grand-mother promises to knit Jane a red hat for Christmas, but then, Christmas is a long way off.

70.   Kennedy, Richard.   COME AGAIN IN THE SPRING.   New
             York: Harper and Row, 1976.   Illus. by Marcia Sewall.
             47pp.   Grades 1-3.

        When Death with his inexorable ledger comes to call on Old Hark, the laconic old man is too busy making winter preparations for his feathered friends to be bothered to submit.   Death, a bureau-crat of the first water, is annoyed and considers administering Hark a violent end but has to go by the book which ordains "means of de-parture" as "quiet, gentle, peaceful. "   With Machiavellian cunning he tries to outwit Old Hark into putting 'paid' to his life, but the old man's faithful birds keep him one step ahead of the Grim Reaper whose frustration mounts as Hark goes purposefully about his chores. Then Death asks one final question which even the birds can't answer, and suddenly Hark feels hopeless and spent and takes to his bed docilely.   Just as Death is about to gloat over his apparent victory, Hark's old spirit returns for an instant and he blurts the very words the old vulture doesn't want to hear, "Open the window.   Let the birds sing. "   Death stalks off in high dudgeon, and Old Hark bounds from bed with a new lease on life.

70a.   Kirk, Barbara.   GRANDPA, ME AND OUR HOUSE IN THE
             TREE.   New York: Macmillan, 1978.   Illus. by the author.
             Unpaged.   Grades K-3.

        In this photo story, a young boy and his robust grandfather enjoy romping with the dog, playing ball, tilling a garden, and build-ing a tree house.   Later, the boy is stunned by his father's sober news that Grandpa has been very ill and his speech and motor co-ordination impaired.   He wonders if they will ever have fun again, recalling that when his grandmother went to the hospital he never saw her again.   His mother brings Grandpa home looking frail and wan.   For many days he does nothing but sleep while the boy mopes. Then one day he confides that the boy is now the chief contractor on their construction project, while he is now the consultant, and when he gains sufficient strength, the two sally forth slowly to rig a tin can telephone between tree house and ground control.

71.   Knotts, Howard.   GREAT-GRANDFATHER, THE BABY AND
             ME.   New York: Atheneum, 1978.   Illus. by the author.
             30pp.   Grades K-3.

A small farm boy is apprehensive when his father announces he is going to bring Mommy and his new baby sister home from the hospital, because he is uncomfortable with strangers.   Great-grandfather alleviates his fears by telling him of the summer when he was a boy of 16 harvesting wheat in Canada.   One of the memorable events in that wide, empty country was an arduous ride to a distant house to pay a call on a new baby who anticlimactically slept through the ceremonious occasion.   Great-grandfather and great-grandson go out hand-in-hand to greet the new baby.

71a.   Langner, Nola.   FREDDY MY GRANDFATHER.   New York: Four Winds, 1979.   Illus. by the author.   Unpaged.   Grades 2-3.

To his small granddaughter, Freddy seems remarkably youthful.   Hungarian-born, his pronunciations are odd, but his meanings are unmistakable.   A retired tailor, he still makes coats especially for her.   He likes to tease but only playfully.   His room in her parents' house smells of cigars and lemons.   There he teaches himself Spanish through newspapers and radio.   Freddy sometimes angers his daughter by staying out late or taking his granddaughter to a Hungarian restaurant where there is music and dancing into the night.   They also enjoy visiting his many friends.   Blizzards and thunderstorms don't daunt him at all.   In the sanctuary of Freddy's room, his granddaughter is ensconced in love and security.

71b.   Lapp, Eleanor J.   IN THE MORNING MIST.   Chicago: Whitman, 1978.   Illus. by David Cunningham.   Unpaged. Grades K-2.

The grandfather wakes the boy at daybreak to catch trout for breakfast.   Hand in hand they float through billows of aqueous mist, while ghostly apple trees, sheep and horses loom eerily as they cross orchard, pasture and meadow.   A dead elm is festooned with lacy spiderwebs beaded with dewy diamonds.   They remark on blue jays, salamanders, mushrooms and deer as they move through the woods in the muffling fog.   At the trout pool they flush a great blue heron, and Grandfather lands three beautiful fish.   Returning home past the barn, the mist starts to lift, and finally the sun burns through.

72.   Lasky, Kathryn.   I HAVE FOUR NAMES FOR MY GRANDFATHER.   Boston: Little, Brown, 1976.   Illus. by Christopher G. Knight.   46pp.   Grades K-1.

Tom alternately calls his grandfather Poppy, Pop, Grandpa or Gramps, but he's always the same grandfather to Tom, and a photogenic one, too.   Because he is bald, he owns hats for fun, sun, snow and show.   Tom is as tall as Poppy's pocket, and his shoe is the size of his hand, but Gramps' nose is as long as Tom's

finger. They run, fish, hammer, plant, make funny faces, and
visit the railroad museum together.   When Tom is mad or bad, he
always calls Pop for understanding.   And when he is sad, Grandpa
hugs him close and says, "I love you, Tom. "

72a.   Lasky, Kathryn. MY ISLAND GRANDMA. New York:
            Warne, 1979. Illus. by Emily McCully. Unpaged. Grades
            2-3.

        Grandma's hands, strong from unshuttering her cabin win-
dows each June, digging her summer garden, pumping water from
the well, and carrying logs for the stove, hold her granddaughter
Abbey securely while she learns to swim.   Together they go beach
combing, berrying, and sailing, concocting stories suggested by the
shifting cloud formations.   At night they search for the star pictures
of constellations, and on rainy days they make moss dish gardens
and moon cookies.   All winter long when Grandma wears the trappings
of a cosmopolite, Abbey thinks of her as her Island Grandma and
associates her with all the happy memories of summer in Maine.

73.   Lawson, Robert. THEY WERE STRONG AND GOOD. New
            York: Viking, 1940. Illus. by the author. Unpaged.
            Grades 2-4.

        Author/illustrator romanticizes his proud and colorful fore-
bears from his maternal grandparents, a Scottish sea captain and a
New Jersey Dutch girl, to his Minnesota-born, convent-educated
mother.   He traces his paternal lineage from his fiery Indian-fighter-
turned-evangelist grandfather to his staunch and battle-scarred Con-
federate father.

74.   Lenski, Lois. DAVY GOES PLACES. New York: Walck,
            1961. Illus. by the author. 47pp. Music. Grades K-1.

        Davy's means of locomotion include tricycle, wagon and
scooter, but one day Daddy takes him by car to the railroad station
to travel by train, taxi, bus and truck to Grandpa's house in the
country.   There he rides a horse, a goat-drawn cart, a tractor, a
hay wagon, and a wheelbarrow.   And on a special outing, Grandpa
takes him on boat and airplane rides.   "Davy liked this the best of
all!"

75.   Lexau, Joan M. BENJIE. New York: Dial, 1964. Illus.
            by Don Bolognese. Unpaged. Grades K-2.

        Benjie is the most bashful boy his black Granny has ever
seen, and she despairs of him when he starts school in a few weeks.
He hates to talk to anyone, and always peeks to see if the coast is
clear before venturing outside the door alone.   He is especially

intimidated by the formidable bakery lady.   One day after church,
Granny loses one of her keepsake earrings.   While she is napping,
he goes out to search for it again, remembering that nobody looked
in the bakery where they stopped after church.   He slips in the
back room while the bakery lady is engaged, but when she discovers
him, he is compelled to explain his mission to prevent her from
calling the police.   Then she even helps him sift through the trash
till the earring is found.   Granny is overjoyed to get it back but
notes with a twinkle that something else is missing: his bashfulness.

76.   Lexau, Joan M.   BENJIE ON HIS OWN.   New York: Dial,
           1970.   Illus. by Don Bolognese.   Unpaged.   Grades K-2.

          When Benjie's grandmother (see 75) is not there to meet
him after school as usual, he is concerned about her but not sure
he can find his way home alone through the ghetto streets.   He is
chased by a dog and accosted by teenage toughs but finally arrives
home to find her desperately ill.   Resourcefully, he calls for an
ambulance from the police emergency box.   He doesn't want to leave
her alone while he waits outside to guide the ambulance team but has
no one to turn too.   Finally in desperation he yells, "HELP!   Please
somebody HELP!"   At last the impassive neighborhood rallies 'round,
and helping hands reassure Granny that he will be well cared for
while she is in the hospital.

76a.   Lexau, Joan M.   I HATE RED ROVER.   New York: Dut-
           ton, 1979.   Illus. by Gail Owens.   56pp.   Grades 2-3.

          Jill is smaller and less aggressive than her classmates and
hates to be ridiculed for her impotence when they all play Red Rover
at recess.   She confides her humiliation to her grandfather who returns the confidence by telling her he is to have all his teeth ex-
tracted and is also afraid of derision.   His fortitude encourages her
to hold the line when her team is on defense and eventually to breach
the opposing line on offense, and when Grandpa sports his new teeth,
they both laugh at their old trepidations.

77.   Lim, John.   AT GRANDMOTHER'S HOUSE.   Montreal:
           Tundra, 1977.   Illus. by the author.   Unpaged.   Grades
           3-4.

          Author/artist Lim depicts lavishly and Orientally the life
on his grandmother's Singapore farm in the prewar years of his
youth.   A widow, Grandma had tried city life with her grandchildren
but missed the country and especially her independence, so returned
to her thatched-roof plantation house.   Johnnie herds ducks, feeds
pigs, catches ornamental fish, races boats, plays hide-and-seek in
the bamboo grove, observes bats at dusk, listens to Grandma's ghost
stories, and watches the extensive cultivation of exotic tropical fruits,
for Grandma is a good manager with many workers.   While their

customs and language are British, the family also enjoys traditional Buddhist celebrations.

78.   Loof, Jan. MY GRANDPA IS A PIRATE. New York: Harper and Row, 1968. Illus. by the author. Trans. by Else Holmelund Minarik. 48pp. Grades 1-2.

A boy and his grandfather sneak away from napping Grandma and sail off on a pirate adventure fantasy in which Grandpa's archenemy Omar and his Arabian corsairs scuttle their ship and take Grandpa prisoner to Omar's island stronghold. The boy smuggles Grandpa a spade with which he tunnels out of the dungeon and duels Omar. They capture his treasure chest and hijack his private zeppelin, also making off with the magic carpet pool so the pirates can't pursue. They are forced to jettison carpets and treasure in a storm but reach home safely without Grandma being any the wiser. The boy hopes Grandpa will don his pirate attire again soon.

79.   Low, Alice. DAVID'S WINDOWS. New York: Putnam, 1974. Illus. by Tomie dePaola. Unpaged. Grades K-2.

David wants to stop and look in all the fascinating city windows they pass, but his mother hustles him along because they are late for the train that will take him to grandmother's house. On the train he has plenty of time to look out the windows, and when Grandma meets him, she, too, takes time for window-watching as she does her errands. David likes the stained glass window at Grandma's house, and when he hears an owl hoot beyond his own bedroom window, he is too sleepy to mind that the blind is drawn, because there will be lots of time for country-looking tomorrow.

80.   Lundgren, Max. MATT'S GRANDFATHER. New York: Putnam, 1972. Illus. by Fibben Hald. Trans. by Ann Pyk. Unpaged. Grades 2-3.

Mother and Father drive Matt to the "old people's home" in the country to visit Grandfather on his eighty-fifth birthday, admonishing him to be solicitous because "Grandfather is so old that he is almost like a baby again. " Balderdash! That carefully contrived facade of senility grants the crafty old man independence from the patronizing adults who feel compelled by convention to dehumanize the institutionalized. He keeps his snuff in a flower pot on the windowsill and pretends to misunderstand that it is verboten. When Mother and Father disappear to consult the nurses, grandfather and grandson hie off to the garden where the old man shows the boy his other well kept secret: the dapper suit of mufti and dark glasses he keeps in the unused summerhouse which enable him to leave the grounds incognito.

80a.   MacLachlan, Patricia. THROUGH GRANDPA'S EYES. New
        York: Harper and Row, 1979. Illus. by Deborah Ray.
        Unpaged. Grades 2-4.

        John loves to visit Grandpa's house because Grandpa, being
blind, has his own way of seeing and is teaching it to the preschool
boy. The sun warms him awake, and he senses Nana's whereabouts
and the breakfast menu by hearing and smell. Nana arranges Grandpa's food plate like the face of a clock with certain foods at certain
hours. Grandpa plays the cello by touch and memory, but relies
upon John to steer when they walk down to the river. Grandpa
identifies birds by their calls and the direction of the wind by its
feel. He shows John his trick for pouring tea without spilling, and
reads aloud to John and Nana the amusing parts of his Braille books.
He can even follow TV programs by dialogue and type of music, but
at bedtime as he tucks John in, he accidentally turns the light on instead of off and John does not let on. In the dark at last, John
"sees" things the way Grandpa does.

81.   Mahy, Margaret. ULTRA-VIOLET CATASTROPHE! or THE
        UNEXPECTED WALK WITH GREAT-UNCLE PRINGLE. New
        York: Parents, 1975. Illus. by Brian Froud. Unpaged.
        Grades 2-3.

        Sally hates to be scrubbed and brushed for the periodic
visits with fussy, fastidious Aunt Anne, but this time it is different.
Aunt Anne's father is paying her a call, and she sends the two on
a walk together. Although the old man is grotesquely ill-proportioned,
Sally soon discovers he is a kindred spirit who likes to crawl through
hedges, wade in mud, dam a creek, and even get chased by a sharp-
horned cow. But best of all, he likes to assert his individuality by
concocting his own colorful ejaculations just as she does. They return to the quaint English cottage torn and disheveled, to Aunt Anne's
disapprobation, but Uncle Magnus invites Sally and her mother to
his home with the promise that they won't be bored.

82.   Mayer, Mercer. MRS. BEGGS AND THE WIZARD. New
        York: Parents, 1973. Illus. by the author. Unpaged.
        Grades K-2.

        Soon after bespectacled and pompadoured Mrs. Beggs rents
a room to old Mr. Alabasium, strange occurrences begin to frighten
her other boarders. Thunderstorms and blizzards rage through the
house, guests levitate, loathsome reptiles appear in beds, and creepy
creatures inhabit every nook and cranny. Even the constable she
summons turns into a foolish-looking ram. The undaunted landlady
fights fire with fire and dons her own witch costume. The beasties
she conjures up carry off Mr. Alabasium in the middle of the night
to the city dump, but peace at the rooming house may be short-
lived: at dinnertime a sinister shrouded figure with reptilian tail
and clawed appendages rings the bell.

83.   McCloskey, Robert. BURT DOW, DEEP-WATER MAN.
       New York: Viking, 1963. Illus. by the author. 63pp.
       Grades 2-4.

    Beetle-browed Burt has retired from the sea but still keeps
two boats and does odd jobs.   One boat is filled with earth and
planted with geraniums; the other is patched and caulked but still
floats and is painted in multiple hues with leftover paint.   One day
he casts off in the Tidely-Idley to fish for cod.   Instead he snags
the fluke of a very large whale that threatens to scuttle the boat.
As he frees the barb and considerately bandages the whale's tail, he
hasn't noticed that weather is brewing that will surely sink the
Tidely-Idley.   Politely he asks the whale if he can weather the
storm ala Jonah, and the leviathan obligingly swallows him, boat
and all.   By lantern light he explores the cavernous craw and worries that the whale has forgotten that the arrangement is temporary.
To give the whale a bellyache, he empties his paint cans and the
bilges of the boat with indiscriminate abandon about the cetacean interior.   The whale disgorges him--straight into a whole gam of
grumpy grampuses in a riot of colors.   Quickly he senses their
trouble and adorns each of their tails with one of his handy band-
aids.   As the contented whales disappear over the horizon in forma-
tion, imperturbable Burt sets his tiller for home.

83a.   McPhail, David. GRANDFATHER'S CAKE. New York:
       Scribner, 1979. Illus. by the author. Unpaged. Grades
       2-3.

    Two boys and their perverse pony, carrying a basket of
freshly baked cake to their grandfather at their grandmother's be-
hest, are accosted in the foreboding forest by, in turn, a wily and
sinister fox, a menacing and cunning bear, and a barbarous brigand
brandishing a brace of pistols.   When the latter summarily starts
to appropriate the basket of cake, the indignant pony, aware that
the hamper also contains an apple for her, roundly trounces the
bounder with a swift kick to the solar plexus.   The boys finally
catch up with Grandfather and his flock of sheep, and discover that
Grandmother has prudently packed three pieces of cake.

84.   Memling, Carl. OLD MAN RIDDLE. Chicago: Whitman,
       1972. Illus. by John Faulkner. Unpaged. Grades 1-3.

    Down, down the mountain trail runs grizzled Old Man Rid-
dle, followed by plump Grandma Riddle, young Jed Riddle, the
Peddlar Man, and all their Ozark neighbors.   Old Man Riddle is
expecting a package at Deep Hollow Post Office, and the curiosity
of the rest is piqued.   Along the way the chipper old man tosses
out riddle clues.   The surprise parcel, of course, proves to be a
new fiddle.   There's a barn yonder, and the crowd is already assembled; the occasion calls for an impromptu hoedown.

85.   Merrill, Jean.   PLEASE DON'T EAT MY CABIN.   Chicago:
        Whitman, 1971.   Illus. by Frances Gruse Scott.   Unpaged.
        Grades 2-4.

        Adam is a friendly boy with an aptitude for taming animals.
When he goes to visit his grandmother Tessie, who paints nature at
her relaxed camp compound in the woods, he domesticates animals
for her to sketch.   The only wild creatures she objects to are
porcupines which gnaw her cabins for the salt content of human
perspiration.   When Adam finds an orphaned porcupine, he can't resist taming it nonetheless, and Tessie is apprehensive.   The two
prepare to eat a homemade ice cream treat but are interrupted by
the unmistakable sound of porcupine munching.   Adam's pet is chew-
ing on the old tree stump over which Tessie discarded the briny
water from the ice cream freezer.   Her problems are solved: she
can spare her cabins and rid the grounds of stumps by simply
marinating them!

86.   Milhous, Katherine.   THE EGG TREE.   New York: Scrib-
        ner, 1950.   Illus. by the author.   Unpaged.   Directions.
        Grades 2-4.

        On Katy and Carl's first Easter egg hunt on their grand-
mother's Pennsylvania Dutch farm, Katy discovers in the attic a
hatbox full of gaily painted hollow eggs that Grandmom made when
she was a child.   The cousins beg to be shown all the designs
Grandmom used so they can make some of their own, and when
they are finished, they have enough to decorate a large birch tree
and bring spring right into the house.   Their unique egg tree attracts visitors from far and wide.

87.   Moeri, Louise.   STAR MOTHER'S YOUNGEST CHILD.
        Boston: Houghton Mifflin, 1975.   Illus. by Trina Schart
        Hyman.   Unpaged.   Grades 2-3.

        A forgotten old peasant woman wishes one Christmas Eve
for a real Christmas with tree, presents, candles, music, and a
feast.   Up in the heavens, the Star Mother's restless Youngest
Child asks just once to experience Christmas as it is celebrated
on earth before he must take his place in the constellations.   The
old woman wakes to a knock at the door and opens it to an odd-
looking waif she mistakes for a village scamp, but she gruffly asks
him in.   All day her unwelcome visitor tags along behind her asking
inquisitively about the Christmas symbols until she must grudgingly
demonstrate each one.   Gradually she warms to her task of provid-
ing Christmas for the Ugly Child and even produces a homely feast
and a present under the tree.   The starry-eyed youth in his gratitude
gives her the love and memories she is starved for.   Each is replete.

88.   Mosel, Arlene. THE FUNNY LITTLE WOMAN. New York: Dutton, 1972. Illus. by Blair Lent. Unpaged. Grades K-2.

Long ago in Old Japan, a mirthful little woman follows an errant rice dumpling down a crack in the earth and finds herself in a netherworld peopled with talking statues of the gods and wicked, monstrous oni. The fearsome oni capture her and spirit her across a subterranean river to their donjon-keep where they force her to cook for them. The work is not onerous, for they provide her with a magic paddle or spoon, but eventually she longs for her little home. She escapes by boat, but the oni drink the river dry, leaving her in the mud. For once her sense of humor deserts her, but the oni are convulsed. As they open their mouths in derision, the water flows back into the river, and the little woman makes good her escape. Having had the foresight to bring the magic paddle with her, her fortune is assured, "Tee-he-he-he-he!"

89.   North Shore Committee on the Older Adult. GROWING UP, GROWING OLDER. New York: Holt, Rinehart and Winston, 1964. Illus. by Sonia O. Lisker. Unpaged. Grades K-2.

Traces the physical and social development of middle class John from infancy through retirement. He is portrayed learning to walk and talk, playing with others, getting a haircut, and learning to read. He enjoys being a Cub Scout, delivering newspapers, and playing on the football team. As a teenager he earns money with a part time job, develops a career interest, and acquires a girlfriend. He pursues his interest in science through college, and after a stint in the Air Force returns to become a zoo veterinarian and marry his high school sweetheart. His responsibilities increase with the addition of two children and upward mobility at the zoo, and at the age of 50 he is appointed zoo director. Meanwhile, the children have grown up and presented him with grandchildren who visit him at the zoo. Upon retirement, he devotes his time to reading, gardening, walking in the park, talking with old friends, and telling stories to the grandchildren.

89a.   Palay, Steven. I LOVE MY GRANDMA. Milwaukee: Raintree, 1977. Illus. by Brent Jones. 31pp. Grades K-2.

This candid photo story depicts the way in which a small girl and her grandmother, both of Latin-American descent, spend their days while the girl's parents are at work. Grandma always meets her after school and chats with the crossing guard, an old friend. They pause at the playground while the girl climbs the jungle gym and then wait on the front stoop for the mailman. A neighbor walking his dog stops to talk about old times and then accompanies them on an excursion to the park where they feed ducks and watch clouds. Later, Grandma reads to the girl or helps her work a jigsaw puzzle, and sometimes the girl expresses her love by helping Grandma with her chores.

90.   Parish, Peggy. GRANNY AND THE DESPERADOES. New
        York: Macmillan, 1970. Illus. by Steven Kellogg. 40pp.
        Grades 1-3.

        When a pair of hungry and villainous brigands filch feisty,
frontier granny's fresh-baked pie, her dander is raised and she sets
off into the woods with her trusty gun in hot pursuit. Soon she has
them grudgingly picking berries for another pie, rounding up wood
ducks, and mending her roof. Tiring of being flummoxed by a harmless old woman, Hank and Jeb try to grab her gun. To their continuing consternation, she kicks their shins, trips them up, and has
them trussed like turkeys by the time the sheriff arrives. The
docile desperadoes are chagrinned to learn that Granny's old gun is
useful only for reaching things on high shelves and brushing cobwebs
from corners. Granny cheerfully shares her pie with lawman and
outlaw alike and offers the horrified desperadoes honest work when
their terms are up.

91.   Parish, Peggy. GRANNY AND THE INDIANS. New York:
        Macmillan, 1969. Illus. by Brinton Turkle. 40pp. Grades
        1-3.

        Granny Guntry, uncowed even by bears, refuses to leave
her cabin in hostile Indian territory. Under their enraged noses she
unwittingly snatches game for her stewpot that had been destined for
the Indians' own trenchers. She is a grim annoyance, but they cannot shoot her for fear of retribution by the townspeople. When an
errant spark from her hearth burns her little cabin to the ground,
Granny installs herself with the Indians, and when she begins tidying
the camp, they leave in disgust. They return at the end of the day
and drag her away kicking and screaming--to the brand-new cabin
they have spent the day constructing. In gratitude she offers to
cook their meals, but they quickly insist on supplying her staples
instead, in exchange for her steering clear of their woods. Granny
and the Indians live in peaceful coexistence ever after.

91a.   Parish, Peggy. GRANNY, THE BABY AND THE BIG GRAY
        THING. New York: Macmillan, 1972. Illus. by Lynn
        Sweat. 40pp. Grades 1-3.

        Walking through the woods one day, ingenuous Granny Gun-
try comes upon an unattended Indian papoose and decides to take it
home for safekeeping. Farther along she encounters a growling gray
creature whom she subdues with a whomp on its nose with her rifle
and drags it home to be a watchdog for the baby. Vigilant Indian
eyes follow her, and, believing she is going to cook the baby and
feed it to the wolf, the scout spreads the alarm. Granny, meanwhile, dozes off while the wolf gnaws through its restraints. Indians creep up on Granny's cabin while wolf stalks baby, but Granny
wakens in time to spare the baby with another blow of her unfire-
able fowling piece to the lupine snout. She returns the baby but
vows to keep the next one she finds.

92.   Peck, Richard. MONSTER NIGHT AT GRANDMA'S HOUSE.
             New York: Viking, 1977. Illus. by Don Freeman. Unpaged.
             Grades 2-4.

        When Toby visits at Grandma's Victorian house, he enjoys
swinging on the porch swing, filling the old fish pond, and eating
corn-on-the-cob, but facing the dark at the top of the stairs every
night is nightmarish. One night after Grandma has gone to bed and
the house is dark and quiet, he hears the floorboard creak and
imagines a fire-breathing Monster in his room. When it retreats
into the hall, he cautiously follows the "night-crawling, flame-throw-
ing, tail-thumping" creature through the house, heart palpitating
when he comes eyeball to glass-eyeball with the moth-eaten moose
head on the wall. He negotiates the shadowy parlor only steps behind the "wall-eyed, tongue-lolling" hulk to the front porch where the
beast disappears and he falls asleep on the swing. He awakes in
the morning to the return of the Monster swishing its scaly tail, but
it is only Grandma sweeping the walk. She doses Toby with hot
cereal.

92a.   Pinkwater, Daniel M. PICKLE CREATURE. New York:
             Four Winds, 1979. Illus. by the author. Unpaged. Grades
             1-3.

        Conrad likes to spend the night at his grandmother's house
because she lets him stay up as late as he pleases. One night she
sends him around the corner to the all-night market to pick up items
for the following day's lunch. He finds the milk and raisins with
no difficulty, but the only thing that looks like a large loose pickle
moves and resembles a cross among a dinosaur, a large dog, and
a crocodile. It looks friendly and likes raisins, so he purchases
it and coaxes it to grandmother's house. Grandmother is unruffled
and seems to know all about the care and feeding of pickle creatures.

93.   Politi, Leo. THREE STALKS OF CORN. New York:
             Scribner, 1976. Illus. by the author. Unpaged. Recipes.
             Grades 2-3.

        In the Barrio de Pico Viejo near Los Angeles, Angelica
lives with her grandmother who keeps alive for her the legends and
traditions of their Mestizo ancestry, especially the importance of
corn to their culture. Cornmeal forms the staple of their diet, tor-
tillas, and even the husks are saved for tamales and the cornsilk
for tea. Grandmother teaches Angelica to cook and lets her play
with her cherished corn-husk dolls. When a fiesta is planned,
Grandmother is asked to manage a food booth, making her special-
ties, tacos, enchiladas, and bunuelos. Angelica's teacher and principal are so impressed that they invite Grandmother to conduct a cooking class for the boys and girls in her school. For Angelica's help
in the project, Grandmother makes her a gift of the corn-husk dolls,
and the happy girl goes to sleep with the shadowy stalks of corn
nodding in the garden outside her window.

94.   Potter, Beatrix.   THE TAILOR OF GLOUCESTER.   New
         York: Warne, 1968.   Illus. by the author.   64pp.   Grades
         3-4.

"In the time of swords and periwigs and full-skirted coats
with flower'd lappets, " a poor old tailor receives an order from the
Mayor of Gloucester for a Christmas outfit that will make his fortune.   He carefully cuts it out and goes home.   He sends his faithful feline out for "twist, " but while he is gone, the tailor discovers
the cat's cache of live mice under teacups and releases them.   The
ired cat refuses to give the tailor the necessary silk, and the tailor
falls ill, thrashing in delirium for days.   Unbeknownst to him, the
grateful mice seek out his shop and industriously stitch the garment
except for a single buttonhole for which the twist was intended.   The
tailor recovers on Christmas Eve, and the repentant cat gives him
the thread.   On Christmas Day the tailor is stunned to see the coat
completed on time but for the buttonhole.   With a modicum of effort, his future is secure.

95.   Prather, Ray.   NO TRESPASSING.   New York: Macmillan,
         1974.   Illus. by the author.   Unpaged.   Grades K-2.

The ball-playing boys of the black suburban neighborhood
are terrified of old Miss Riley who has barricaded her property
behind the only fence on the block.   They cajole a younger boy to
help them retrieve their ball from her shrubbery, but every effort
is foiled by the inhospitable, cane-wielding, hobnail-booted, shrill,
wizened, waspish character until quick-witted Charlie deploys a
diversionary maneuver he has seen on TV.   The ball is quickly recovered, and Charlie is rewarded with team status.

96.   Robbins, Ruth.   BABOUSHKA AND THE THREE KINGS.
         Berkeley: Parnassus, 1960.   Illus. by Nicolas Sidjakov.
         Unpaged.   Grades 2-3.

On a chill winter's night the Three Wise Men stop at
Baboushka's snug hut and invite her to join them in their search
for the Christ Child.   At the first light of dawn, the gentle and
generous peasant woman feels a new awakening and knows she must
follow the kings in their pursuit of the Babe.   She packs a few poor
but precious gifts and sets out, but the snow has covered the
strangers' tracks.   She asks at every village, but no one has seen
them.   Still she never falters.   Russian legend has it that every
Christmas Eve the children await Baboushka's coming and take joy
in the little treasures she leaves behind in the silent night.

97.   Robinson, Adjai.   FEMI AND OLD GRANDADDIE.   New
         York: Coward, McCann and Geoghegan, 1972.   Illus. by
         Jerry Pinkney.   Unpaged.   Grades 2-3.

Orphaned by the flood that sweeps over his West African home, young Femi subsists by working in the nearby village but longs to start his own cassava plantation.   No sooner does he plant his first roots than a grown pig comes along and destroys them.   A kind old woman gives him a huge cassava root, but before he can take it home, a wily and importuning ancient begs most of it and steals the rest, giving him a useless riddle in exchange.   The following morning, the hungry boy is drawn by promises of feasting to the headman's compound where the headman is auctioning off his daughter to the young man who correctly guesses her name.   All of the more eligible swains try and fail, but ragged Femi, remembering the old man's riddle, wins the hand of the dusky maiden. As the bridal party approaches the river for the ceremony, Femi spots his fraudulent old beggar of the previous day; he is one of the headman's retainers.

98.   Rockwell, Anne.   BEFANA, A CHRISTMAS STORY.   New York: Atheneum, 1974.   Illus. by the author.   Unpaged. Grades 1-3.

Old Befana has lived in seclusion since the death of her husband and baby, when strangers, three finely dressed men and a poor shepherd, intrude upon her, seeking Bethlehem.   Curiosity about the Nativity and a desire to see the Babe impel her to join them, but she is afraid of darkness.   Dazzling angels appear to light the night sky, and she changes her mind, bringing along her small horde of treasures.   She never catches up with the shepherd, though her feet seem tireless and fleet, but she stops in every home she passes to leave a gift from her basket, which is never empty, for a new gift replaces each one she gives.

99.   Rockwell, Anne.   GIFT FOR A GIFT.   New York: Parents, 1974.   Illus. by the author.   Unpaged.   Grades K-2.

A humble old Oriental grasscutter hoards his life savings and blows it on a gold and emerald bauble which he delivers anonymously to a beautiful princess.   She responds by sending him a prancing palfry.   Having no use for the horse, he has it presented to a courageous prince, who, not to be outdone, returns a brace of camels laden with precious spices which also finds its way to the princess.   The ever-escalating gift exchange between prince and princess incurs their curiosity and results in an eventual meeting. They fall in love and marry, unaware of the unwitting old man who set the events in motion.

100.   Roy, Ronald.   A THOUSAND PAILS OF WATER.   New York: Knopf, 1978.   Illus. by Vo-Dinh Mai.   Unpaged. Grades 1-3.

Small boy questions why his father must kill whales for a

living and is told that he knows no other trade. His grandfather
tells him to ask his questions of the sea. On the beach he finds a
stranded whale, and single-handedly he tries to keep the leviathan
wet until the tide turns. When he is too exhausted to continue, his
grandfather relieves him, and soon the whole Oriental whaling village
rallies 'round, led by the boy's father.

101.   Ryan, Cheli Duran. HILDILID'S NIGHT. New York: Mac-
        millan, 1971. Illus. by Arnold Lobel. Unpaged. Grades
        K-1.

        Old Hildilid hates owls, bats, moths, stars, moon, shadows
and sleep, anything associated with night. She tries to sweep and
scrub the darkness away, burn it off, tie it in a bundle, shear it
like a sheep, toss it to her wolfhound to devour, tuck it into her
bed, duck it in the well. No amount of appeasement or abuse will
banish the night, and weary from battling it, she sleeps the daylight
hours away to be refreshed for the following night's fray. "Good
Night. "

102.   Sawyer, Ruth. JOURNEY CAKE, HO! New York: Viking,
        1953. Illus. by Robert McCloskey. 45pp. Grades K-2.

        Old woman Merry, old man Grumble, and buoyant Johnny,
the bound-out boy, live in a log cabin on Tip Top Mountain, each
attending to his chores according to his disposition, until misfortune
strikes. Gradually the livestock and larder are depleted and Johnny
must reluctantly be given his walking papers. The old woman lugu-
briously outfits him for the road, adding on top the large, round,
crusty Journey Cake for sustenance. Not far down the road the
Journey Cake bounces out of his pack and rolls down the road, at-
tracting a hungry cow, donkey, ducks, sheep, pigs and hen who
chase it until it runs out of steam--back in Merry and Grumble's
barnyard where they are quickly corralled. The lucky Journey Cake
has restored their good humor and good fortune, and as the old
woman rustles it up for supper, she dubs it Johnny Cake.

103.   Say, Allen. ONCE UNDER THE CHERRY BLOSSOM TREE.
        New York: Harper and Row, 1974. Illus. by the author.
        32pp. Grades 2-3.

        A miserly, misanthropic old Japanese landlord begrudges
his oppressed tenants the only thing he can't control, their merri-
ment. One day he swallows a cherry pit that travels to the top of
his head and sprouts into a full-grown tree. When the poor peasants
gather 'round to marvel at its beautiful blossoms, he imagines that
they are deriding him and tears the tree out of his scalp by its roots,
leaving a gaping hole that soon fills with rainwater. The pond
spawns carp for the skinflint. One day the village boys creep up
while he is napping to poach fish from his cratered cranium. A

splash awakens him, and in routing the boys, he trips on a rock and crashes to earth, leaving nothing but a tranquil fishpond.

104.   Schick, Eleanor. CITY IN THE SUMMER. New York: Macmillan, 1969. Illus. by the author. Unpaged. Grades K-1.

It is hot in the noisy, bustling city with no place to escape the heat but the apartment house roof.   Jerry spends a lot of time there feeding the pigeons with the old man who is his friend, but he dreams of cool places with wind, water, and room to play.   The old man grew up near the ocean and offers to take the boy there, riding the subway to the last stop.   They arrive before the crowds and spend the day, partaking of the myriad sights, sounds, smells and activities of the beach.   A thunderstorm scatters the people, but afterward there is a lovely sunset.   In the cool dark they take the subway train back home.

105.   Schick, Eleanor. CITY IN THE WINTER. New York: Macmillan, 1970. Illus. by the author. Grades K-2.

Jimmy awakes in the morning to find that schools are closed because of the blizzard, but his mother must still go to work while he stays home with Grandma.   After breakfast he helps Grandma straighten the apartment and makes a barn out of a cardboard box.   He eats his prepacked school lunch as an indoor picnic and feeds the birds bread crumbs on the windowsill.   He and Grandma make a sortie through the snow to buy milk but find the corner grocery store closed.   Jimmy prepares the vegetables and sets the table for their soup supper, and recounts the day's events for his mother when she gets home.   She tucks him tenderly to bed.

106.   Schlein, Miriam. BOBO, THE TROUBLEMAKER. New York: Four Winds, 1976. Illus. by Ray Cruz. Unpaged. Grades K-2.

An old man named Bobo with nothing better to do mischievously makes his neighbors nervous by prognosticating that the moon will not return, that the river is draining away because the world is tilting, and that the sun is being devoured by a gigantic serpent.   He purports to get his information from a talking monkey and a mammoth bird.   The simple villagers eventually get wise to Bobo's attention-getting tactics and cure him by beating him at his own game.   They force him to spend the night in a tree, ostensibly standing guard against the voracious serpent of his imagination. His acrophobia completes the therapy.

107.   Segal, Lore. TELL ME A MITZL New York: Farrar, Straus and Giroux, 1970. Illus. by Harriet Pincus. Unpaged.   Grades K-2.

When Martha asks for a story, her mother tells about a preschooler named Mitzi who changes, feeds and dresses her baby brother in the predawn hours for a trip to her grandmother's apartment. The doorman hails a taxi, but it is a short-lived junket, because Mitzi doesn't know her grandmother's address. In another Mitzi tale, the whole family contracts colds simultaneously and has no one to nurse them till Grandma arrives. When they recover, it is Grandma's turn to be sick while all of them tend her.

108.   Sharmat, Marjorie. REX. New York: Harper and Row,
        1967. Illus. by Emily McCully. 32pp. Grades K-2.

A retiree, complete with pipe and slippers, answers a knock on the door to find a small bespectacled boy who claims he is a dog looking for a new home. "Why did you pick my house?" the man asks. "I see you sitting alone on your front porch. You look like you need a dog," replies Rex who extols his canine qualities by fetching the man's newspaper in his teeth and barking to frighten off an imaginary robber. He accepts a dog biscuit (cookie) and a pat on the head. While rocking and talking, the man gently and tactfully probes Rex's reason for running away and then walks Rex home, hand-in-hand for reassurance, to a happy reunion with his mother. He departs with an invitation from her to return.

109.   Shortall, Leonard. JOHN AND HIS THUMBS. New York:
        Morrow, 1961. Illus. by the author. 48pp. Grades 2-3.

Everyone says John is "all thumbs." He tries to help in his father's grocery market but topples a pyramid of cans. Efforts to assist in his cousin's service station go awry. Disconsolately he heads for home past his grandfather's farm where Grandfather is planting peppers and tomatoes. John makes such a good job of planting and tending the tomatoes that he earns a new sobriquet; now everyone says that John has a "green thumb."

110.   Skorpen, Liesel Moak. MANDY'S GRANDMOTHER. New
        York: Dial, 1975. Illus. by Martha Alexander. Unpaged.
        Grades 1-3.

Grandmother's first visit to Mandy's house starts inauspiciously. Grandmother believes little girls should wear frilly dresses, play with dolls, and eat oatmeal and eggs for breakfast. Mandy favors blue jeans and a floppy hat, plays with her pet toad in a makeshift fort, and always has peanut butter and banana sandwiches for breakfast. She decides that grandmothers are boring and mean, while Grandmother retires to her room with a case of the vapors in disappointment over her alien granddaughter. Then they discover a common ground, rocking and lap-sitting, and their relationship is retrenched in compromise. Grandmother teaches Mandy to knit, while Mandy tutors Grandmother in whistling. Together they whistle and knit a blanket for Mandy's horse.

111.   Snyder, Agnes. THE OLD MAN ON OUR BLOCK. New
        York: Holt, Rinehart and Winston, 1964. Illus. by Donald
        Lynch. Unpaged. Grades K-1.

Told entirely in pictures, this story encourages children to
make up their own words. The opening spread depicts a lonely
silver-haired gentleman dejectedly rocking in his drab and shabby
living room. He registers pleasant surprise when three children
call on him, and hand-in-hand they walk down to the harbor to wave
to the boats. Later in the park he umpires a baseball game and
then pauses to rest over a game of checkers on a park bench with
a balding man while the children gambol. They admire the mastodon
at the natural history museum and visit a toy shop. After he regales them with a story, the children bring him home with them for
dinner. As he departs, mother and the children present him with
a bouquet of flowers. Back home in his rocking chair, he smokes
his pipe contentedly in a room that is visibly brighter and less
shabby.

112.   Snyder, Anne. THE OLD MAN AND THE MULE. New
        York: Holt, Rinehart and Winston, 1978. Illus. by Mila
        Lazarevich. Unpaged. Grades 2-3.

The cantankerous, snaggle-toothed, stubble-chinned, wart-
nosed Georgia mountain man, Zeke, and his equally ill-favored, foul-
tempered mule, Tully, belong to a mutual aggravation society.
When Zeke throws a bucket of cold water on Tully, the mule re-
taliates by planting the old man in the icy trough and turning the
laugh back on him. Zeke longs to be rid of Tully but has no one
else to help him on the farm; Tully dreams about running away but
has no one else to feed him. When Zeke inherits a tractor, he
sees his opportunity and unloads Tully on a neighbor widder woman.
Neither has had it so good, but both are lonely. Zeke retrieves
Tully who perversely destroys the tractor. Zeke maliciously ties
Tully under a hole in the roof all night in the rain. In the morning
Tully kicks over the outhouse with Zeke sitting in it. Neither has
been happier. Hee haw.

112a.   Sonneborn, Ruth A. I LOVE GRAM. New York: Viking,
        1971. Illus. by Leo Carty. Unpaged. Grades 2-3.

Ellie's mom works late and her big sister is always busy
with homework, so it is Gram who is always there to meet Ellie
after school, give her snacks, and play with her. But one day
Gram is hospitalized, and the bewildered and frightened black inner-
city child wonders if she might die like Joey's grandmother did.
The days drag hollowly as the three try to cope without Gram, but
when Mom announces that Gram is coming home tomorrow, Ellie
exultantly draws her a welcoming picture and asks the preschool
teacher to emblazon her message across the top.

113.   Stevenson, James. "COULD BE WORSE!" New York:
         Greenwillow, 1977. Illus. by the author. Unpaged. Grades
         K-1.

         Grandpa's routine never varies, and no matter what befalls
him he replies, "Could be worse. " When he overhears the children
explain that he is dull because nothing interesting happens to him,
he says something different: "Guess what?" Then he launches a
flight of fancy in which a monstrous bird plucks him from his bed
and carries him into a mountain encounter with the abominable
snowman; a desert confrontation with a stupendous ostrich and rep-
tile; and an undersea run-in with a colossal goldfish, lobster, squid
and turtle. He floats to dry land on a piece of toast and folds a
discarded newspaper into a paper airplane which he flies home to
bed. "Now, what do you think of that?" "Could be worse!" shout
the kids.

114.   Swayne, Sam and Zoa Swayne. GREAT-GRANDFATHER IN
         THE HONEY TREE. New York: Viking, 1949. Illus. by
         the authors. 53pp. Grades 1-3.

         Great-grandfather and Great-grandmother were newlyweds
on the Indiana frontier. Weary of their hominy diet, Great-grandmother persuades Great-grandfather to go to the lake to bag a bird.
He nets so many geese he can't hold them down and is airborne.
He drops off and plummets into a hollow tree filled with honey where
he is mired until a bear comes along for a sweet treat. He hitches
a ride out of the tree with the startled bear who becomes the first
candidate for Great-grandmother's pantry. In washing off the goo in
the lake he inadvertently snags a fish and stuns a partridge. Before
long, a deer, two dozen geese, and twelve turkeys have fallen to
fate, and only one shot has been fired! For good measure he drains
off a barrel of honey before bearing his booty triumphantly home.
In addition to the food, Great-grandmother makes good use of hides
and feathers.

115.   Tabrah, Ruth. THE OLD MAN AND THE ASTRONAUTS.
         Norfolk Island, Australia: Island Heritage, 1975. Illus.
         by George Suyeoka. Unpaged. Grades K-3.

         In the New Guinean village of Bongu, everyone listens to the
news broadcasts in pidgin English. Jun and his grandfather Kandege
listen in awe to the report of men walking on the moon and collecting
rock samples. That night when they paddle far out beyond the reef
to net the big red fish that can only be caught under a full moon,
they return empty-handed. In growing anger Kandege reasons that
the astronauts' activities are dimming the moon's luminosity and
stalks to the headman with his complaint. The headman scoops a
hole in the sandy beach and tells the old man to fill it with water.
When Kandege realizes he can never fill the hole nor empty the sea,
he understands that the removal of a few moon rocks will not disturb

the balance of the universe nor his livelihood.   Jun wonders if there
are crocodiles on the moon.

116.   Takahashi, Hiroyuki.   THE FOXES OF CHIRONUPP ISLAND.
          New York: Dutton, 1976.   Illus. by the author.   Trans. by
          Ann King Herring.   Unpaged.   Grades 2-3.

          Every summer the old Japanese fisherman and his wife re-
turn to the inhospitable and uninhabited northern island to ply their
trade, and one summer they are adopted by a friendly little vixen
fox cub.   At the end of the season they send the cub back to her
family in the forest.   In their absence, soldiers come to the island
and kill or wound the little vixen's family and leave her fast in a
steel trap.   While there is still life in the mother fox, she feeds
and tends her cub, but when her strength fades, she enfolds the cub
to impart her waning warmth as the snows of winter cover them and
they sleep to eternity.   When the kind old couple returns at war's
end, they find the rusted trap.   A profusion of fox-roses commemo-
rates the final resting place of the wild victims of humankind as
dust returns to dust.

117.   Talbot, Toby.   A BUCKETFUL OF MOON.   New York:
          Lothrop, Lee and Shepard, 1976.   Illus. by Imero Gobbato.
          48pp.   Grades 2-3.

          One bright night, a sprightly old woman is carrying the
moon home in her bucket of water when she trips and the moon
spills out.   She spies it in the sky and grabs a passing windmill
sail to ride up and recapture it but grows dizzy and falls to the
ground.   When she revives, she sees it reflected in the eyes of a
goat, and when she tries to snatch those, the enraged animal butts
her onto the miller's doorstep.   Seeing the moon in the miller's
windowpane, the foolish woman breaks the glass to reach it, causing the miller to douse her with water.   Next she spots it atop a
statue and climbs up for it but overreaches and falls into the river.
There it drips through her fingers when she tries to clutch it, so
she resourcefully hails a passing bucket-maker, corrals the elusive
moon, and continues merrily home.

118.   Tapio, Pat Decker.   THE LADY WHO SAW THE GOOD SIDE
          OF EVERYTHING.   New York: Seabury, 1975.   Illus. by
          Paul Galdone.   Unpaged.   Grades K-2.

          When rain spoils her picnic, the sporting old lady reminds
herself that it will be good for the flowers, and when ensuing floods
sweep away her home and cast her and her cat adrift on a log down
the river to the sea, she rationalizes her losses and misfortunes
cheerfully and declares that she always wanted a vacation at sea.
After bobbing for weeks, she makes landfall on the shores of China
where she realizes her dream of seeing the Great Wall.   Finding an

empty cottage nearby, she moves in, but no sooner is she settled than it begins to rain again.   "Oh, well, " she sighs, "The rain will make the rice grow better. "

119.   Taylor, Mark. THE OLD WOMAN AND THE PEDLAR.
        San Carlos: Golden Gate, 1969. Illus. by Graham Booth.
        Unpaged. Music. Grades 2-3.

The author speculates on how the old woman of the Mother Goose rhyme came to have her petticoats snipped short.   A jocular, rubicund and independent bachelor woman weekly markets her succulent mulberry delicacies.   When she fails to bow to the blandishments of importunate Pedlar Stout, who tells her she needs a husband to look after her but who in reality has a proprietary interest in her material assets, the chauvinistic swain sabotages her cart on market day and, while she sleeps in exhaustion by the roadside, churlishly slashes her dignity and self-esteem in causing her deshabille. Smugly and condescendingly he lets her redeem them only when she meekly concedes that she seems to need his protection after all.

120.   Teal, Val. THE LITTLE WOMAN WANTED NOISE. New
        York: Rand McNally, 1943. Illus. by Robert Lawson.
        Unpaged. Grades 2-3.

An old woman who has spent all her life in the bustling, vibrant city is bequeathed a country farm by her cousin but finds no rest or peace of mind because of the unaccustomed silence.   A neighbor advises her to buy animals to give the place some animation, but a cow, dog, cat, pig, and assorted poultry aren't noisy enough, so she purchases an "old rattlety-bang car with a good loud horn" and goes in search of more cacophony.   She finds it in two small boys who provide the farm with all the bedlam she desires. The little woman still has no rest, but she has plenty of peace of mind.

121.   Tresselt, Alvin. THE MITTEN. New York: Lothrop, Lee
        and Shepard, 1964. Illus. by Yaroslava. Unpaged. Grades
        K-1.

In Grandfather's boyhood, his grandmother sends him into the forest to gather firewood on the coldest day of winter where he loses his mitten in a snowdrift.   A mouse spies it and takes up residence in its snug interior.   One by one the mitten becomes refuge to a frog, owl, rabbit, fox, wolf, and boar.   Then a bear comes along and stretches the poor mitten to the very limit of its endurance, and the next creature to squeeze in, a tiny cricket, causes it to burst its seams, sending the animals flying in all directions.   When the boy returns for the mitten all he finds are scraps, but his grandmother makes him a new pair, "And my grandfather says he never did know what really happened to his mitten. "

122.   Tresselt, Alvin. THE OLD MAN AND THE TIGER. New
         York: Wonder, 1965. Illus. by Albert Aquino. 60pp.
         Grades 1-3.

Indian folk tale retold as an easy-to-read play. Kind-
hearted old man frees trapped tiger who repays him by offering to
eat him. Two inanimate objects, a tree and a road, and a beast of
burden, an ox, all who feel they have been misused by man, counsel the old man to let himself be eaten. A wily fox comes to his
aid when his fate seems sealed by tricking the tiger back into the
trap and securing it.

123.   Trez, Denise and Alain Trez. THE BUTTERFLY CHASE.
         Cleveland: World, 1960. Illus. by the authors. Unpaged.
         Grades 2-3.

"Freddy's best friend is his grandfather, but Freddy's grandfather is not like most grandfathers. " He is a French scholar with
an imposing uniform and full white beard who is searching the land
for a butterfly in the colors of the French flag. At a convenient
butterfly crossing, they leave their car in pursuit of a flight of butterflies, leapfrogging over sheep, crawling through caves, swinging
from trees, and disguising themselves as bushes, only to discover
the elusive tri-colored butterfly hovering over the car. They impress the venerated membership of the erudite Academy and then
give the patriotic lepidopteran its liberté, égalité, fraternité.

124.   Tripp, Wallace. SIR TOBY JINGLE'S BEASTLY JOURNEY.
         New York: Coward, McCann and Geoghegan, 1976. Illus.
         by the author. Unpaged. Grades 1-3.

Old Sir Toby's prowess at slaying dragons, not to mention
griffins, trolls, ogres, wild boars, bears, tigers and wolves, is
fading fast, but before his legend in the environs of Grimghast Forest
pales and he can hang up his blade honorably and grandiloquently, he
must perform one final feat relying on wit alone. On his trusty
steed he dauntlessly penetrates the perilous forest preserves and
quickly attracts a pack of the most fearsome and reprehensible
monsters and miscreants ever to darken a darkling wood, who skulk
behind bent on revenge for past indignities, snarling voice-balloon
asides. They attempt to bury him, crush him, and drown him, but
to their growing agitation he innocently and miraculously escapes
unscathed until the retinue reaches the portals of Sir Toby's own
castle. Stepping aside to let them enter first, he deftly locks the
courtyard door behind them and retires to rest on his laurels as he
rakes in the gate of the most exotic zoo in the land.

125.   Trofimuk, Ann. BABUSHKA AND THE PIG. Boston:
         Houghton Mifflin, 1969. Illus. by Jerry Pinkney. 40pp.
         Grades 2-3.

Babushka rocks alone day after day, wishing she had something to do and someone to do it for.   One day a gypsy rides by and sells her a tiny piglet which soon grows to porcine proportions under her coddling till she can no longer afford it or cater to it.   One day it runs away and wreaks havoc in the neighbors' gardens.   They chase it down at the Fair near where the Prince has just bought a kitten.   The Prince is overwhelmed at the pig's size and must have it for himself, vowing to treat it regally.   In exchange he gives Babushka the kitten and a bag of gold.   Babushka can live comfortably the rest of her days with a lap-sized pussy to pamper.

126.   Udry, Janice May.   MARY JO'S GRANDMOTHER.   Chicago: Whitman, 1970.   Illus. by Eleanor Mill.   Unpaged.   Grades 2-3.

Mary Jo loves to visit her grandmother's old house in the country with its woods and fields, baby chicks, and good food to look forward to.   This Christmas vacation of deep snow and frigid cold, Grandma slips and breaks her leg in the pantry.   After making her comfortable on the floor, Mary Jo courageously and foresightedly trudges more than two miles to the main road over the unplowed country lane to summon assistance, because there is no telephone in the farmhouse.   Left unresolved is the problem of whether the warm and independent black woman will eventually return to her isolated home or move to town, as her children have been urging her to do.

127.   Van Woerkom, Dorothy.   BECKY AND THE BEAR.   New York: Putnam, 1975.   Illus. by Margot Tomes.   Unpaged. Grades 1-3.

When Father and Ned go hunting that lean Maine spring in colonial days, Becky, 8, grouses to Granny that she wishes she could be a brave hunter, too.   Granny only laughs and assigns her the task of stirring hasty pudding while she hurries off to help a neighbor in an emergency.   Picking huckleberries for supper, Becky is startled by a ravenous, slavering bear who chases her home. Thinking quickly to save the vulnerable piglets in the barn, she concocts a flip of rum and molasses with which she doses the bear who falls into a drunken torpor.   When Father and Ned return empty-handed, Becky and Granny have bear-on-the-hoof neatly trussed.

128.   Van Woerkom, Dorothy O.   TIT FOR TAT.   New York: Greenwillow, 1977.   Illus. by Douglas Florian.   56pp. Grades 1-2.

An altruistic old woman with no earthly possessions but a small house, a scrawny cow, and an apple tree, gives away her meager produce to the children of the village.   Nearby lives a parsimonious old man in a fine house with every comfort.   On a bitter winter's night when a tattered stranger knocks at his door, the old

man refuses him shelter and gives him but a niggardly repast.
The man offers him good luck in exchange for it, the old miser
scheming all the while to get still richer with the proffered luck.
At the humble home of the cheerful old woman, the stranger is wel-
comed to partake of her lean board and hearth, and at the promise
of good luck, she dreams of doubling her charity. Her reward is
wealth beyond imagination which she characteristically shares, while
all the irascible skinflint gains is a bad cold.

129.   Vogel, Ilse-Margret. DODO EVERY DAY. New York:
         Harper and Row, 1977. Illus. by the author. 42pp.
         Grades 3-4.

         A traditional grandmother called Dodo peels apples so art-
fully that her young granddaughter forgets to be sad and invents such
an imaginative game that the girl's boredom evaporates. Dodo dispels the girl's jealousy when Uncle Karl is too engrossed in his
Mozart book to pay attention to her drawing, and she assuages her
contrition when she throws a rock at the cat for killing a mouse.
When Dodo is frightened of a snake in the garden, the girl takes
pride in telling her that garter snakes are harmless, and on Dodo's
birthday she's happy because Dodo likes her modest gift and has one
for her in return. She doesn't have to wait for special occasions
to see her grandmother; she has "Dodo every day. "

130.   Wahl, Jan. GRANDMOTHER TOLD ME. Boston: Little,
         Brown, 1972. Illus. by Mercer Mayer. 32pp. Grades
         K-2.

         Many small boys see monsters lurking in lonely places, but
this boy claims that his grandmother sees "things that were never
seen by me. " They are things like trolls in the garden, mermaids
in the hollow oak, singing lions in the woods, dancing alligators in
the alley, Eskimos in the night, and bears in the old mill. Never
mind that Grandfather drives a flivver or that Grandmother wears
a nightcap and shawl, her eyes still twinkle behind her granny
glasses.

131.   Williams, Barbara. KEVIN'S GRANDMA. New York: Dut-
         ton, 1975. Illus. by Kay Chorao. Unpaged. Grades K-2.

         Kevin, a budding flower child, has an avant garde grand-
mother who tools around town on a motorcycle; grooves on yoga
exercises, mountain climbing, and sky diving; sends out for pizza at
midnight; repairs her own wheels, not to mention her roof; teaches
karate; hitchhikes across country, sleeping in haystacks; and used to
work as an acrobat and lion tamer in the circus. His best friend's
grandmother seems to pale by comparison as a purse-carrying, conventional, middle-class senior adult and clubwoman who drives a
sedate station wagon, plays checkers and bridge, shells peas, gives

piano lessons and birthday gifts to her young grandson, and stays in motels on motor trips.   The prosaic grandmother is more attentive to her grandson than is the flamboyant one, because Kevin can't participate in some of his grandmother's more adventurous activities.

132.   Williams, Jay.   A BAG FULL OF NOTHING.   New York:
          Parents, 1974.   Illus. by Tom O'Sullivan.   Unpaged.   Grades
          1-3.

          A bit of whimsy in which Tip finds an empty paper bag and tries to convince his father it is magic.   It serves first to gather berries, then as a disguise to prevent an officious and portly old woman who resembles the Marzipan Shepherdess from chucking his cheek.   When he finally explodes the bag to frighten off a vicious dog, Tip's dad has to concede its supernatural qualities.

132a.   Wittman, Sally.   A SPECIAL TRADE.   New York: Harper
          and Row, 1978.   Illus. by Karen Gundersheimer.   Unpaged.
          Grades K-2.

          When Nelly is very small, her aging neighbor Bartholomew pushes her stroller down the block every day, warning her of bumps, charging through sprinklers, and petting nice dogs or rebuffing mean ones.   When she learns to walk he lends a helping hand, teaches her to roller skate, and consoles her when she falls.   The neighbors call them "ham and eggs" because of their constant companionship.   After Nelly starts school, she notices that sometimes Bartholomew needs aid in crossing streets, and she willingly obliges.   Then one day Bartholomew is hospitalized after a fall, and when he finally returns in a wheelchair, he sadly tells her that their walking days are over.   Nelly knows better.   Down the block they go, over the bumps, through the sprinklers, past the dogs, with Nelly at the controls and a smile back in Bartholomew's eyes.

133.   Wood, Joyce.   GRANDMOTHER LUCY GOES ON A PICNIC.
          Cleveland: Collins World, 1970.   Illus. by Frank Francis.
          Unpaged.   Grades K-2.

          Grandmother Lucy and her granddaughter prepare to take a picnic to the river.   They pass through a tall beech copse and by the rubble of an old chapel.   Near the river they exult with the swallows and butterflies, and Grandmother shows the girl how to skip stones and make daisy chains.   After lunch they scatter the crumbs for the birds and bury their apple cores, and finally walk home slowly the other way around.   The girl helps Grandmother Lucy up the steep hill toward home, and Grandmother calls the cat for supper.

134.   Wood, Joyce.   GRANDMOTHER LUCY IN HER GARDEN.
          Cleveland: Collins World, 1974.   Illus. by Frank Francis.
          Unpaged.   Grades 1-3.

On the first day of spring, the little girl helps Grandmother Lucy down the mossy steps into her garden because of her winter-creaky knees.   There they admire the daffodils, goldfish and frog spawn in the reflecting pool; plant rosebushes; collect pussy willow boughs; visit the beehive; check on the hibernating hedgehog; and watch the chickadees build a nest.   Tom, the cat, is not welcome on their nature walk, but back in the house they placate him with milk.

135.   Zemach, Margot.   IT COULD ALWAYS BE WORSE.   New York: Farrar, Straus, Giroux, 1976.   Unpaged.   Grades K-3.

A peasant's hut in winter is too confining for a fractious family of six children, parents and mother-in-law, so the harassed husband asks advice of the Rabbi who counsels him to bring his barn-yard fowl into the hut and add, in turn, his goat and his cow.   When the turmoil grows so great that the poor man can stand it no longer, he returns to the Rabbi who directs him, after due deliberation, to remove all the livestock.   The hut is so peaceful and quiet by con-trast that the grateful man believes the Rabbi has accomplished a great miracle.

136.   Zolotow, Charlotte.   MY GRANDSON LEW.   New York: Harper and Row, 1974.   Illus. by William Pene DuBois.   32pp.   Grades K-2.

Unexpectedly, Lewis, 6, tells his mother he misses the grandfather who died when he was 2.   His startled mother asks him what he remembers.   They share fond reminiscences of a brisk, bright-eyed, bearded man of warmth and vitality who used to stay with Lewis when his parents were out of town.   The boy has never asked about him because he has been waiting for him to come back. "But you made him come back for me tonight by telling me what you remember, " says Lew's mother.   ". . . now we will remember him together and neither of us will be so lonely as we would be if we had to remember him alone. "

137.   Zolotow, Charlotte.   WILLIAM'S DOLL.   New York: Harper and Row, 1972.   Illus. by William Pene duBois.   32pp.   Grades K-1.

Tow-headed William yearns for a doll to cuddle and nurture like a baby.   His brother calls him a creep, and the boy next door tells him he's sissy.   His father succeeds in interesting him in basketball and electric trains, but those activities do not take the place of a doll to love.   When his visiting grandmother learns of his interest in dolls, she reacts differently.   "Wonderful, " she says and buys him a baby doll with sleeping eyes which he adores.   In response to William's distressed dad, his grandmother explains, "He needs it . . . so that he can practice being a father. "

Intermediate Grades

137a. Adler, C. S. THE SILVER COACH. New York: Coward,
       McCann and Geoghegan, 1979. 122pp. Grades 5-7.

As the older daughter, Chris, 12, feels that her newly
divorced mother imposes upon her and loves her less than her cute
but temperamental little sister Jackie, 7. Now Mother has enrolled
in intensive nurse's training and has brought the girls to spend the
summer with the paternal grandmother they have never met in her
retirement home in the Vermont wilderness. Chris is apprehensive
and plans immediately to leave with her father when he comes to
visit. Grandmother turns out to be pleasant, frank, reassuring, in-
tuitive and imaginative, and even shares with Chris the delicate fili-
greed ornamental coach that she has found useful for dispelling gloom
when she is lonely. Chris takes many flights of fancy aboard the
magic coach, always to blissful adventures with her father. Daddy
eventually appears--but with his new girlfriend and her three bump-
tious boys--and reveals himself as the shallow, selfish, immature
person he is, a disappointment to his mother and a bitter disillusionment to Chris and even Jackie. In helping her sister adjust emotionally, Chris loses her jealousy of Jackie and learns to be more
tolerant and cooperative with her mother through Grandmother's in-
sightful guidance. Mother is quick to appreciate the transformation
in her girls.

138.   Alexander, Anne. TROUBLE ON TREAT STREET. New
       York: Atheneum, 1974. Illus. by John Jones. 116pp.
       Grades 5-7.

Clem gets off to an inauspicious start when he moves to the
San Francisco ghetto with his righteous but tender grandmother after
his parents' death. Manolo, also 10, lives in the same building but
takes an instant dislike to Clem simply because he's black, not Chicano like himself. In school they are paired together but maintain
their unsheathed hostility until a gang of older toughs of mixed race
tries to play the two against each other. Just as they achieve mutual trust and friendship, Clem's grandmother and Manolo's mother
jump to the erroneous conclusion that the other boy is a bad influence on hers through circumstantial evidence. Only after Clem's
Granny saves the life of Manolo's baby brother does the true story
unfold. Mrs. Gomez, in gratitude, invites the newcomers to a party,
and Clem stands up to the bullies.

139.   Alexander, Lloyd. THE WIZARD IN THE TREE. New
         York: Dutton, 1975. Illus. by Laszlo Kubinyi. 138pp.
         Grades 5-6.

At the dawn of the Industrial Revolution, rapacious Squire
Scrupnor evicts his cottagers to exploit the coal beneath their small-
holdings, and drafts a usurious contract with the browbeaten inn-
keeper and his unctuous wife to whom the orphan Mallory is kitchen
maid. Mistreated by Mrs. Parsel, imaginative Mallory spends her
free time in the woods where she discovers and frees a Wizard who
has been imprisoned in a tree since that legendary day when he was
to join his fellow necromancers in Vale Innes. She befriends the
tattered and acerbic old man whose powers have been sapped by his
long captivity. When the nefarious Squire, who murdered to acquire
his sinecure, learns of the old man's presence, he sees him as the
scapegoat for his crimes. In trying to escape the Squire's clutches,
Arbican accidentally assumes a variety of amusing animal guises
with his diminished powers, but finally he and Mallory seem ir-
revocably doomed until Mallory spies the gold ring that is part of
the Squire's ill-gotten gains. It restores Arbican's powers, and the
Squire meets an electrifying demise. Arbican convinces Mallory to
accept the privileges and responsibilities of administering the estate,
as he sails off for his belated rendezvous.

140.   Allen, Robert Thomas. THE VIOLIN. Toronto: McGraw-
         Hill Ryerson, 1976. Illus. by George Plastic. 78pp.
         Music. Grades 3-5.

Chris saves a jarful of pennies and dimes to buy a battered
violin and tries to play it for his friend Danny but produces nothing
more than a strident squawk. Deciding that the violin is no good,
he dumps it in a trash bin in the park. He is startled when an old
man retrieves it, tunes it, and plays beautiful music. Thus begins
a friendship à trois and for Chris the expert tutelage he needs. One
day the boys are playing, and the violin is inadvertently smashed.
A stricken Chris vows he will never play again. Hearing of the accident, the old man leaves his own invaluable violin for Chris before
departing the city. Chris knows the only way to express his gratitude and appreciation is by learning to play the fine instrument
creditably. Danny is sad at their friend's departure, but Chris tells
him, "nobody ever says goodbye who leaves the world beautiful music. "

141.   Anastasio, Dina. A QUESTION OF TIME. New York: Dut-
         ton, 1978. Illus. by Dale Payson. 90pp. Grades 4-5.

Sydell Stowe, 11, is convinced that she will hate living in
the small town in Minnesota that her great-grandfather, 95, grew
up in and left at 18 to become an actor. Through her love of dolls,
she becomes embroiled with an old dollmaker and his granddaughter,
Syd's only friend, in a 1901 corpseless murder mystery. Careful

detective work at the library reveals that Syd's very lively great-grandfather was the purported victim. Further sleuthing discloses that the very corporeal dollmaker and granddaughter are actually turn-of-the-century shades who have returned to absolve the "murderer," also deceased, and set the records straight through Syd, who decides to become an investigative reporter on the kids' community newspaper staff and to teach the local girls her skateboard skills in exchange for learning their jump rope games. The ghosts, their mission accomplished, dematerialize.

142.   Anckarsvard, Karin. AUNT VINNIE'S INVASION. New
        York: Harcourt, Brace and World, 1962. Illus. by William
        M. Hutchinson. 128pp. Grades 5-6.

The six Hallsenius children are sent to stay with their independent, sensible, unsentimental, elderly Aunt Lavinia in a Stockholm suburb while their parents are on assignment in Africa. Aunt Vinnie will not tolerate dogs, but Lollie, 12, is determined to bring her mutt Piazzo along and ingeniously smuggles him in and out of her room until Aunt Vinnie catches on and lets her keep him. She further captivates the youngsters when Per, 9, wanders away from school in a reverie, and she squares his truancy with school authorities with a white lie. The greatest test of her patience and wisdom comes when belligerent Sam, 13, accidentally stuns his brother Anders, 16, in an altercation, believes he has killed him, and runs away from the scene of the crime. Later he redeems himself by heroically forestalling an act of arson. The children demonstrate their appreciation and affection for Aunt Vinnie on her birthday.

143.   Anckarsvard, Karin. AUNT VINNIE'S VICTORIOUS SIX.
        New York: Harcourt, Brace and World, 1964. Illus. by
        William M. Hutchinson. 155pp. Grades 5-6.

Annika, 15, and Anders are absorbed with members of the opposite sex as spring comes to Nordvik (see 142), and Lollie is mortified when she accidentally breaks Aunt Vinnie's best antique crystal bowl and goes to great lengths to replace it. But it is Per who causes the greatest stir in his beloved aunt's life, instructing her how to enter the soccer pool, entreating her to help him with his homework at the crack of dawn in the bushes behind the school, and causing great concern when the shy little African boy he has befriended disappears and is feared drowned. The boy is found unexpectedly, but even more surprisingly, Aunt Vinnie wins the soccer pool and abides by the Hallsenius' family motto, "One for all and all for one."

144.   Angelo, Valenti. NINO. New York: Viking Press, 1938.
        Illus. by the author. 244pp. Grades 5-8.

This is the heartwarming story of the first eight years in

the life of Nino, an Italian peasant boy living with his mother in his
62-year-old grandfather's comfortable cottage, awaiting money from
his father who is in America working for their passage to join him.
It is also the saga of the ebb and flow of Italian village life as it
has throbbed for centuries, ordained by the seasons, the crops, the
religious traditions, and the folk customs.   Nino is a clever and
imaginative boy whose ambition is to become an artist in emulation
of the village woodcarver.   He is reared with wisdom and compassion in an atmosphere rich in intangible values if lacking in materi-
alistic appurtenances.   Their eventual bittersweet departure is tempered by the fond memories they are free to take and the looming
expectations that fill their horizon.   Grandfather accompanies them
on their journey.

145.   Babbitt, Natalie. THE EYES OF THE AMARYLLIS. New
        York: Farrar, Straus and Giroux, 1977. 128pp. Grades
        5-7.

        Witnessing his seafaring father's death at sea when he was
a boy so unnerved Jenny's father that he moved inland when grown
and never returned to his mother's seaside New England home. Now,
at 75, she has broken her ankle and needs Jenny's help; her father
reluctantly agrees.   But the resolute and absorbing old lady is not
an invalid.   She needs Jenny only to search the beach at high tide
every day for a sign from her drowned husband aboard the sunken
Amaryllis.   Another mysterious beachcomber is singlemindedly determined to throw back to Father Neptune anything the sea disgorges
or forfeit his life.   When Jenny finds the marvelously intact figurehead of the lost ship, Gran is fiercely bent on keeping it out of
Seward's clutches, but the sea has the final word.   It spawns a
deadly hurricane that breaches the very house in search of its own,
and Gran almost sacrifices herself to it.   She is saved by Jenny's
father's courageous intervention, an act which is cathartic to his
fear.   The figurehead is lost, but the capricious sea brings Gran a
tropical amaryllis blossom, and Jenny and her romantic grandmother,
kindred spirits, draw a sense of strength and freedom from the
eternal, restless sea.

146.   Baker, Betty. THE SHAMAN'S LAST RAID. New York:
        Harper and Row, 1963. Illus. by Leonard Shortall. 182pp.
        Glossary. Grades 4-6.

        Great-grandfather arrives from the reservation to spend the
summer at the same time that Uncle Red Eagle, entrepreneur and
ghost town souvenir shop proprietor, arranges for a Hollywood film
crew to begin shooting a TV western.   The ancient Apache medicine
man eschews anything modern and "not Indian, " and dreams of re-
capturing bygone glories when he rode as a boy with Geronimo.
The means becomes available when he spots the film company's
remuda, and twins Ebon and Melody become unwilling conspirators
in his quixotic adventure. From the venerable and taciturn shaman,

Ebon learns desert endurance and survival skills, ceremonial rituals, and craftsmanship, but he worries about the legal consequences of rustling Mr. Donnelly's cattle. His efforts to circumvent the scheme fail, and the crusty and crafty old warrior steals the steers under the very eyes of the cameras. Only Ebon with his recent training can track them into the mountains and recover most of the herd. The shaman has his victory celebration, and Uncle Red emerges as another sort of hero. Ebon realizes that everybody has to be his own kind of Indian; he wants to be the herpetologist kind.

147.   Barber, Antonia. THE GHOSTS. New York: Farrar, Straus and Giroux, 1969. 189pp. Grades 5-8.

An elderly apparition from the 1800's returns to the present to atone for a sin of omission in the past which resulted in the deaths of two innocent children. These children, ghosts themselves, appear to Lucy and Jamie and show them how to travel the Wheel of Time back to their era before the fatal fire. With the help of Jamie and Lucy, their hapless fate is averted, and old Mr. Blunden's spirit makes expiation and is laid to rest. Back in the present after a harrowing transversal, it is miraculously discovered that Jamie and Lucy are the great-great-grandchildren of one of the ghost children (who lived happily to a ripe old age). Her country estate is legally theirs, and their widowed mother's future is secure.

148.   Baudouy, Michel-Aime. OLD ONE-TOE. New York: Harcourt, Brace and World, 1959. Illus. by Johannes Troyer. Trans. by Marie Ponsot. 190pp. Grades 5-6.

Piet, Lina, and twins Genevieve and Gerard are sent to their aunt's home on the edge of a vast French primeval forest where Tatie raises chickens. One night a fox raids the henhouse, endangering Tatie's livelihood, and the children vow revenge. They set traps but are remorseful on learning that the fox has escaped with a maimed foot. Their philanthropic neighbor and Tatie's landlord, the lonely old Commandant, retired from the sea, teaches intense Piet the art of woodsmanship, and he tracks the fox with its unique spoor until he learns its habits and comes to respect the noble and intelligent creature. The Old Gentleman also stalks Reynard, but not with conservationist impulses. He is an avid and accomplished hunter who thrills to match wits with his prey. It becomes a contest to defend the fox without losing the friendship of the Commandant. With hair-raising maneuvers the battle is fought to a draw, the old man's face is saved, and old One-Toe lives to sire three more marauders.

148a.   Bawden, Nina. THE ROBBERS. New York: Lothrop, Lee and Shepard, 1979. 155pp. Grades 5-6.

Philip Holbein, 9, has always lived contentedly with his

grandmother in a "Grace and Favour" apartment in a seaside castle provided by the Queen for widows of military commanders while his widowed father, a television newscaster, has followed current events around the globe. His long association with elderly ladies has matured him beyond his years and sensitized him to the physical and emotional problems of the aging, including his grandmother's tunnel vision. Suddenly his cool and remote father remarries, settles down in London, and decides to make a home for the boy. Although he and his grandmother both resent the upheaval in their lives, Philip tries to make the best of it for her sake and makes friends with his stepmother and a neighbor boy, Darcy, whose father is crippled with arthritis and cannot work. When Darcy's brother, the family's sole support, bends the law and is sentenced to prison, the boys try several abortive moneymaking schemes before Darcy persuades Philip to break into a haughty rich woman's house. The two are caught, and Philip's unbending father prescribes harsh punishment. His grandmother indignantly marches to Philip's defense, spirits him back to their castle home, and offers to intercede in a musical career for Darcy.

149.   Bawden, Nina. THE WITCH'S DAUGHTER. Philadelphia: Lippincott, 1966. 181pp. Grades 5-8.

Orphaned in infancy, Perdita, 11, has been reared by compassionate, elderly Annie MacLaren on a tiny island off the coast of Scotland where she has run as free and wild as the wind and grown as shy and stunted as the flowers in their rocky crevices. Annie acts as housekeeper for the enigmatic Mr. Smith who does not allow Perdita to attend school or make friends with the other island children who fear the clairvoyant girl is bewitched. When the steamer brings a vacationing family and a mysterious stranger to Skua, Perdita finds her first friends in blind Janey and her imaginative brother Tim. The children pool their extraordinary capabilities to solve an almost perfect crime and save one another from a hideous demise. Mr. Smith has been kind to Perdita in his clumsy way, and when his complicity is revealed, she warns him to escape and grieves when he loses his life in the attempt. He leaves his house to Perdita, assuring her and Annie of a roof over their heads and an opportunity for education.

150.   Baxter, Caroline. THE STOLEN TELESM. Philadelphia: Lippincott, 1975. 192pp. Grades 5-8.

Spending the summer with their mouselike Aunt Emily in the country, Lucy and David receive an enigmatic invitation to pay an obligatory visit on elderly Miss Fothersby-Bane at the ominous, mouldering Hall. The children are both mesmerized and repulsed upon entering the old woman's oppressive room where she keeps a baboon to do her bidding. They break the spell and escape, only to discover a foreboding, bottomless pool on the grounds and near it a pathetic captive foal with a mysterious stone around its neck. They

rescue Telesm, nurse him to health, and watch him sprout powerful wings. It soon becomes horrifyingly apparent that the malevolent
witch means to destroy the magnificent creature by sending packs of
slavering wolves after it and unleashing the forces of Darkness that
are pent in the pool, imprisoning the district in the grip of an arc-
tic blizzard. The children entrench themselves with Telesm to face
the furious onslaught of the demons, but when their defenses are
breached, they escape upon the back of the winged horse to the
chamber of the benevolent wizard behind the waterfall who charges
them with the final chilling showdown with the old witch. Aunt Emily adopts the hapless baboon.

151.   Beatty, Patricia. BILLY BEDAMNED, LONG GONE BY.
        New York: Morrow, 1977. 223pp. Grades 5-8.

        In the summer of 1929, Mom and Grandmother Quiney, both
vivacious redheads, plan an adventuresome cross-country motor tour
from San Diego to Louisiana with Merle, 13, and Graham, 10.
They are delayed in the very hamlet where two of Grandmother's
numerous brothers, Hoyt and Rudd Quiney, live. Hoyt is friendly
and likable, but Rudd is obviously the black sheep of the Texas
Quineys, illiterate, cantankerous, boorish, and mendacious. In
five days he tells seven different versions of how he lost his left
ear lobe, each more outrageous than the last, and each prefaced
by once-upon-a-time in cowboy parlance, "Billy bedamned, it's long
gone by...." Literal Merle is repelled by her great-uncle's vul-
garity and impatient with his fabrications. She can't understand
why Graham is fascinated and even Mother and Grandmother seem
tolerantly amused by his tall tales, until her mother explains that
the banty rooster is not only a has-been but a never-was who pre-
varicates to entertain others and enhance his own stature. When
he tells the truth at last, they don't believe him.

152.   Behn, Harry. THE TWO UNCLES OF PABLO. New York:
        Harcourt, Brace, 1959. Illus. by Mel Silverman. 96pp.
        Grades 4-6.

        Improvident, illiterate, disreputable, but ebullient Uncle
Silvan, his mother's uncle, volunteers to take Pablo from his isolated family farm in Mexico and underwrite his education in the
town of San Miguel. Pablo quickly learns that Uncle Silvan's
promises are nothing but fantasies, but the compassionate, philosophical boy accepts and forgives the old man's deception, lassitude,
and fraud, because he knows his nature will never change, though
he always means well. To his astonishment, he also discovers that
San Miguel's leading citizen, Don Francisco, is his father's uncle,
a wealthy but aloof and lugubrious poet whom Pablo also pities.
The two uncles have been feuding for years, but because of the boy's
generosity of spirit, Uncle Silvan lives up to his responsibilities for
once, and lonely Don Francisco unbends. After Pablo returns to
the farm for the birth of his baby brother (whom he names Silvan)

and to help his father with the crops, he will return to San Miguel and live with Don Francisco to pursue his education belatedly.

153. Bellairs, John. THE TREASURE OF ALPHEUS WINTER-
BORN. New York: Harcourt, Brace, Jovanovich, 1978.
Illus. by Judith Gwyn Brown. 180pp. Grades 5-8.

An eccentric millionaire archaeologist builds a rococo town library as a monument to himself, lives in it for a week before it opens, then dies two weeks later. There is wide speculation that he has cached a treasure in the building, but he has taken the secret to his grave. Anthony Monday, a lonely boy whose father has been idled by a heart attack, is given a job as library page by the sympathetic but stereotypic aging librarian, and he is determined to track down the treasure after finding a hidden clue. Though skeptical, Miss Eells helps him in his probe, and they soon discover that the old man's pompous, unscrupulous banker nephew is himself hot in pursuit of the cache and will stop at nothing to acquire it. On a night as dark as Erebus when the town has been evacuated because of flooding, Hugo forces Anthony to scale the precipitous escarpment of one of the library's parapets in a dizzying denouement. Mr. Winterborn's stash proves to be Biblical treasure for which a museum pays handsomely, and Anthony's father's financial concerns are over.

154. Blue, Rose. GRANDMA DIDN'T WAVE BACK. New York:
Watts, 1972. Illus. by Ted Lewin. 62pp. Grades 3-5.

Her grandmother's encroaching senility causes Debbie, 10, increasing anguish. She remembers the good times since Grandma, at her husband's death, came to live with her and her professional parents: the warm cooking smells, having friends in for refreshments, the shared confidences after school. Now Grandma no longer waves to her from the balcony after school or provides snacks and meals, but worst of all, she forgets who Debbie is and fails to get dressed all day. Debbie's friends are embarrassed to come over. A sudden return to lucidity convinces Debbie that she has recovered, as from a virus, but the memory lapses return, and one night she is found wandering in the street. An adult family council decides reluctantly to place her in a nearby nursing home. Debbie is distraught that she will be "put away" like an infirm animal and wishes that her malady were merely being hard of hearing like the elderly woman next door. Visiting her at the nursing home, Debbie finds her alert once more. ". . . you think of your grandma. But not always," says the aging woman. At home Debbie says, "You know, Mom, when you start to grow up there are lots more used-to-be's. "

155. Bolton, Evelyn. DREAM DANCER. Mankato: Creative,
1974. Illus. by John Keely. 31pp. Grades 3-5.

Caroline spends every summer with her grandfather in the
company town of Santa D'Oro, California, owned by Mr. Judd,
where she looks forward to riding Mr. Judd's horse, Dandy.   Grandpa looks a trifle frailer and more stooped this year, and indeed, he
breaks the news that he has reached the mandatory retirement age
of 65 and that Mr. Judd is relieving him not only of his job as
skilled cabinetmaker but of his house, as well.   An incensed Caroline goes off to ride in the Fourth of July parade, but spying an
aging gray horse in the corral, she foreswears riding Dandy that
day in favor of staging a protest demonstration against Mr. Judd's
arbitrary dismissal policy.   Stirred by the martial music, Dream
Dancer lives up to his former reputation, surprising everyone.   Mr.
Judd, who can't abide waste, reads Caroline's message loud and
clear.

156.   Boston, L. M.   THE CHILDREN OF GREEN KNOWE.   New
         York: Harcourt, Brace and World, 1955.   Illus. by Peter
         Boston.   157pp.   Grades 4-6.

Shy, sensitive Tolly comes to spend the Christmas holidays
with his great-grandmother and discovers that he has a natural affinity for the sprightly, conspiratorial old lady and her ancient ancestral castle that is peopled with the spirits of children who in-
habited it centuries before and with the wild birds she befriends.
It is no surprise to Granny Oldknow that Tolly begins to hear the
voices and see the forms that she revivifies in her wonderful stories
of Green Knowe's history, how it got its name, and of the topiary
trees that are sometimes curiously and once terrifyingly animate.
At the end of the holiday, Granny tells him that he need not return
to his intimidating old boarding school but may attend one close to
home and spend all his holidays with her.

157.   Boston, L. M.   TREASURE OF GREEN KNOWE.   New
         York: Harcourt, Brace and World, 1958.   Illus. by Peter
         Boston.   185pp.   Grades 4-6.

Tolly returns to his partridge-like great-grandmother at
Green Knowe (see 156) for the Easter holiday, meets two new apparitions, Susan and Jacob, and learns from Granny Oldknow the
eighteenth century history of the estate when a Georgian manor
house was built to surround the old stone keep.   It is a story of
knavery, conflagration, and the heroism of Jacob, blackamoor companion to blind Susan who saved her life by leading her down one of
Green Knowe's impervious stone flues.   Curiosity piqued, Tolly finds
the fortune in fabulous jewels that was lost at the time of the fire
in a long-abandoned chimney.   It enables his great-grandmother to
make necessary repairs to the old house without selling their favorite
painting.

158.   Boston, L. M.   A STRANGER AT GREEN KNOWE.   New

York: Harcourt, Brace and World, 1961. Illus. by Peter Boston. 158pp. Grades 4-6.

Ping, a Chinese Displaced Person, has been taken for the summer by diminutive Mrs. Oldknow in place of her great-grandson, Tolly (see 156 & 157). Ping is agitated over the escape of the gorilla Hanno with whom he empathizes as another uprooted creature and who, like a genie, is now free. He builds a hideout in the bamboo thicket that Mrs. Oldknow maintains as her bird sanctuary to which it is foreordained that the gorilla will gravitate for refuge resembling his natural habitat. The behemoth accepts the delicate boy as naturally as he would any non-threatening jungle denizen, and Ping helps him appease his gargantuan appetite from Green Knowe's kitchen and garden. But officials become suspicious of the thicket and Ping's evasions, even though he is staunchly defended by Mrs. Oldknow. It is unfortunate Hanno who finally makes his own decision between returning to captivity or dying violently. When astute Mrs. Oldknow sees Ping's reaction to Hanno's choice of death, she offers him the liberty of a permanent home with her.

159. Boston, L. M. AN ENEMY AT GREEN KNOWE. New York: Harcourt, Brace and World, 1964. Illus. by Peter Boston. 156pp. Grades 4-6.

Tolly and Ping have joined forces at Green Knowe with Granny Oldknow (see 156, 157 & 158) just in time to fight for the very possession of the venerable estate against satanic forces. A malevolent witch in the guise of an unctuous professor, Dr. Melanie Powers, tries to gain access to the castle to search for an ancient manuscript. When Mrs. Oldknow politely but firmly refuses, Melanie uses hypnotism, chicanery, and then a Mephistophelean panoply of plagues to drive them out. The three defend themselves with some countermagic, and the boys, delving under the roof, discover the crumbling book, The Ten Powers of Moses, which, when translated by their own resident professor, proves to be the salvation of Green Knowe and the destruction of Melanie. The enchanted Persian looking glass that mirrors the immediate future shows that Tolly's father is returning and bringing a friend who also happens to be Ping's father.

160. Brady, Esther Wood. TOLIVER'S SECRET. New York: Crown, 1976. Illus. by Richard Cuffari. 166pp. Grades 5-6.

When Grandfather sprains his ankle in British-occupied Philadelphia in 1776, there is no choice but for timid Ellen Toliver, 10, to deliver his secret message, baked into a loaf of bread, to Washington's couriers in New Jersey, dressed as a boy. What should be a simple and straightforward transaction is complicated when she is chased by bullies and misses the patriot boats. Instead, she is hijacked by rough British soldiers, bent on eating the

fresh loaf, and sailed to the wrong port.   There she escapes the
Redcoats but must find her way through unfamiliar and hostile countryside to her destination while maintaining her alien identity.   The last
part of the journey is made in Stygian darkness, but she stubbornly
perseveres and eventually delivers the battered bread to the proper
agent, earning the accolades of her grandfather and General Washington after his victory at Trenton.   With new courage and self-
respect, she stands up to the bullies.

161.   Bragdon, Elspeth. THAT JUD! New York: Viking Press,
        1957.   Illus. by Georges Schreiber.   126pp.   Grades 4-6.

        Some say it crossly, some admiringly, some lovingly.
"That Jud" is a trial and tribulation to everyone in the Maine fishing village except laconic old Captain Ben whom the town appointed
his guardian after his parents' death. Jud, 12, can be rebellious
and heedless from time to time but never deliberately mean or dishonest.   He did break Homer's boathouse windows in a fit of pique,
but he helped replace them.   His greatest source of satisfaction is
the cabin he is building on a tiny island.   The opportunity arises to
earn money toward it when a wealthy summer resident, Mr. York,
hires him to care for his outboard motorboat.   Suspicion is pointed
at Jud when a mysterious fire erupts in Mr. York's shed which Jud
just happens to be on hand to extinguish, but many voices rise to
his defense, the true culprit confesses, and Jud is exonerated and
touted as the hero he is.   Captain Ben's faith in him has never
faltered.

162.   Branscum, Robbie. JOHNNY MAY. Garden City: Double-
        day, 1975.   Illus. by Charles Robinson.   135pp.   Grades
        5-8.

        Living in the Ozarks with her toothless Grandma and
tobacco-chewing Grandpa while her mother lives licentiously in the
city, Johnny May, 10, is preoccupied with the scatological concerns
of the pubescent, in general, and the earthy, uninformed hillbilly,
in particular, and with means of preventing Aunt Irene from marrying the mean and shifty Mr. Berry.   Her days are engaged with the
attractive new boy, Aron, and in the simple country pleasures of
swimming nude, fishing, and box suppers.   She can't afford shoes or
a dress but is too proud to admit it to Aron and so exaggerates her
tomboy image when he teases her about her appearance.   Her im-
petuous and mischievous behavior raises pangs of guilt, because Grandma says that she is old enough to pay for her own sins or be saved
at revival meeting.   She is convinced that the flood that nearly
claims her life is God's retribution for enviously ruining her city
cousin's dress.   She begrudges Grandpa her hard-earned clothing
allowance when an emergency arises, but when her mother sends
her a windfall, she is generous with it and earns the approbation
of her family and a kiss from Aron.

163.   Branscum, Robbie. THREE BUCKETS OF DAYLIGHT.
          New York: Lothrop, Lee and Shepard, 1978. Illus. by
          Allen Davis. 125pp.   Grades 4-6.

          Jackie Lee, 11, lives with his grandparents deep in the
Arkansas hills.   He and his youngest uncle, Jimmy Jay, 13, are
inseparable companions who rove the hills together but have a
healthy respect for the ominous old "holler," so gloomy and overgrown that one would have to import sunlight like well water to live
there.   When they snitch apples from the witchy old Blackgrove
sisters' orchard, one of them puts a curse on them.   In trepidation
they turn to religion as an antidote, but just in case, they bribe
another toothless old woman with gifts of food to invoke a reverse
curse.   The unusually harsh winter is rife with sickness and starvation, exacerbated by an illicit still which supplies the men with
moonshine at the expense of the women and children.   On an expedition to get an ingredient for the magic potion, the boys stumble
upon the still, and Jackie Lee is captured by the Blackgrove sisters
who have been operating it in the holler.   He is rescued by Grandpa, with some help from the sheriff, and the last of their fear and
suspicion of the curse and the holler is allayed.

164.   Branscum, Robbie. TOBY, GRANNY AND GEORGE.
          Garden City: Doubleday, 1976. Illus. by Glen Rounds.
          105pp.   Grades 4-6.

          A bastard left on her grandmother's doorstep, enterprising
October (Toby), 13, grows up in an atmosphere of subsistence and
quiet acceptance along with her canine companion, George, among
their Ozark neighbors where life revolves around crops and church.
Complacency dissolves when an obese parishioner drowns during
baptism.   One faction, led by penurious Deacon Treat, believes that
Preacher Davis maliciously held her under.   The other faction, led
by sensible and respected Granny, an herbalist, maintains that Deacon Treat was negligent in dredging the baptismal hole.   Then Deacon is discovered dead, and the Treat baby is missing.   Toby is
bound to solve the mystery and absolve Preacher.   She makes
friends shyly with the mute eldest of the Treat tribe whose father
had starved and enslaved them for his own gain.   When she hears
Granny's tale of child abuse and finds the small grave hidden deep
in the woods, she knows intuitively that her new friend killed his
father in defense of the baby.   Preacher Davis assures them that
the boy will not be prosecuted.   Toby is afraid of having to go to
the city with her mother, but strict but loving Granny reassures
her that she will always have a home with her, to be the succor of
her old age.

165.   Brodie, Deborah. STORIES MY GRANDFATHER SHOULD
          HAVE TOLD ME. New York: Bonim, 1977. Illus. by
          Carmela Tal Baron. 113pp. Glossary. Grades 4-6.

This is a collection of stories excerpted from books by
famous children's authors on the Jewish experience.   Holidays represented include a Bar Mitzvah, a P'Idyon Ha-ben, Purim, Passover,
and a wedding.   The Diaspora is reflected in episodes from European
villages, Palestine, immigrant America, and the modern state of
Israel. Tales are eclectically amusing, poignant, triumphant, traditional, and contemporary.

166.   Bulla, Clyde Robert. MARCO MOONLIGHT. New York:
         Crowell, 1976. Illus. by Julia Noonan. 104pp. Grades
         3-5.

         Marco, 13, has only a dim recollection of the time before
his mother died when he was brought to his grandparents' great
manor house.   When their old gardener is disabled by thugs and
forced to retire, Flint, his incongruous replacement, makes friends
with Marco and one day takes him to a bleak and isolated beach cottage.   Dropping his mask of respectability, Flint stuns Marco with
the embodiment of his waking dream, his twin brother Matt.   The
boys' dastardly and avaricious uncle, Flint has had custody of Matt
since their father died.   He now plots to cop Marco's inheritance
for himself and Matt, his impenitent dupe.   The plan is chillingly
successful, but Flint has not reckoned on an instinctive brotherly
bond nor on the effect of the grandparents' unwitting kindness to the
imposter.   Learning that Flint is coming to kill Marco, Matt helps
him escape in a harrowing cliff chase.   Marco offers to share and
share alike, but a reborn Matt must first make certain restitutions
before he can take his rightful place alongside Marco with his grandparents.

167.   Burch, Robert. TWO THAT WERE TOUGH. New York:
         Viking, 1976. Illus. by Richard Cuffari. 80pp. Grades
         3-5.

         At the Yorks' farm a defiant and perverse chick is hatched
of their most independent hen.   Mr. Hilton, the old miller who lives
nearby, observes the feisty gray fowl's progress as he forages for
spilled grain.   When the brood is "frying size, " Mrs. York snares
them one by one, all but the wary gray.   Deftly he eludes predators
and picnickers whose lunches and fishing worms he plunders.   When
the Yorks move away, he remains behind in the woods of the deserted farm.   With a little assistance from Mr. Hilton, who dubs
him Wild Wings, he weathers the worst of the winters.   But one
year Mr. Hilton nearly dies of flu, and his daughter urges him to
move to Atlanta with her.   The redoubtable old man postpones retirement for a year, citing his duties at the mill and to the bird.
In that year business falls off, and a new family moves into the
farm.   He decides to take Wild Wings with him and sets about winning his confidence so he can trap him.   He succeeds, but in doing
so he suffers a mild heart attack, then wonders if chickens can die
of fright, too, or pine away in confinement.   He sets Wild Wings
free but enlists the new family at the farm to look after him.

168. Byars, Betsy. AFTER THE GOAT MAN. New York:
Viking, 1974. Illus. by Ronald Himler. 126pp. Grades
4-6.

Harold is a self-indulgent, egocentric, obese boy who takes
lugubrious pleasure in wallowing in his own misery. His only friend
is Ada who is totally unselfconscious, tolerant, thoughtful, and sympathetic. Then diffident, defensive Figgy moves in, and Harold,
with Ada's guidance, learns to become sensitive to the misfortunes
of others. Figgy lives with his grandfather, Ira Gryshevich, the
taciturn "Goat Man, " an eccentric recluse whose cabin has been
condemned to make way for a superhighway. The broken old man
cannot adjust to city life in the row of concrete block houses where
he has been relocated, and he returns to the cabin to defy the bull-
dozers. Figgy's injury in a bike mishap en route to his grandfather's defense with his new friends forces his grandfather to abandon his campaign but not his dignity. Ada's father promises to find
them a suitable home in the country.

169. Byars, Betsy. THE CARTOONIST. New York: Viking,
1978. Illus. by Richard Cuffari. 119pp. Grades 5-7.

Pap, Alfie's grandfather, curses the bureaucracy by day
and reminisces incessantly by night. His mother watches TV
ceaselessly except when she's haranguing Pap to shut up. His sister, Alma, bears the brunt of household responsibility, and Alfie
escapes the discord by retreating to his windowless, raftered attic
crawl space, reached only by trap door, where he keeps the tools
of his cartooning obsession. There he covertly draws wry scenes
from the acerbic life around him. Then one day his mother informs him that his larcenous, unemployed, scapegrace older brother,
Bubba, his mother's favorite, and his expectant wife are coming to
live with them, and she plans to fix up his private domain for them.
Stricken and angry, Alfie barricades himself in the attic, and no
threat or entreaty will bring him down, though Pap and Alma secret-
ly side with him. When Bubba's plans change and Alfie is reprieved,
his mother taunts him that he has not been victorious but has won
only by default. He decides to bring his cartoons out of conceal-
ment and work in public.

170. Byars, Betsy. THE HOUSE OF WINGS. New York: Viking, 1972. Illus. by Daniel Schwartz. 142pp. Grades
4-6.

Youngest of eight children, Sammy, 10, has been allowed
to rear himself in unfettered freedom. Now his parents have just
cast him off on his mother's long-widowed father at his big, derelict house in Ohio where odd fowl roam at will. Incredulous and
outraged at the perfidy, the boy visits his anger and frustration on
the grizzled old man, calling him names and leading him on a
gruelling chase through a culvert and up a rocky hillside. His

desperate flight is halted by the haunting cry of a stranded and injured crane.   His grandfather's determination to save the afflicted
creature puzzles but fascinates the callous, self-centered boy.   Because the bird is blind it must be hand fed; their personal comfort
must wait.   Sammy learns that while his grandfather cannot sort
out his own children, he has no problem recalling each of his succession of avian acquaintances.   He finally makes peace with his
grandfather, whose unorthodox lifestyle he finds appealing, especially
his disregard of bathing or changing clothes.   He hopes that when
he eventually tries his own wings, his grandfather will remember
him as he has his other departed wildfowl.

171.   Callen, Larry. THE DEADLY MANDRAKE.   Boston: Lit-
          tle, Brown, 1978.   Illus. by Larry Johnson.   163pp.
          Grades 5-6.

An angry, broken old man puts a curse on the ignorant,
superstitious Louisiana backwater town of Four Corners and dies before he can be persuaded to rescind it.   A cow drops dead after
giving birth to a gray calf, the calf jumps into a rowboat and becomes alligator bait, a hen begins crowing, a cistern springs a
leak, but worst of all, Pinch Grimball's mother takes deathly ill.
The alienated old man's mysterious black box that contains the
source of the curse is missing, and his mute daughter, Sorrow Nix,
Pinch's best friend, won't renege on her promise to her dying father not to divulge its whereabouts.   When the secret is told and the
box comes to light, the deadly mandrake root it contained is gone,
and only Sorrow can lead them to where it is growing and exuding
its malignancy.   The adults are too frightened to uproot it, and the
task devolves upon the quaking children.   The mutant calf eats the
weed with no ill effect, but Pinch's mom recovers miraculously.

172.   Cameron, Eleanor. JULIA AND THE HAND OF GOD.
          New York: Dutton, 1977.   Illus. by Gail Owens.   168pp.
          Grades 5-7.

When her improvident journalist father was killed in World
War I, Julia Redfern and her mother and brother moved into her
maternal grandmother's cramped house in Berkeley.   Gramma's
open favoritism of Greg has always rankled, but now that Julia is
11, their antagonism flairs into conflict.   Julia, who is imaginative
and absent-minded like her father, is judged irresponsible by her
pragmatic fundamentalist grandmother.   When she is punished for
burning a pot in trying to cremate a dead mouse, Julia meets a
retired professor who encourages her to write creatively of her impressions and daydreams.   She further distresses her family when
she disappears on the day Berkeley burns in a disastrous brush
fire and in one of her abstractions is almost caught by the flames.
Gramma calls it the hand of God that saved her, but Julia knows it
is her sixth sense that spared her.   She ponders this and other
"strangenesses," and when she, Mother, and Greg finally move to

a little house of their own, Julia is inspired to begin filling the
pages of the journal that sympathetic Uncle Hugh gave her. (Julia's
story is continued in A ROOM MADE OF WINDOWS in which a cultured elderly woman plays a pivotal role.)

173.   Carlson, Natalie Savage. ANN AURELIA AND DOROTHY.
         New York: Harper and Row, 1968. Illus. by Dale Payson.
         130pp. Grades 4-5.

Her mother's new husband doesn't like her, so Ann Aurelia
has been shunted to a succession of foster homes. Her new foster
mother, old Mrs. Hicken, is as comfortable as an old shoe and
seems genuinely fond of her, even getting involved in PTA, and
she has found her first bosom buddy in Dorothy, a black girl who
is in her fifth grade class. She and Dorothy have fun concocting
weird snacks, shopping in the supermarket, being in the Safety
Patrol together, being heroines on a field trip, and staging a surprise party for their teacher. When her natural mother turns up
unexpectedly, having divorced Mr. Lacey and avowing her mistake,
Ann Aurelia initially refuses to leave Mrs. Hicken and return to
her until Dorothy helps her to empathize with her mother's loneliness. Mrs. Hicken finds them an apartment near school, and she
and Dorothy go to visit Mrs. Hicken and her new foster child.

174.   Carlson, Natalie Savage. THE FAMILY UNDER THE
         BRIDGE. New York: Harper, 1958. Illus. by Garth
         Williams. 97pp. Grades 3-5.

The jaunty old hobo, Armand, who has an antipathy for
both children and work, returns to his roost on the quay under one
of Paris' famous bridges, only to find that his niche has been ap-
propriated by three homeless, fatherless moppets. The little
"starlings" suffer him to stay, although their mother is mistrustful
of the disreputable beggar. The children quickly endear themselves
to him, and he takes them to visit Father Christmas, a friend
seasonally employed at a fancy department store. They ask for
nothing but a real home. When two officious society matrons
threaten to send the children to an orphanage and their mother to
jail, Armand hastily removes them to the camp of gypsy friends,
to their mother's initial horror. When the gypsies move on, he is
forced to consider gainful employment. Transformed by a bath and
a mend, he is engaged as concierge of an apartment house, the
perfect sinecure because the emolument includes living quarters
where he can nest his brood.

174a.   Carlson, Natalie Savage. A GRANDMOTHER FOR THE
         ORPHELINES. New York: Harper and Row, 1980. Illus.
         by David White. 91pp. Grades 4-5.

In this fifth Orpheline story, naughty, ingenuous, endearing, persistent, vivacious Josine, youngest of the twenty French orphan girls, has her heart set on acquiring a grandmother to keep her company when the older girls are in school and Madame is busy. Their new nursemaid tells them marvelous Breton tales of imps, goblins, enchanted rocks, and of how the beasts in the stable talk in human tongues at midnight on Christmas Eve, but Josine is still so desperate for a grandmother that she entraps the gardener's old mother in the dungeon of their venerable castle in hopes that she can be prevailed upon to join en famille, but the idea backfires. Josine is contrite but longs to hear the animals speak, so on Christmas Eve she creeps out to the barn. What she overhears causes her to summon superstitious Madame. They discover a shabby and starving but respectable elderly couple who have been mistreated by their son and daughter-in-law. In true Orpheline tradition they adopt the Dupuys, and when their new nursemaid leaves, the Dupuys take their place, completing their menage.

175.   Carpenter, Frances. TALES OF A CHINESE GRAND-
         MOTHER. Garden City: Doubleday, 1937. Illus. by
         Malthe Hasselriis. 261pp. Grades 5-8.

In traditional China where the aged are revered, everyone wishes to be thought as old as possible. Ah Shung and Yu Lang's wealthy, aristocratic grandmother, 70, likes to be called Lao Lao or "Old Old One." She rules her large compound imperiously, inspecting each court herself, allotting spending money to her grown sons, and being served special, exotic foods to keep up her strength. After evening meals, the extended family gathers in Grandmother Ling's apartment, where she pragmatically keeps her own coffin, for poems and stories about dragons, unicorns, phoenixes, deities, spirits, immortal men, beautiful maids, and anthropomorphic animals. The children love these sessions, and on Lao Lao's birthday, hundreds of friends call to make obeisance.

176.   Cate, Dick. NEVER IS A LONG, LONG TIME. Nashville:
         Nelson, 1976. Illus. by Trevor Stubley. 92pp. Grades
         3-5.

When their faithful old dog dies, Billy's mum says they will never get another because it breaks one's heart when they die, but Mum's mother, 75, says that "never" is a long, long time. Billy's married sister, Sandra, is expecting, and Grandma enlists Billy's help in refinishing an old crib for the baby. As they labor over the crib, they watch TV, chat, snack, and Grandma smokes her pipe. But the crib is never completed, because Grandma is taken ill while housecleaning for Christmas, has a relapse, and is hospitalized. The prognosis is grim, but the mettlesome old lady recovers enough to spend Christmas with them and is back in her own home by the New Year. It proves to be the happiest holiday season ever. Sandra has a baby girl, and the crib, finished by a neighbor, is received admiringly. As spring approaches, Billy's dad hints that they may add another pup and baby to the growing family circle.

177.   Catherall, Arthur. PRISONERS IN THE SNOW. New York: Lothrop, Lee and Shepard, 1967. Illus. by Victor Ambrus. 128pp.   Grades 4-6.

Moments before the small plane that triggers the avalanche crashes into the steep slope above their Austrian farm, Toni and Trudi see the pilot parachuting to earth. Grandfather, in whose care their parents left them, knows just how to buttress the sturdy old farmhouse against the onslaught of tons of snow. They are safe, even though the three-story house is completely buried, but the cowshed is damaged. To save the animals they bring them into the house, and in forking down hay from the sagging, groaning loft because Grandfather's legs are unsteady, Toni hears a moan from the snow above him and realizes that the downed airman is miraculously alive and within reach. Under Grandfather's direction he heroically extricates him and aids rescue workers in tunneling down to the attic window. The injured flier is airlifted out by helicopter, the children are joyfully reunited with their parents, and Grandfather is not loath to be taken to comfort in the village where, over a pipe, he can relate their adventure to cronies.

177a.   Christopher, Matt. DIRT BIKE RACER. Boston: Little, Brown, 1979. Illus. by Barry Bomzer. 149pp.   Grades 4-6.

Ronnie Baker, 12, salvages a small dirt bike from the bottom of a nearby lake and plans to restore it to working order. To earn money for replacement parts, he hires on as an odd job boy to a wealthy, elderly, blind gentleman, Mr. Perkins, who, before he lost his sight, happened to be a noted automobile and motorcycle racer. Mr. Perkins applauds Ronnie's enterprise and ambition, but Ronnie senses immediately that Mr. Perkins' dilettante nephew Mark resents Ronnie's incursion into his uncle's good graces. At Ronnie's first meet, Mark hires another racer to sabotage Ronnie and warns the younger boy to steer clear of his uncle. But when Mr. Perkins falls ill and seems to languish, Ronnie ignores Mark, who is poised like a vulture over his sick uncle, and tries to cheer his ailing friend and benefactor. At his next meet, Ronnie courageously bests the bully and is heartened by the news that Mr. Perkins has rallied enough to attend the following meet.

178.   Clark, Ann Nolan. SECRET OF THE ANDES. New York: Viking, 1952. Illus. by Jean Charlot. 130pp.   Grades 5-7.

Cusi, 8, has lived for as long as he can remember high in the Andes in the solitude of Hidden Valley with wise, ancient Chuto,

his mentor, herding the sacred flock of Inca llamas.   From an over-
hanging rock he can look down and see a family with three children
like ants far below, and he yearns to be part of a family.   Two unexpected visitors to their mountain sanctuary change his bucolic life
and give him the opportunity he seeks.   Because he wears the golden
earplugs of Inca royalty and is being groomed to be keeper, after
Chuto, of the ancient treasure and traditions, the time has come for
him to make his pilgrimage to Cuzco, bringing the symbolic gift of
llamas.   His dream comes true when he is asked to join a large,
rollicking Indian family on holiday in the city, but he is quickly dis-
enchanted with their Spanish corruptions.   He recognizes that his
place is with Chuto, father of his choice, as guardian of the gold
and llamas.   He returns home, takes his vows, is shown the secret
cave, and is told the story of his blood parents.

179.   Clark, Margaret Goff.   MYSTERY OF SEBASTIAN ISLAND.
         New York: Dodd, Mead, 1976.   159pp.   Grades 5-8.

         Dena Foster, 15, returns to her island home off the coast
of Maine on vacation, resentful of her new stepfather who sent her
to boarding school and usurped her private aerie in her absence.
Among other changes are the influx of off-islanders, including mysterious and attractive Guy O'Neill, and the wave of petty crimes
which are making the insular natives nervous.   Most perplexing
and aggravating of all is the harassment of "Gramp," a recent
widower and respected, guileless lobsterman who tenaciously refuses
to sell his property to the Bangor agent who is offering a grossly
inflated price for it.   When heroin is discovered, and Gramp's boat
is almost scuttled and his dog poisoned, they know that the per-
petrators are dangerous.   Dena suspects that her father is in league
with them.   When she and Barney, Gramp's grandson, learn the
chilling truth, all of their lives are in danger, and they must trust
in Guy, nephew of an underworld kingpin, for deliverance in a suspenseful sea chase.   Dena is reconciled with her stepfather, a
double agent, and he returns her tower room.

180.   Cleaver, Vera and Bill Cleaver.   QUEEN OF HEARTS.
         Philadelphia: Lippincott, 1978.   158pp.   Grades 5-8.

         Granny Lincoln, 79, is autocratic, egotistical, sarcastic,
peevish, obstinate, and obnoxious.   When she suffers a mild stroke,
she adamantly refuses to leave her home or accept a housekeeper/
companion, impetuously choosing her granddaughter, Wilma, 12, to
be her live-in lackey for the Florida summer.   They are anathema
to one another, although Wilma strives stoically to meet her grandmother's demands and discharge her responsibilities to both Granny
and her little brother, Claybrook.   She is astonished to learn that
choleric Granny was a popular dance hall girl in her youth.   When
Granny unforgivably insults Claybrook, an efficient new housekeeper
is hired until Granny churlishly chases her away and they return to
their former arrangement.   Suddenly Granny refuses to eat, bathe,

or take medication, and with pontifical patience, Wilma casts about
to find an activity that will make her feel useful. Conspiratorially,
but in armed truce, they begin baking Granny's famous rolls, and
Wilma peddles them door to door. Eventually she wearies of doing
most of the work and getting none of the credit and longs for the
start of school when she can return home. With a jolt, she learns
that Granny has belligerently alienated yet another companion, and
resignedly she resumes permanently her love/hate post of matching
wills with the tyrant who will not abdicate her independence.

180a.   Clifton, Lucille. THE LUCKY STONE. New York: Dela-
         corte, 1979. Illus. by Dale Payson. 64pp. Grades 3-5.

         Tee and her great-grandmother, Mrs. Elzie F. Pickens
(the F stands for Free), love to sit and rock on their wraparound
porch on hot summer days while Great-grandmother relates the
stories about her lucky stone. The first one tells how she acquired
the stone from the daughter of a runaway slave whose life it saved
before Emancipation. The second recounts how it saved its owner
from being struck by lightning at a gospel meeting. Succeeding
stories disclose the stone's comical intercession when Great-grandmother met her future husband and how Tee herself acquires the
lucky stone while Great-grandmother is recuperating from pneumonia
in the hospital. All are told in the lilting parlance of the black
South.

181.   Clymer, Eleanor. THE GET-AWAY CAR. New York:
         Dutton, 1978. 149pp. Grades 4-6.

         Maggie, 11, has lived contentedly for six years with her
maternal grandmother, whose motto is Fun First, Work Later, in
her inner-city apartment. Now her paternal Aunt Ruby, who has
read books on nutrition, psychology, and education, is getting married and wants to put Grandma in an old-age home and give Maggie
a proper suburban home and schooling. To escape Aunt Ruby,
Grandma quits her job and borrows an old touring car to visit her
cousin on her Upstate estate, taking with her a motley lot of multi-
cultural neighbor children. They are certain Aunt Ruby is on their
trail when they hear a description of their car broadcast on the
radio, so they leave the beaten track. They find the estate derelict
and Cousin Esther cynical, but with a lot of teamwork from friends
made along the way and a run of good luck (antiques in the attic
and thieves' booty stashed in the car, for which there is a handsome
reward), they restore the estate to its former opulence. Cousin
Esther agrees to let Grandma and Maggie move in permanently,
and even Aunt Ruby puts her seal of approval on the new arrangement.

182.   Clymer, Eleanor. MY BROTHER STEVIE. New York:
         Holt, Rinehart and Winston, 1967. 76pp. Grades 4-6.

Annie Jenner, 10, and her brother Stevie, 8, live with
their grandmother on welfare in a housing project in New York.
Grandma can't control Stevie by excoriation, and Annie becomes increasingly worried over his delinquent behavior. A dedicated new
teacher, wise and sympathetic Miss Stover, briefly reverses this
trend by channeling his energy into constructive and meaningful activities, but when she is summoned home by a family emergency,
Stevie drifts back to his old ways and unsavory companions. In
desperation Annie seeks Miss Stover's address in the country and
borrows money for round trip tickets for Stevie and her. An overnight visit in the pleasant bustle of the rural foster home in which
Miss Stover grew up and now helps manage has a cleansing and up-
lifting influence on both children, and they return to the city with
the promise and inspiration of future visits. Grandma develops
greater patience and personal involvement.

183.   Coatsworth, Elizabeth. GRANDMOTHER CAT AND THE
         HERMIT. New York: Macmillan, 1970. Illus. by Irving
         Boker. 85pp. Grades 3-5.

Dave's aging cat leads him into a remote canyon beyond his
home in the San Bernardino Mountains where he is startled to find
a grizzled old man who invites him to visit his "Peaceful Kingdom."
There he has tamed animals from birds and rabbits to coyotes and
mountain lions. Dave looks forward to returning on the infrequent
occasions the hermit permits him to come. But one day, the
recluse, growing restless, forewarns him that all good things must
come to an end, that "only change never changes," preparing him
not only for his cat's eventual death but also for his own imminent
departure. Dave, a loner too, knows that his memories of the
special summer are the one thing that won't change.

184.   Coatsworth, Elizabeth. MARRA'S WORLD. New York:
         Greenwillow, 1975. Illus. by Krystyna Turska. 83pp.
         Grades 3-5.

Despised and mistreated by her scathing grandmother, tol-
erated by her taciturn father, ostracized by her island classmates,
and ignored by her teacher, bewildered, undernourished Marra is at
home only in the isolation of the outdoors and has no friend until
Alison, daughter of the island's first doctor, arrives, and her
wretched life begins to improve. Alison's mother remakes Marra's
ugly, misfitting clothes, and Marra picks up quickly the social
graces practiced in Alison's home. And when Granny observes that
respectable family befriending Marra, her attitude toward the waif
softens subtly and grudgingly. Exploring a new part of the island,
Marra hears poignant, mystical music. That night she has a strange
vision of her mother, of whom she knows only that her grandmother
drove her away, as a seal. On an excursion to a neighboring island with Alison, they are enveloped by fog at sea. Marra calls
her mother's name in distress, and a seal appears to guide them

safely ashore where, uncharacteristically, Granny is waiting with hot chocolate and biscuits.

185.   Cohen, Barbara. THANK YOU, JACKIE ROBINSON. New York: Lothrop, Lee and Shepard, 1974. Illus. by Richard Cuffari. Grades 4-6.

Sam, 10, lives and breathes baseball the summer of 1950, has memorized the record books, and roots for the Brooklyn Dodgers but has never attended a game, because his mother and sisters do not share his enthusiasm. When the elderly black, Davy, becomes chef at the inn his mother manages, shy Sam finally finds a friend and boon companion. Davy is a fan of Jackie Robinson, in particular, and together they travel to as many games as time permits. When a heart attack hospitalizes Davy, Sam courageously makes the pilgrimage to Ebbets Field alone to get a ball autographed for Davy. The ball isn't a powerful enough panacea to spare his friend, and Sam is inconsolable. He turns on the radio just as Jackie comes to bat and whispers, "Hit it for Davy," and is rewarded for his faith. Positive messages on race, religion, and death.

185a.   Cone, Molly. THE AMAZING MEMORY OF HARVEY BEAN. Boston: Houghton Mifflin, 1980. Illus. by Robert MacLean. 83pp. Grades 4-6.

The summer that his parents decide to split up, Harvey, 11, already abstracted and depressed, is especially bedeviled because neither parent seems to want him. Letting each think he has gone with the other, he sets off on his own and soon encounters a very stout but friendly older man, Mr. Katz, scavenging in a supermarket dumpster. Mr. Katz invites the boy to his home which is a motley aggregate of materials scrounged from junkyards. The garage is crammed to overflowing with others' useful discards. Mrs. Katz is an equally amiable dumpling, just as forgetful as Harvey himself, who creates appetizing viands from her husband's gleanings. She is also a walking encyclopedia of mnemonic devices who gladly teaches Harvey her system of memorization. When the health department threatens to evict the Katzes because of their untidy garage, Harvey quickly reorganizes it. And when his parents finally track him down and accuse the Katzes of kidnapping him, Mr. Katz rebuts that as a salvager, he hates to see anything go to waste, including a scrap of a boy. Happy to know that he is wanted and loved, Harvey decides to spend school days with his mother, weekends with his father, and vacations with the Katzes.

186.   Cooper, Elizabeth K. THE WILD CATS OF ROME. San Carlos: Golden Gate, 1972. Illus. by Don Freeman. 70pp. Grades 4-5.

Angelo, dauntless leader of Rome's thousands of wild cats,

has made it his life work to provide the city with a fountain for
felines only. He finds a partner for his project in Nonno, a small,
bent old man who was an artisan in his youth until a slab of marble
fell on him and addled his wits but enabled him to communicate
with cats. Observing birds building a nest, Angelo makes up an
"ancient motto, " "We find what we need and we use what we find, "
and organizes all the cats to locate bits of glass, ceramics, and
other treasures which Nonno collects at night. Then Nonno begins
constructing a fountain, recalling his old skills and improvising.
The finished product is wonderful to behold but is unfortunately dry,
and Angelo loses his credibility among the cats. Then Nonno's employer unwittingly provides a solution, and Nonno's ingenious fountain
becomes a mecca for the thirsty cats of Rome.

187.   Corcoran, Barbara. THE LONG JOURNEY. New York:
         Atheneum, 1970. Illus. by Charles Robinson. 187pp.
         Grades 5-7.

         An orphan, Laurie makes her home with her tough and in-
dependent grandfather in an Eastern Montana ghost town. Grandpa
has taught her self-reliance, grooming, manners, culture, and especially love, while a correspondence school has handled her lessons,
but because of Grandpa's abhorrence of institutions and the authorities who might place her in an orphanage, Laurie has had no experience with humankind or civilization. Now Grandpa is going
blind and charges Laurie with the awesome task of riding her horse
the breadth of the state to summon Uncle Arthur from Butte. Being
alone against the elements of nature does not alarm her, but the
novelties of modern plumbing and restaurant meals are perplexing,
and the encounters with the religious maniac and the trigger-happy
rancher are terrifying. She meets generous and sympathetic individuals, also, who try to belay her mistrust. When she finally
reaches Butte, and Grandpa has had surgery for his cataracts,
Laurie eschews a comfortable home with Uncle Arthur and Aunt
Helen to resume the rigors of the primitive life with her beloved
grandfather, but she promises to visit often to continue her accul-
turation.

188.   Curry, Jane Louise. THE LOST FARM. New York:
         Atheneum, 1974. Illus. by Charles Robinson. 137pp.
         Grades 5-6.

         Petey MacCubbin's larcenous father, Trashbin, rattles the
wrong cage when he pockets Professor Lilliput's gold watch. A
malfeasant himself, the charlatan has invented a Wart and Malignant
Growth Reducer, in need of refinement, with which he has shrunk
a whole town and its inhabitants to display in his Marvelous Museum
of Miniatures. Now he turns the machine on the MacCubbins'
Pennsylvania farm. Trashbin soon pines away, but Pete, 12, and
Granny cheerfully and inventively make do with what they have in
protecting themselves and their Lilliputian livestock and crops from

Brobdingnagian predators and elements with Granny's philosophy of
"no harm trying." The spirited old lady finally succumbs at the
age of 105, and Pete, a strapping adult, carries on. At the age
of 62, when he is reconciled to his life of solitude and diminution,
he is abruptly delivered by a woman whom he recognizes as one
of the mountebank's Miniatures of his youth. He and Samantha,
both restored to full size now, have a lot to catch up on.

189.   Dahl, Roald. CHARLIE AND THE CHOCOLATE FACTORY.
        New York: Knopf, 1964. Illus. by Joseph Schindelman.
        162pp. Grades 4-6.

        Charlie Bucket's family is poor and starving. His four
grandparents are so old and feeble that they lie in bed all day,
two at the head, two at the foot. One day Mr. Willy Wonka, proprietor of the world's most fabulous chocolate factory, announces
that five lucky children will be given a guided tour of his mysterious premises. Miraculously, Charlie qualifies. He chooses his
suddenly spry Grandpa Joe, 96-1/2, to be his chaperon. Fellow
tourists include an insatiable glutton, an odious, overindulged brat,
a marathon gum chewer, and an uncontrollable TV addict. The factory is as enthralling as its reputation, and one by one the other
four children succumb to its temptations and receive a clever and
diabolical comeuppance that fits each of their excesses. Only
Charlie obeys eccentric old Mr. Wonka's rules and is rewarded by
being named heir to the factory. In his magical great glass elevator, Mr. Wonka goes to fetch the rest of the deserving family
from their hovel to live with him in the chocolate factory.

190.   Dahl, Roald. CHARLIE AND THE GREAT GLASS ELE-
        VATOR. New York: Knopf, 1972. Illus. by Joseph
        Schindelman. 163pp. Grades 4-6.

        Charlie, his parents, Grandpa Joe, and his other three
still-bedridden grandparents (see 189) board Willie Wonka's incredible glass elevator for the return trip to the chocolate factory but
are accidentally detoured deep into space where they dock with a
deserted orbiting space hotel that has been invaded by insidious and
invincible Vermicious Knids. The elevator is impervious to the
Knid attacks, but three U. S. astronauts and their passengers are
not so fortunate. Intrepid and ingenious Mr. Wonka spectacularly
saves them, while the three grandparents cower in weightless terror.
Back in the bowels of the chocolate factory, Mr. Wonka offers the
oldsters the fountain of youth so they can arise from their twenty
years of self-imposed repose. They become greedy and overdose,
reverting to infancy, and Grandma Georgina regresses to minus two
and vanishes altogether. After Charlie and Willy Wonka rescue her,
riding the elevator in reverse, and Mr. Wonka has restored them
all to their proper ages by secret formula, they receive heroes' invitations to the White House. Only the prospect of being left behind
galvanizes the three into shedding their bed, and off they skip, arm
in arm.

191.   Dahlstedt, Marden. THE STOPPING PLACE. New York:
        Putnam, 1976. Illus. by Allen Davis. 160pp. Grades
        5-6.

        Lissa Evorssen is appalled when her peripatetic parents
decide to drop out of the ratrace in teeming Brooklyn and move to
the Pine Barrens of South Jersey. The woods are lonely and oppressive, the natives are insular and backward, and she is far from
her best city friend. Then she meets a forbidding elderly woman,
Mrs. Gilfillan, who proves to be her port in a storm. A former
school teacher, Mrs. G., who now hooks rugs for a living, tells
her the local history and introduces her to herbalism. She learns
to her amazement that attractive Jess Cowperthwaite and his friend,
Helen-Ann, are not aloof but shy. One night when her parents are
away, a forest fire routs Lissa and Helen-Ann from the Evorssen
cabin, and Lissa reacts bravely in saving Mrs. G. In response
to Lissa's ambivalence to the Pine Barrens, Mrs. G., a former
outsider herself, tells her she must accept a place for what it is
and has to give, that life is change and should be appreciated one
day at a time. When her parents begin rebuilding, Lissa feels an
affinity for the Pine Barrens and hopes it will not be just another
stopping place.

192.   Daringer, Helen F. ADOPTED JANE. New York: Har-
        court, Brace and World, 1947. Illus. by Kate Seredy.
        225pp. Grades 4-6.

        Modest but self-respecting Jane Douglas, oldest resident of
her orphanage, is ecstatic over not one but two invitations to spend
the summer away. Practical Matron decides it will be more advantageous to accept that of the reputedly wealthy widow who may
be inveigled to endow an infirmary. Jane is uncomfortable and
tongue-tied with dignified Mrs. Thurman, concerned at being a
financial burden on her because her old-fashioned furnishings hint
of genteel poverty, and preoccupied with the difficulty of making
friends among the class-conscious girls of the turn-of-the-century
town. Nevertheless, she experiences mixed emotions when her visit
ends and Matron says she may spend a week with the Scotts, as well,
who are a warm-hearted, down-to-earth farm family with a niece
just her age. Jane enjoys the most wonderful week of her whole
drab life. She is thunderstruck when both Mrs. Thurman and the
Scotts, who might even send her to college, bid to adopt her. After
careful soul-searching she opts for Mrs. Thurman who is lonely and
who can teach her to become a lady. The first lesson should be
one on fine antiques. Mrs. Thurman can afford to build the infirmary and also send Jane to college.

193.   Dickinson, Peter. ANNERTON PIT. Boston: Little,
        Brown, 1977. 175pp. Grades 5-8.

        Jake Bertold is an asset to his family, because, while blind

from birth, his acutely developed hearing is advantageous, and he
navigates with the assurance of a sighted person. He and his older
brother Martin are scouring the north of England for their grandfather, a retired mining engineer who has disappeared pursuing his
hobby of debunking ghost stories. Their sleuthing leads them to a
reputedly haunted mine where they find their grandfather a prisoner
of a militant ecology group who are planning to blow up an oil rig.
The three soon realize that their captors are not only willing to die
but to kill for their cause. Granpa, accustomed to the robust exercise of outdoor life, contracts pneumonia in the damp confinement
of the shaft, and Jake, to whom the darkness is no handicap, starts
exploring to find an adit. He leads Martin in a gripping, groping
odyssey through the bowels of the earth to daylight. It is while he
is returning through the mine to await rescue with Granpa that he
senses another presence in the tunnel, panics and falls, coming
face to face with the phantom. Their rescue is anticlimactic, Granpa recovers, and Jake realizes that the vision he had was psychological.

194.   Enright, Elizabeth. GONE-AWAY LAKE. New York: Har-
          court, Brace and World, 1957. Illus. by Beth and Joe
          Krush. 192pp. Grades 4-6.

          Cousins Portia, 10, and Julian, exploring in the woods,
come upon a swamp and bordering it a dozen anomalous, mouldering
Victorian mansions. Even more surprising is their discovery of the
pair of antiquaries, brother and sister Pindar and Minnehaha, who
wear turn-of-the-century costumes and inhabit the lost world.
"Uncle" Pin and "Aunt" Min explain that the bog was once a beautiful lake where wealthy families summered until a new dam caused
it to drain in 1906, leaving the exclusive retreat worthless and forgotten. The two elders, former summer residents fallen on hard
times, return to Gone-away to subsist on the bounty of the bog and
the furnishings of the abandoned houses. The children return daily
to Gone-away to learn of the glorious history of the summer colony
and the flora and fauna of the swamp. They establish a clubhouse
in one of the erstwhile elegant houses and keep Gone-away a secret
until Portia's little brother, Foster, follows them one day and becomes mired in the quicksand the old folks call the Gulper. The
families are introduced, and the club expands as the idyllic summer
comes to a close.

195.   Enright, Elizabeth. RETURN TO GONE-AWAY. New York:
          Harcourt, Brace and World, 1961. Illus. by Beth and Joe
          Krush. 191pp. Grades 4-6.

          Portia and Foster Blake's parents decide to purchase the
least decrepit of Gone-away Lake's once-imposing summer residences,
Villa Caprice (see 194), formerly owned by imperious and flamboyant
Mrs. Brace-Gideon who perished in the San Francisco earthquake,
leaving no heirs. The mansion is overgrown, dust-choked, and

vermin-ridden, but it is still sound and filled with priceless antiques.   They spend the summer restoring it to its former grandeur,
aided by Aunt Min and Uncle Pin who lived there in the colony's
heyday and have a story about every treasure they unearth.   There
is also a dumb-waiter and a suit of armor that yields the combination to a safe which, when finally found, disgorges heirloom jewelry.
During a hot spell, Uncle Pin guides them to an abandoned quarry
to swim.   At the end of the summer, Dad decides to live year
'round at the refurbished showplace they have re-christened Amber-
side, so they can watch the march of the seasons across the swamp
with their insouciant elderly neighbors.

196.   Estes, Eleanor. THE MIDDLE MOFFAT. New York: Har-
        court, Brace and World, 1942. Illus. by Louis Slobodkin.
        317pp.   Grades 4-6.

The self-proclaimed "mysterious middle Moffat, " shy, sensitive Jane, concocts her own cures for the middle-child syndrome.
Blind faith and the luck o' the Irish help her muddle through them
triumphantly.   Her chief mission is to preserve the health of Cran-
bury's "oldest inhabitant, " Mr. Buckle, who shows her his stereop-
ticon slides and trounces her at double solitaire, in anticipation of
the spry and spirited fellow's hundredth birthday.   An organ recital
and a play at the Town Hall are rescued from the brink of disaster
by wry and spectacular quirks of fate, and when she ventures into
basketball she virtually cannot miss.   Together with her best friend,
Nancy, as gregarious and vivacious as Jane is bashful, she witnesses a solar eclipse and bathes stray dogs.   The centenary birthday celebration inadvertently brings honor and glory to the modest
Moffats through Jane.

197.   Ewing, Kathryn. A PRIVATE MATTER. New York: Har-
        court, Brace, Jovanovich, 1975. Illus. by Joan Sandin.
        88pp.   Grades 4-5.

The people moving in next door are a friendly retired
couple who have plenty of time to give Marcy Benson, 9, the attention she lacks because her divorced father lives in California
and her realtor mother works most of the time.   Marcy tags along
everywhere with Mr. Endicott as he putters about his house and
garden, and he gives her little tasks to do to make her feel important.   Soon she begins to fantasize in school compositions that
he is her missing father.   When her real father and his new wife
want to take her on a weekend trip, she tries unsuccessfully to
circumvent it and is relieved to return to Mr. Endicott and the school
project he is helping her with.   Mrs. Endicott dies suddenly, and Mr.
Endicott cannot handle his grief in the house they shared.   When
he moves away, Marcy experiences the same sense of bereavement
and at the same time must adjust to the prospect of a new stepfather and the move to a new home.

198.   Farjeon, Eleanor.   THE OLD NURSE'S STOCKING BASKET.
New York: Walck, 1965.   Illus. by Edward Ardizzone.
102pp.   Grades 3-5.

Indefatigable Old Nurse, whose charges at one time included
the children's mother and grandmother, and who claims to have
nursed the Brothers Grimm, knows no end of yarns which she spins
for Doris, Ronald, Roland, and Mary Matilda every evening before
bed while she darns their stockings.   Large holes demand long
stories and vice versa.   Her international parables include the foot-
step, the choleric Indian prince, the haughty Spanish infanta, the
little French duke who wanted to trade places with the ragpicker's
son, Lipp the Lapp who was too tiny to be found and therefore required no care, the veiled Persian princess who was too stunning to
be seen, the minuscule princess of China who loved butterflies, a
Swiss miss, boys of ancient Greece and Rome, and more, all
former wards.

199.   Fenton, Edward.   DUFFY'S ROCKS.   New York: Dutton,
1974.   198pp.   Grades 5-8.

Gran Brennan reared the son on whom she doted, Timothy's
father, so permissively that he grew up to be wild, restive, and irresponsible, stirred with the wanderlust that only brought him to
visit motherless Tim, 13, once.   Gran is determined not to make
the same mistake with Tim, who loves her in spite of her stringency
that precludes him from having friends outside of their dingy milltown suburb of Pittsburgh during the Great Depression.   But Tim
is anguishing to know this magnetic, enigmatic man who is his father.   By stealth, he finds Bart Brennan's last known address, already two years old, among his grandmother's effects.   Boarding a
bus to New York, he traces Bart to a dead end, gaining insight into
his character from two kind women he has discarded.   Returning
home, he finds his grandmother's heart failing.   She has waited to
succumb only to extract his promise not to follow in his father's
footsteps, a pledge easily vowed.

200.   Fitzhugh, Louise.   THE LONG SECRET.   New York:
Harper and Row, 1965.   Illus. by the author.   275pp.
Grades 5-7.

Beth Ellen's patrician grandmother, with whom she has
lived in luxury for all of her 12 years, has tutored her to be a lady
at all times, and she has grown up timid, indolent, and insipid.
Her friend, Harriet, is of the opposite temperament, brash, abra-
sive, and ambitious.   She is determined to expose the author of
the barbed, Biblical-sounding notes that have been surfacing around
the summer colony.   Beth Ellen is unprepared for the descension
of the chic, brittle, and sybaritic mother she hasn't seen in seven
years and her vacuous, sycophantic, and parasitic new husband.
When Beth Ellen expresses a tentative desire to pursue an art

career and be a productive member of society, they are first amused
and then alarmed and decide to remove her from her grandmother's
influence.   She asserts herself histrionically at last, they lose interest, and her strait-laced grandmother even condones her single
breach of etiquette.   Harriet finally finds her evidence, but the long
secret has served its purpose.

201.   Fox, Paula. A LIKELY PLACE. New York: Macmillan,
        1967. Illus. by Edward Ardizzone. 57pp. Grades 3-5.

        Lewis, 9, is out of step with the rest of his urban world.
His unduly protective parents hover in concern over his apparent
apathy and irresponsibility.   An indifferent student, he is thinking
of running away until his parents introduce him to his new baby-
sitter.   Miss Fitchlow is another original who is into Yoga exercises and health foods.   She doesn't turn a hair when he casually
requests to go to the park alone.   There he meets a restless, retired shoemaker from Barcelona whose son-in-law has ignominiously
sidelined him, and Lewis helps Mr. Madruga compose a letter of
polite protest to the son-in-law, with whom he lives.   The boy is
left in limbo when Mr. Madruga fails to appear at the park for several days, but when he does reappear the old man is jubilant.
Their letter has been astonishingly successful.   The son-in-law has
found him skilled employment, and Mr. Madruga bestows on Lewis
his highly prized umbrella in gratitude.   When his parents return,
Miss Fitchlow praises his outstanding motor coordination, and his
flagging ego is twice bolstered.

201a.   French, Dorothy Kayser. I DON'T BELONG HERE. Phila-
        delphia: Westminster, 1980. 102pp. Grades 5-8.

        "Gram's a modern old lady! She's got lots of bounce."
But when Mary, 16, arrives in her grandmother's one-horse California town to spend her senior year while her parents are on
assignment in the South American jungle, she discovers that the
fretful, confused, incompetent and stingy old woman living there is
not Gram anymore.   In the year since her husband died, her mind
has begun to slip in and out of gear, but mostly she lives in the
past, waiting for her husband to return, eating only canned foods,
forgetting to take her medication and change her underwear, and
driving recklessly.   In panic Mary wants to leave but cannot contact
her parents.   Olga, her grandmother's enduring old cleaning woman,
and Ken, the attractive and sympathetic young temporary ticket
agent at the bus depot, are the only people to whom she can turn.
Accustomed to being indulged by her mother, Mary is resentful and
sulky at having to do chores for the first time.   Then Gram falls
and is hospitalized with a broken ankle, and a geriatric specialist
finally explains her grandmother's condition, its causes and treatment.   With Mary's help in controlling Gram's medication, cooking
nutritious meals, and making her feel useful, needed and loved,
Gram's memory and coordination are expected to improve.   With
Ken to support and inspire her, she accepts the challenge gracefully.

202.   Gage, Wilson. BIG BLUE ISLAND. Cleveland: World,
         1964. Illus. by Glen Rounds. 120pp. Grades 5-6.

         Darrell, 11, is sent from Detroit to live with his only
known relative, a great-uncle who lives alone on a river island in
Tennessee without plumbing or electricity. He is resentful of the
lack of amenities, the imposed solitude, and especially the old
codger's acerbity. He plans to run away to Florida, but he lacks
both money and opportunity, being a virtual prisoner on the island
because the old man padlocks his rowboat. When his uncle bets
him a dollar he can't catch one of the great blue herons that winter
there, he sees his chance to earn pocket money and sets about the
task with determination until he learns that it is impossible, illegal,
and dangerous to trap the creatures when his uncle stumbles on the
snares and hurts his back. The ranger convinces the boy that it
is actually desirable to live on the island like a sort of permanent
camping trip and persuades the curmudgeon to buy the boy an old
motorboat so he will have some mobility.

202a.   Garner, Alan. GRANNY REARDUN. New York: Collins
         and World, 1978. Illus. by Michael Foreman. 61pp.
         Grades 4-6.

         Written in the arcane idiom 'of nineteenth century Cheshire,
this story tells of the day young Joseph decides his future. Because his father is dead and he lives with his grandparents, he is
known as a "granny reardun. " His grandfather, a "Sunday saint
and Monday sinner, " is also a master stonemason, and evidence of
his craft stand like living monuments to him about their village.
But Joseph does not want to follow in his footsteps as is customary.
He is embittered that good neighbors have been evicted from their
substantial stone house so that the structure can be recycled as a
garden wall at the whim of the rector's wife. On the last day of
his formal schooling, he ponders the trade he must soon choose.
In a flash of insight he decides to become a blacksmith, who, on
his anvil, forges the weathervanes, clocks, lightning rods, and
bells that grace the steeples of church and chapel, as well as the
tools of the stonemasons. His grandfather applauds his choice.

202b.   Garner, Alan. TOM FOBBLE'S DAY. New York: Collins,
         1979. Illus. by Michael Foreman. 72pp. Grades 4-6.

         When a bigger boy "Tom Fobble's" his homemade crate
sled, the abstruse Cheshire equivalent of declaring "dibs" on it, and
then wrecks it against a tree, William goes for solace to his Gran-
dad, the lad of GRANNY REARDUN (see 202a). The time is now
World War II, and the Battle of Britain is in full sway. At his
forge, the silver-haired, rosy-nosed smith deftly fashions runners
for a new sledge, all the while reminiscing about his part in the
Boer War and Kaiser Bill's War. Back at his cottage, he puts the
finishing touches on the solid ash sled while explaining to William

the ancestral significance of the pair of horseshoes hanging within
the chimney.   After tea, the village boys gather to go sledding in
the dark, searchlights lashing the leaden sky, anti-aircraft artillery
arcing, and spent shrapnel fizzling into the snow.   On his perfectly
crafted coaster, William has the nerve and exhilaration to go to the
top of the hill and take the course full tilt, pretending he is piloting
a Spitfire.   Returning to the cottage, he finds a crowd of adults
surrounding the bed where his beloved grandfather lies dying.   Silently, but with great emotion, he discards his shrapnel souvenirs
and Tom Fobble's the old horseshoes his grandfather intended for
him.

202c.   Gates, Doris.   A MORGAN FOR MELINDA.   New York:
          Viking, 1980.   189pp.   Grades 5-7.

          Melinda Ross, 10, does not share her father's fancy for
horses, and when he announces his intention of buying her one and
making a horsewoman of her, she is terrified but determined not
to disappoint him.   A fine Morgan gelding miraculously becomes
her property, but she keeps her distance until a well-to-do elderly
author, Miss Zinn, who has a passion for Morgans, approaches her
father for riding lessons, her lifelong dream, and becomes a family friend.   Missy, as Melinda familiarly dubs her, encourages her
ambition to become a writer but also imparts to Melinda her enthusiasm for both the breed of horse and competitive equitation.   In
assuming the care of her Morgan, and by remembering Missy's
favorite aphorism, "What you fear will come to pass," Melinda conquers her fear of horses and learns to love riding.   Missy, in her
mid-seventies, enters the "Jack Benny" class in the Golden West
championship at Monterey and wins, but later suffers a massive
coronary.   She lingers long enough in the ICU to read Melinda's
manuscript and recommend it to her publisher, and when she dies,
she bequeathes to Melinda her horse and dog.   But most precious
to Melinda is the living memory she leaves.

202d.   Gerson, Corinne.   TREAD SOFTLY.   New York: Dial,
          1979.   133pp.   Grades 5-7.

          Since her parents were killed in an auto accident when she
was 4, Kitten Tate, now 10, has lived with her staid and prosaic
maternal grandparents who speak in antiquated adages, axioms, and
quotations.   To compensate for her lack of a normal, nuclear family, Kitten has created a fantasy Family, complete with baby sister,
with whom she holds imaginary conversations.   Only once does she
refer to her Family aloud, and that secures her a summer job as
mother's helper to a doctor and his wife.   She likes her young
charge Tommy, enjoys the family's swimming pool, makes friends
with Lulu, a new girl in town, and even shares an idyllic vacation
at a Maine lake with Tommy's family and Lulu.   But at the end of
their stay, Kitten quarrels with Lulu over a lie Lulu tells, and Kitten's own probity hangs precariously in the balance because of her

continuing deception to substantiate her Family. When her true
homelife is finally bared, Tommy's mother sanctimoniously tells
Kitten's grandparents that the girl is a pathological liar who needs
psychiatric care. The compassionate pair know better, however,
and defend their granddaughter staunchly and eloquently with lines
from Yeats. Kitten, in turn, forgives Lulu.

202e.   Girion, Barbara. MISTY AND ME. New York: Scribner,
          1979. 139pp. Grades 5-7.

     When her mother takes a full-time executive position and
encumbers her with the after school care of her first grade brother
Willie, not only does it curtail Kim's critical sixth grade social
life, but it also scotches her expectation of getting a new puppy.
Stubbornly, she decides to get one anyway without her parents' permission and sacrifices her babysitting money, Willie's school milk
money, and her mother's PTA dues to redeem a puppy from the
animal shelter. The problem of where to keep Misty is solved by
an ad in the paper run by an elderly lady who takes odd jobs to
supplement her Social Security income. Mrs. Macvey helps them
train Misty, and her delapidated home becomes a haven to the
children after school, even freeing Kim to participate in the disco
dance lessons sponsored by the PTA. Mrs. Macvey's sudden heart
attack exposes their secret, the puppy comes to live with Kim's
family, and Mrs. Macvey's daughter arrives to close her house.
When Mrs. Macvey is released from the hospital to go live with
her daughter, Kim surprises even herself by magnanimously giving
her precious Misty to Mrs. Macvey to compensate for her loss of
independence and companionship.

203.   Godden, Rumer. MR. MCFADDEN'S HALLOWE'EN. New
          York: Viking, 1975. 127pp. Grades 5-7.

     Because her willful pony detours into Mr. McFadden's turnip
field, shy Selina Russell makes the acquaintance of the perverse and
cantankerous old Scot and his intimidating guard dog and aggressive
gander. Slowly she perceives that beneath his irascible, misanthropic crust, Mr. McFadden has a gentle and vulnerable soul.
The townspeople hate him because he refuses to sell an insignificant
portion of his land for use as a recreation center. When the old
man breaks his foot, doughty Selina braves his acrimony to make
him comfortable and see to his chores. She and a neglected orphan
boy, Tim, gradually worm their way into his callous heart, but for
their defense of "the enemy" they are reviled in town, and on Halloween night, village bullies vandalize Mr. McFadden's house and
brutally assault Selina. Belatedly recognizing that her persistent
loyalty and his own intransigence have both ostracized and jeopardized
her, Mr. McFadden, with Selina's inspiration and encouragement,
atones in spades to the community and officially adopts Tim. The
following Halloween he and Selina, by acclaim, bashfully dedicate
the new park.

204.   Goffstein, M. B.   TWO PIANO TUNERS.   New York:
         Farrar, Straus and Giroux, 1970.   Illus. by the author.
         65pp.   Grades 3-5.

         Reuben Weinstock, who has tuned pianos for the immortals,
takes on a new vocation, that of capably parenting his small orphaned
granddaughter, Debbie.   He is grooming her to be a concert pianist,
but she wants nothing so much as to follow in his footsteps and tags
along on all his jobs, alertly observing.   One day Mr. Weinstock is
scheduled to tune the concert grand for Isaac Lipman, with whom he
used to tour, but remembers that he has also promised to tune a
neighbor's piano.   He sends Debbie with a message for Mrs. Perlman, but Debbie, with childish confidence, decides to tune the piano
herself with her grandfather's discarded instruments.   When Grandpa
and Mr. Lipman come to collect her, they find that it is only the
antiquated instruments that have betrayed her efforts.   Mr. Lipman
invites her to play for him, and he and Mrs. Perlman agree that
Mr. Weinstock should train her instead to be the piano tuner she
has the proclivity for being.   Mr. Weinstock is in accord.

205.   Gonzalez, Gloria.   THE GLAD MAN.   New York: Knopf,
         1975.   160pp.   Grades 5-6.

         In investigating a derelict bus hidden near the city dump,
Mellissa and Troy are startled by the menacing old man and his
snarling dog who are obviously its occupants.   On closer acquaintance,
they find that the old codger is friendly and his dog obsequious.   The
bus was once a mobile flower shop with which Eddie, a widower,
made his living, specializing in gladiolas.   Mellissa concludes that
not all old people are grouchy and dull and writes a school compo-
sition about their experience which her teacher sends to the newspaper, stirring up a hornet's nest.   The officious Housing Commissioner insists on evicting Eddie from city property and relocating
him in a subsidized senior citizen's project.   The independent old
man is stricken.   Mellissa and her classmates, with their teacher's
and parents' collusion, refurbish the bus in the hope of changing
the Commissioner's mind, but he is adamant, and Eddie and his
mastiff are doomed to be parted and confined.   The old recluse
takes the matter into his own hands by driving off in the rejuvenated
bus.   He promises to write when he has found a more hospitable
location.

205a.   Gordon, Shirley.   THE BOY WHO WANTED A FAMILY.
         New York: Harper and Row, 1980.   Illus. by Charles
         Robinson.   90pp.   Grades 3-5.

         One of his few possessions is a battered suitcase, because
Michael, 7, is an orphan who has bounced from one foster home to
another.   Like a wish come true, his social worker tells him there
is someone who wants to adopt him.   Miss Graham turns out to be
a single, aging, gray-haired writer who asks him to call her Mom.

Michael likes having a room to himself and a large yard to play in at her suburban Southern California home, but he's afraid that he will miss the camaraderie of other children. He is also anxious that his new mom will not find him acceptable. The older boys down the block are sometimes impatient with him, but the boys in his class like him immediately. Mom, moreover, has many fascinating friends, including the retired Navy man who builds ships in bottles. Mom has imagination and a good sense of humor, and plans many Saturday adventures for the two of them. After a year in which he adopts a cat, wins a goldfish at the school carnival, celebrates an intimate Christmas and an extraordinary birthday, his adoption becomes final, and all his reservations are expunged. His old suitcase will prove useful on a round trip to meet his new grandfather.

206.   Gottschalk, Elin Toona. IN SEARCH OF COFFEE MOUN-
        TAINS. Nashville: Nelson, 1977. 203pp. Grades 5-8.

Having survived the horror of the war in fear of bombings and strafings, German and Russian concentration camps, and especially the brutalities of retaliatory German children, Lotukata, her mother, grandmother, and uncle are assigned a tiny room in a houseful of refugees at a DP camp for Estonians. When she is among others of her own kind, her nightmares recede and she loses her diffidence, wins the acceptance of the gang she admires, and learns the disillusioning techniques necessary for survival in a hostile, dehumanizing environment. Her mother is soon evacuated to England where they are to join her, and debonair, dissolute Unki departs for Brazil, leaving Lotukata and her grandmother, her last remaining pillar of strength, to face the rigors of interminable boxcar rides to reach a series of appallingly pestilential transit camps. When she becomes separated from her grandmother, she is saved from panic only by the reassuring herding of her fellow refugees and a sympathetic English soldier. When they are suddenly reunited, her joy and relief are so unbounded that she only dimly appreciates the luxuries of soft white bread and porcelain plumbing fixtures.

207.   Goudge, Elizabeth. LINNETS AND VALERIANS. New York:
        Coward-McCann, 1964. Illus. by Ian Ribbons. 290pp.
        Grades 5-8.

In the year 1912, Father brings the four spirited, inquisitive Linnets, Nan, 12, Robert, 10, Timothy, 8, and Betsy, 6, home to England to live with his mother while he returns to his regiment in India. Life with Grandmama and Miss Bolt, her housekeeper, is stifling and intolerable, and the four lose no time in running away-- straight into the arms of bombastic old Uncle Ambrose, a formidable curmudgeon, retired headmaster, and vicar of the village church. But the children sense that he is a benevolent tyrant and accept the challenge and adventure of living with him, adjusting to

strict discipline and tough lessons.   They also encounter danger and
excitement with such colorful characters as reclusive Lady Alicia
Valerian of mysterious Linden Manor and her monkey valet, gentle
Daft Davie, wicked sorceress Emma Cobley, supernatural bees, and
superstitious Ezra whose strong countermagic ends the skulduggery
and enchantments and restores Lady Alicia's loved ones.   Father
also returns and all live happily, immortally, and Edwardianly ever
after.

208.   Green, Phyllis.   MILDRED MURPHY, HOW DOES YOUR
         GARDEN GROW? Reading: Addison-Wesley, 1977.   Illus.
         by Jerry Pinkney.   89pp.   Grades 4-6.

A newcomer to California, Mildred Murphy, 10, misses her
friends in New Jersey, and whiles away the lonely summer hours by
confiding to her diary and spying on her elderly neighbors.   There
is the graying black maid next door who takes her to San Francisco,
Mrs. Murchison who does volunteer work, Old Man Porter and his
lemon trees, and the Calloways, a childless working couple.   One
day she sees a mysterious stranger creep into the Calloway's vacant
garage apartment.   Curious and bold, she confronts the old woman
and learns that she is destitute and unwanted.   Mildred aids and
abets Gertie, 67, in her pathetic bid to live independently and clandestinely until she discovers that the garage apartment is riddled
with termites and has been condemned.   Gertie's daughter arranges
to put her in a retirement home, but before she can leave, Mildred's
mother finds her diary and Gertie's plight is dramatically aired.
Mrs. Murchison takes her in, and the neighborhood pitches in to
find suitable employment for the castoff grandmother.

209.   Greene, Constance C.   A GIRL CALLED AL.   New York:
         Viking, 1969.   Illus. by Byron Barton.   127pp.   Grades
         4-7.

When Al first moves to Apartment 14C, she is a conscious
non-conformist, compensating for her broken home.   Her chic,
svelte mother works all day and dates most evenings, and her father
sends her plenty of money but never writes, calls, or visits.   Left
to her own devices, the lonely and intense seventh grader gorges
herself to obesity, wears a homely hairstyle, and hates being called
Alexandra.   She and the amusingly ingenuous narrator of the story,
a classmate who lives down the hall, become firm friends.   With
the tactful help of the inimitable building superintendent, Mr.
Richards, a retired bartender, armchair philosopher, and novel
floor polisher, Al begins to think positively about herself, make the
best of the situation, and improve her appearance.   Mr. Richards'
sudden heart attack and untimely death sobers and matures both
girls, but memories of shared camaraderie buoy their spirits once
more.

210.   Griffiths, Helen. RUNNING WILD. New York: Holiday,
          1977. Illus. by Victor Ambrus. 192pp. Grades 5-7.

          Left on his grandparents' primitive farm in Spain since in-
fancy by his parents who are working in a German factory, Pablo,
8, has been reared happily and beneficently, but he pines for companionship. Grandfather brings home a puppy, but Pablo makes a
pet of her instead of training her to guard Grandmother's fowl from
forest predators, and she rapidly grows to mastiff size. Grandfather drowns Neska's puppies because he can't support more than
one dog, but Pablo's resentment is ameliorated by the news that
his parents are returning. Mother and Grandmother quarrel, however, and when his parents move to the city, Pablo, his loyalty
divided, opts to remain on the beloved farm. Next time he hides
Neska's puppies deep in the woods. Only months later, when a
neighbor's daughter is attacked and he himself witnesses the ferocity
of animals he recognizes as Neska's offspring, does he realize they
have gone wild. Believing them to be wolves, the fear-frenzied
villagers fire the forest and murder the innocent and endangered
wolf population. Grandfather's wisdom has penetrated to Pablo too
late, and he returns to his parents sadder but wiser.

211.   Hamilton, Virginia. THE HOUSE OF DIES DREAR. New
          York: Macmillan, 1968. Illus. by Eros Keith. 246pp.
          Grades 5-8.

          Thomas Small is 13 when his family leaves Great-grand-
mother Jeffers' home in North Carolina and moves to the small Ohio
college town where his father will teach black history and where he
has leased a historic house that was once a major station in the
Underground Railroad. The house is built over a series of subterranean caves and passageways, as Thomas learns when he accidentally falls into one and is scared witless. It is also the object
of considerable intrigue involving the malicious Darrow brothers and
the ancient black man, Pluto, a reputed devil, who is caretaker of
the house and who seems bent on frightening them off the premises.
When their kitchen is barbarously vandalized, Mr. Small's hackles
are raised, and he and Thomas set off to confront Pluto in his cave.
Deep in the bowels of the earth they locate the old man and only
then learn of the priceless treasure he guards and of his suspicious
alter ego. As cohorts, they orchestrate a phenomenal and fitting
revenge on the kitchen vandals.

211a.   Hanson, June Andrea. SUMMER OF THE STALLION. New
          York: Macmillan, 1979. Illus. by Gloria Singer. 108pp.
          Grades 5-7.

Janey's maternal grandparents lease from Janey's father the
Montana ranch where she spends her summers.   She adores Grandpa who taught her to ride superbly, and she eagerly anticipates the
summer of her twelfth birthday there.   Grandpa, however, is moody
over a quarrel with Daddy about money, and, stern and unyielding,
expects Janey to cross the open range and flooding river with him
to bring in a vicious, untamed stallion.   Terrified, Janey almost
bungles the perilous and grueling assignment but develops an awesome respect for the wild and free spirit of the magnificent mustang.
Grandpa's ruthless method of humbling the horse appalls Janey, and
she begins to understand the allegations that her grandfather was unstable in his youth and something of a maverick himself.   When she
sees the broken and pathetic shadow of the horse, she vows to rear
his newborn foal, the image of his formerly proud sire, to fulfill
his full potential.   Janey's grandmother remains loyal and sympathetic to both her husband and granddaughter.

212.   Hartling, Peter. OMA. New York: Harper and Row, 1977.
         Illus. by Jutta Ash. Trans. by Anthea Bell. 95pp. Grades
         4-6.

Kalle is 5 when he is orphaned and goes to live in the tiny,
old, sixth floor Munich apartment of his paternal grandmother, 67.
The events of their lives for the next five years are chronicled from
Kalle's point of view in fifteen chapters, following each of which Oma
briefly soliloquizes, soul-searchingly and heart-warmingly, her views
of the same events: confronting the welfare office for Kalle's orphan's
allowance to augment her meager pension; her modesty at bath time;
her need of an occasional relaxing nip of brandy when she is frightened about inflation; his embarrassment when Oma breaks up his
fight with a playmate; her inability at helping him with homework;
her defense to the officious welfare worker who comes to investigate;
and her interest in his soccer team.   Their only serious clashes
occur over the memory of Kalle's mother whom he sanctifies.   Still,
their love and affection blossom feelingly.   Oma, though he has kept
her young in spirit, knows she must prepare him for a time when
she is gone.   He copes very capably when she is hospitalized for
angina, and on his tenth birthday, they discuss seriously but not
morbidly the prospects that may lie ahead for both of them.

212a.   Hellberg, Hans-Eric. GRANDPA'S MARIA. New York:
         Morrow, 1974. Illus. by Joan Sandin. Trans. by Patricia
         Crampton. 189pp. Grades 4-6.

This is the astute and empathetic observation of 7-year-old
Maria's abstractions, emotions, and exploits, captured by her grandfather who has the expert eye of the professional photographer focused fondly upon his favorite subject.   The perplexities of childhood appear humorous to him, but his amusement is always en rapport with Maria.   The small Swedish girl has been christened Maria
Charlotta, and though the usually obedient and poetic Maria predom-

inates, sometimes her naughty alter ego Charlotta surfaces.   Maria
believes that Grandpa is her father until a neighbor girl blurts that
she has no daddy.   Then Mama has to go away to a rest home because of a nervous breakdown.   Adults' explanations of these unsettling situations are most mystifying, but Maria takes comfort in
Grampy's solid and philosophical presence.   Mama sends her a gift
certificate for a bicycle, and Grandpa helps her pick one, though
she must teach herself to ride it (with occasionally comical and
chaotic results) because Grandpa has a lame leg and walks with a
stick.   One day she meets her real father and a half-brother she
didn't know existed, which adds to her bafflement.   Finally Mama
returns, and Grandpa's photos chronicle for her Maria's development
in her absence.

213.   Herman, Charlotte.   OUR SNOWMAN HAD OLIVE EYES.
         New York: Dutton, 1977.   103pp.   Grades 5-7.

         Sheila, 10, has a room of her own at last and is prepared
to be resentful at having to share half of it with her grandmother,
Bubbie, 79, but even though she keeps her teeth in a glass on the
windowsill at night, Bubbie proves to be a boon companion and a
staunch ally when her irritable adolescent sister, Muriel, 15, provokes her.   Bubbie bakes cookies, shares her photo album, and
shows her how to take plant cuttings.   But the two get into trouble
with Mother when Bubbie volunteers to sleep on the davenport when
Sheila has an overnight guest and when the two of them spend a
cold but contented afternoon making a snowman on the lawn.   Mother's misguided and abortive efforts to provide contemporary companionship for her mother result in Bubbie's sneaking off to find a
friend on her own.   Because of Sheila's well meant meddling, Bubbie's new male companion is frightened off and Sheila is remorseful,
but it is her mother's overprotective interference that causes Bubbie's frustration and discontent.   She decides to move in with her
farm son's family where she will be needed.   Before she leaves,
she gives Sheila a special hiding place for her new journal to remember her by.

214.   Hickman, Janet.   THE STONES.   New York: Macmillan,
         1976.   Illus. by Richard Cuffari.   116pp.   Grades 5-8.

         Dad is missing in action in France in 1944, and Garrett,
11, and his rural hamlet chums amuse themselves playing war games
against the eccentric and excitable old immigrant they call Jack
Tramp.   Their hooliganism escalates when their imaginations convince them that the hapless and taciturn man is a German spy.
Garrett wants to prove to the older boys that he is not a sissy, especially because his pontifical Great-aunt Em, who keeps house for
his grandfather and working mother, has charged him with the care
of his baby sister.   When the old man is provoked into firing his
old rifle at them, all the boys are grounded, but one malicious one
sneaks out and burns the old man out.   In covering for his com-

panion, Garrett calls his sister a liar and she runs away hurt.   The
search for her takes on grim overtones as darkness drops and rain-
swollen floodwaters rise.   Garrett finds her clinging precariously
to a rock outcropping.   Jack Tramp comes to his assistance, but
Garrett alone must save her courageously and ingeniously.   When
he recovers from the ordeal, he learns the bad news that the
fiercely independent Jack had to go to the County Farm against his
will, but the good news is that Dad is alive.   With greater self-
reliance he realizes that nothing is certain but change.

214a.   Holland, Isabelle.   NOW IS NOT TOO LATE.   New York:
        Lothrop, Lee and Shepard, 1980.   159pp.   Grades 5-7.

        While her father and stepmother tour Europe, Cathy Bar-
rett, 11, spends her vacation with her paternal grandmother at her
summer home off the coast of Maine.   Cathy is independent, headstrong, outspoken, and perverse, but her grandmother is sensible,
perspicacious, and flexible enough to give her the latitude to come
and go as she chooses.   In Cathy's meanderings she meets a reclusive and mysterious painter, Elizabeth, and agrees to pose for
her, but remains secretive about visiting her.   When she impulsively hurts one of Elizabeth's cats she runs away in remorse, badly
frightening her grandmother.   Following one of her recurring nightmares, she accepts the solace of sleeping in Granny's bed.   Later
she learns the source of those nightmares with the accidental and
stunning revelation that Elizabeth is Cathy's natural mother, a
former alcoholic who vituperatively abused her when she was 4.
Again she runs and hides in her confusion, shame and panic in a
narrow cave above treacherous shoals from which she is eventually
rescued by her elderly fisherman friend who risks his life to save
hers.   From her grandmother she learns the reason for her defensiveness and dislike of animals, and, that it is not too late to
make friends with her own mother.

215.   Hunt, Irene.   UP A ROAD SLOWLY.   Chicago: Follett,
        1966.   Illus. by Don Bolognese.   192pp.   Grades 5-8.

        Julie Trelling is 7 when her mother dies and she and her
brother, 9, are wrenched from their home to live in the country
with their reserved, cultivated maiden aunt, 65, and suave, sarcastic, alcoholic uncle, 55, leaving their sister, 17, to keep house
for Father.   Aunt Cordelia is also their school teacher, and Julie
is frequently bitterly resentful of her inflexibility and devotion to
duty.   She longs for a future when she can return to the security
of her own home and family.   But when her brother is sent to
boarding school, her sister marries and has children of her own,
and Father remarries, she realizes that Father's house is no longer
the home she remembers.   Over the years she has become fond of
her undemonstrative aunt and chooses to remain with her, com-
muting to high school in town.   An unfortunate infatuation with a
boy who exploits her almost spoils her relationship with her child-

hood beau, but Uncle Haskell intervenes before it goes too far, one
of his few constructive acts before he dies of liver sclerosis.   Julie and Danny finally declare their mutual affection, and Julie, class
valedictorian, prepares to go off to the state university, secure in
the knowledge of her aunt's pride.

215a.   Hurmence, Belinda.   TOUGH TIFFANY.   Garden City,
         N. Y.:   Doubleday, 1980.   166pp.   Grades 5-7.

         Youngest of six children of a poor black North Carolina
family, Tiffany Cox, 11, is cheerful about her lot, curious about
life, and an innate problem solver.   Her grandmother, a skinflint
who grudgingly doles out used plastic bags and bits of string, is
caustic with her criticism, but she owns her own home and has
money saved for a rainy day.   Tiffany's mother, conversely, is a
spendthrift who buys on whim and nonchalantly juggles her creditors.
Tiffany, moreover, must share a tiny bedroom with her sisters,
one a beauty queen, another pregnant out of wedlock, and a pair of
twins.   Tiff's major concerns this summer are with her pregnant
sister's well-being, saving the new bunkbeds from repossession, and
coexisting peacefully with Granny the week she must spend with her
during the annual family reunion.   From her grandmother's cadenced
argot she learns of her family's proud and independent traditions in
their community, but her greatest achievement is convincing unlettered and sometimes forgetful Granny to deposit her considerable
savings in the bank.   When her sister goes into labor unexpectedly
while the town is deserted, Tiff proves her mettle in saving the
baby, and for her part she is allowed to name it.   She calls it
Turner, after Granny.

216.   Hutchins, Pat.   THE HOUSE THAT SAILED AWAY.   New
         York: Greenwillow, 1975.   Illus. by Laurence Hutchins.
         150pp.   Grades 4-5.

         Grandma is an active and peripatetic senior, temporarily
sidelined by a slip on the dance floor, when she comes to visit
Morgan's family of caricatures: a father who makes unflattering
remarks about his mother-in-law, a rattle-brained mother, and a
baby who torments the cat.   Grandma herself is a frumpy, dumpy
winebibber, but fatuity does not end here.   A sudden deluge inun-
dates London and casts their house adrift on a South Seas adventure
complete with pirates, messages in bottles, tropic isles, castaways,
cannibals, and buried booty.   Of course, Grandma is invited for
dinner by the natives where she flirts with the chief before being
rescued   Then she is kidnapped by the pirates because of her weakness for the treasure, which proves to be the missing Crown Jewels.
When all seems lost, the luxury liner Queen Elizabeth II materializes, and passengers and crew join in the fray.   The captain of
the QE2 falls in love with Grandma, and they are all given a royal
welcome upon their return home.

216a.   Irwin, Hadley.   THE LILITH SUMMER.   Old Westbury,
        N. Y.:   Feminist Press, 1979.   109pp.   Grades 4-6.

Desire to earn money for a ten-speed bike is all that induces Ellen Groves, 12, to spend the summer as a daytime companion to Lilith Adams, 77.   Old age seems to her to make people
boring, regimented, retrospective, imperious, and forgetful.   Then
the two learn to their mutual mortification that while Ellen is being
paid to "lady-sit" Lilith by Lilith's daughter, Lilith is also being
paid to babysit Ellen by Ellen's mother.   This duplicity creates the
atmosphere for compromise.   When Ellen conquers her resentment
and hostility, she opens her mind and heart to appreciation of the
venerable, independent, intelligent and caring lady.   Lilith firmly
but gently guides Ellen to accept and tolerate her other elderly
friends and acquaintances--one an alcoholic, another Lilith's perennial suitor, and a third who is a veritable vegetable in a nursing
home.   Lilith supervises a canoe outing, defends a racy book, helps
Ellen overcome her fear of storms and an impulse to shoplift, and
finally prepares Ellen to accept death as part of life.   Together
they successfully parry an attempt to send Lilith to a retirement
home, and at the end of the summer they agree that they have both
benefitted.

217.   Justus, May.   GABBY GAFFER.   Minneapolis: Dillon,
        1975.   Illus. by Inese Jansons.   106pp.   Grades 3-5.

Gabby Gaffer, diminutive, puckish, hirsute, and ruddy and
wrinkled of countenance, roams the roads of Unlucky Village, spread-
ing good will and well being among its plaintive inhabitants, and tactfully breaking their selfish habits and substituting magnanimous ones
in twelve short stories.

218.   Kleberger, Ilse.   GRANDMOTHER OMA.   New York:
        Atheneum, 1968.   Illus. by Wallace Tripp.   124pp.   Grades
        4-6.

While the other German village children boast of owning the
most land or livestock, the five children of Schoolmaster Pieselang,
poor but respectable, brag of their most cherished possession,
Grandmother Oma, who looks like a traditional granny but who be-
haves in a most sporty fashion by roller skating for both exercise
and transportation and ice skating for pure pleasure.   A master of
practical psychology, Oma knows just how to convince Peter, 3, to
eat porridge and spinach and Jan, 10, that running away to America is both impractical and dangerous.   She is resourceful and indefatigable in nursing the whole family through measles and a village
heroine for rescuing the mayor's exhibitionist son from thin ice on
the pond.   But best of all is the way she parlays a personal invitation from her zoo director brother, who hates children, into an
exciting month's vacation for all but the baby at Uncle Ludo's zoo.
Of course the old misanthrope is charmed by the children, and the

children are entranced with the animals, especially Ingeborg, 14, who will remain with Uncle Ludo.   When Oma is chided by her punctilious son for being the Peter Pan of the geriatric set, she retorts, "You're as old as you feel!"

219.   Kleberger, Ilse.   TRAVELING WITH OMA.   New York: Atheneum, 1970.   Illus. by Hans Behrens.   Trans. by Belinda McGill.   Grades 4-6.

Redoubtable, roller-skating Grandmother Oma (see 218) subdues an inept burglar, rehabilitates him, then commandeers his conveyance, a bright green gypsy caravan drawn by a peculiar horse named Max, for a glorious, hilarious summer of adventure and misadventure with her three young charges, Jan, Peter, and Bridget. Along the way, with Oma's guidance, daydreamer Peter learns to separate fact from fancy, and adolescent Jan learns that smoking does not necessarily make the man.   The quartet plus Max finally succeed in reuniting despondent burglar/magician Mario with his circus family.

220.   Konigsburg, E. L.   FROM THE MIXED-UP FILES OF MRS. BASIL E. FRANKWEILER.   New York: Atheneum, 1968. Illus. by the author.   162pp.   Grades 4-6.

Claudia, 11, has decided to run away from home to teach her family a lesson in "Claudia appreciation" and has chosen her brother Jamie, 9, to be her companion and bankroll.   Their destination is the Metropolitan Museum of Art in New York City where, with a little luck and a lot of ingenuity, they manage to camp out for a full week undetected.   During that period, the museum acquires a statue of an angel, purportedly an unknown work by Michelangelo, from the collection of one wealthy and eccentric Mrs. Frankweiler, 82, and the experts are arguing its authenticity.   It becomes Claudia's obsession, also, to establish its validity before returning home so that she can claim a real accomplishment.   When the exchequer runs dry before she succeeds, she decides to go directly to Mrs. Frankweiler to discover the truth.   Loving intrigue and excitement, the lady challenges them to a detective game in her filing cabinets. They do not disappoint her, and she rewards them with exceedingly valuable documentation and a ride home in her chauffeured limousine in exchange for the exclusive story of their adventure.

220a.   Konigsburg, E. L.   THROWING SHADOWS.   New York: Atheneum, 1979.   151pp.   Grades 4-6.

In one of five short stories, "At the Home," protagonist Phillip fractures his arm and coincidentally visits the old folks' home where his mother volunteers, a fortuitous event that alters his life and that of the residents.   Because of his ubiquitous tape recorder, he attracts the attention of the provocative Miss Ilona,

an elderly Hungarian Jew, who spellbinds him into daily visits with
her intriguing tale, told in suspenseful installments, of surviving
the Holocaust in Europe, the Communist coup after the war, and
the 1956 rebellion when she escaped to the U. S.   Her purpose is
to stave off the debilitating boredom that already seems to have en-
gulfed the other residents whom she calls the Beige and Grays.
Soon all the residents and patients are clamoring to have Phillip
record their stories, but he is already overextended.   When his
arm heals, he convinces Miss Ilona that she must overcome her
prejudice against other old people and continue recording the others'
experiences as therapy for both herself and them.   He teams her
with an old Ukrainian gentleman whose folk songs Phillip has taped,
and the volunteer staff preserves copies of their recorded tapes in
the home's library.

221.   Kruss, James.   MY GREAT-GRANDFATHER AND I.   New
         York: Atheneum, 1966.   Illus. by Jochen Bartsch.   246pp.
         Grades 5-7.

         Boy's sisters contract measles, and he is sent across town
on the Island of Helgoland to spend his week's quarantine with his
grandmother and great-grandfather who has retired from the sea to be
a poet.   Grandmother is ever the stern pragmatist and pessimist, but
great-grandfather and boy, 11, are kindred spirits who spend their
time rhyming for one another on pine planks in the old lobster shack.
Great-grandfather is also a gifted storyteller who mesmerizes boy
with fanciful tales of how two lame stammerers lost their handicaps,
how a lowly seaman became king for a fortnight, and how the denizens of Helgoland got their colorful nicknames.   He spins yarns of
a lyrical harbor master, whimsical international semanticists, chor-
eographic millipedes, an enchanted island, and resourceful Turkish
thieves and raconteurs.   As the stimulating week draws to a close
and relatives and friends congregate to celebrate Great-grandfather's
eighty-fifth birthday, erstwhile unimaginative Grandmother astounds
her father with a recital of his poems that she has copied on paper.
She and boy further startle him with new "ABC" poems they have
composed for the occasion, and boy reluctantly returns home.

222.   Lampman, Evelyn Sibley.   NAVAHO SISTER.   Garden City:
         Doubleday, 1956.   Illus. by Paul Lantz.   189pp.   Grades
         5-7.

         Sad Girl, 12, and her poor but industrious grandmother,
She-Who-Knows-Much-Trouble, are pitied on their reservation because they have no surviving family.   Sad Girl is reluctant to go
to boarding school to be Americanized, but Grandmother is adamant,
and Sad Girl is launched upon the most exciting and terrifying adventure of her life.   Her first momentous decision is to choose a
name, Rose Smith, the surname of which Grandmother will share.
Making new friends from other reservations and adjusting to strange
customs, language, food, and modern technology are all major hurdles

to surmount, but there are compensations, too, such as her first
state fair, movie, Christmas, and earnings. Her biggest concern
is her lack of a family and how it will affect her status at school
if it becomes known. Just as she is belatedly assured that it makes
no difference, her long-lost uncle appears, who also happens to be
the father of her best friend and roommate, to give familial stabil-
ity to Rose and her grandmother.

223. Lampman, Evelyn Sibley. THE SHY STEGOSAURUS OF IN-
     DIAN SPRINGS. Garden City: Doubleday, 1962. Illus. by
     Paul Galdone. 220pp. Grades 5-7.

When Huck returns home from Indian boarding school to his
grandfather's hut on the reservation for the summer, he is startled
to discover George the Stegosaurus inhabiting the hot mineral springs
where he does the laundry, but he is delighted to make friends with
Joey and Joan Brown who are spending the summer with their aunt.
Huck has no friends among his own kind because they ridicule his
grandfather, Opalo, a truculent old medicine man who speaks only
the Klickitat tongue. The new Chief enjoins Opalo to board in town
with one of the progressive families the following winter, while
Opalo just as obdurately refuses to relinquish his rigorous traditional
life on the desert. Brainless but instinctive George inadvertently
provides Opalo the spectacular opportunity of restoring his tarnished
prestige at the annual harvest festival by his insatiable appetite for
overripe bananas. A compromise is achieved for Huck's grandfather.

224. LeRoy, Gen. EMMA'S DILEMMA. New York: Harper and
     Row, 1975. 123pp. Grades 5-6.

Emma, 13, practices being grownup by behaving very con-
scientiously, whether she is baby-sitting Herbie in his apartment
next door, doing her homework, or walking her adored sheepdog,
Pearl. Then Emma's maternal grandmother, a stranger, comes to
live in their cramped New York apartment and turns her ordered
existence upside down. Grandmom is allergic to dust and dog hair,
and Pearl must be banished precipitously. Grandmom is distressed
at Emma's despair, but that does not ameliorate the agony and injustice. Emma's attempt to place Pearl with Herbie's unstable
mother fails, and plans proceed to send Pearl to cousins in suburban New Jersey until Herbie, 6, and the dog disappear. Emma
finds them hiding with the misguided notion that they can elude the
long arm of parental authority. Emma sees in Herbie's defiance
her own obstinacy and accedes to the inevitable. She accompanies
her mother in taking Pearl to the country and sees firsthand how
much happier the big dog will be running free. She and Herbie can
visit on weekends, and in the meantime, she will take the lonely
and insecure boy under her wing.

224a. Lowry, Lois. ANASTASIA KRUPNIK. Boston: Houghton
      Mifflin, 1979. 113pp. Grades 4-6.

Anastasia at 10 is an intelligent girl of mercurial temperament. A budding poet like her father, a Harvard professor, she
collects words and ideas in a small notebook. Two of her lists are
comprised of things she likes and things she hates. Among items
on her hate list are her teacher (who doesn't appreciate free verse),
her parents (because they decided to have a baby without consulting
her), babies, and her paternal grandmother who at 92 is far older
than all her friends' grandparents. She is a nursing home resident
because of her advanced senility and speaks in the present tense of
her husband, long deceased, and infant son, Anastasia's father.
Her parents have given Anastasia the privilege of naming the baby,
and she plans to call him something hideous in retaliation for their
saddling her with a name she also despises. Then her father introduces her to a line from Wordsworth, "The inward eye which is
the bliss of solitude, " and explains that her grandmother is happy
living in the past with her memories. When her grandmother dies
peacefully in her sleep, Anastasia decides to name the baby Sam
after the grandfather she never knew, her grandmother's beloved
husband. One by one, she has transferred most of the items on
her hate list to the love column.

225.   MacDonald, Betty. MRS. PIGGLE-WIGGLE. Philadelphia:
        Lippincott, 1957. Illus. by Hilary Knight. Grades 4-5.

Widowed Mrs. Piggle-Wiggle is eccentric and lives in an
upside-down house, but she has her head together when it comes to
handling kids. She is endlessly and amusingly imaginative and resourceful in devising painless panaceas for such common but chronic
and contagious complaints as "Won't-pick-up-toys, Answering-back,
Selfishness, Never-wanting-to-go-to-bed, Slow-eating-tiny-bite-taking,
Fighting-quarreling, Bath-hating, and many, many more in the succeeding books in the series, MRS. PIGGLE-WIGGLE'S MAGIC;
HELLO, MRS. PIGGLE-WIGGLE; and MRS. PIGGLE-WIGGLE'S
FARM.

226.   MacGregor, Ellen. MISS PICKERELL GOES TO MARS.
        New York: McGraw-Hill, 1951. Illus. by Paul Galdone.
        128pp. Grades 3-6.

Upon returning from a visit with her nieces and nephews,
acrophobic spinster lapidarist Miss Pickerell is righteously indignant to find that a space complex, complete with rocket ship, has
mushroomed in her cow pasture in her absence. Intent on berating
the pilot, she climbs into the towering spacecraft, unobserved,
moments before liftoff. She demands to be returned to earth, but
as they have left the absent-minded flight engineer behind, there is
some doubt of their returning at all. Left to her own devices, she
discovers that she likes weightlessness, receives some elementary
physics lessons from a member of the expedition, sets the table for
a space-packaged meal, and even stands navigational watch. While
the crew is exploring Mars, Miss Pickerell becomes a heroine when

she rescues a stranded man. She also loses her acrophobia. Back
on earth, Miss Pickerell enters her Mars rocks in the state fair
and wins an award, and the tardy flight engineer, who has been
caring for her cow, decides to become a veterinarian instead.
(First of numerous Miss Pickerell adventures.)

227.   Majerus, Janet.   GRANDPA AND FRANK.   Philadelphia:
       Lippincott, 1976.   192pp.   Grades 5-7.

Love and loyalty to the grandfather who has been a surrogate father to her since her parents' death enables Sarah, 12, to
perceive what neither Grandpa, recovering from a stroke, nor his
sister, Aunt Martha, will believe, that surly Uncle Frank is planning to commit his father to the County Farm, as he has threatened
to do for years, and have himself appointed conservator of the farm.
Frank is garnering public sympathy for himself over the rural party
line in the year 1949 by exaggerating Grandpa's occasional incon-
tinence and nocturnal perambulations.   Desperately, Sarah enlists
the help of a neighbor boy, Joey, and the two spirit the old man
across the state of Illinois in a derelict Model A truck to Aunt
Clara's home.   Delayed by dozens of unforeseen difficulties, they
reach Chicago to learn despairingly that Aunt Clara has already
been called back to the farm.   Joey is arrested for driving without
a license, and the whole affair hits the headlines, backfiring on
Uncle Frank.   Aunt Clara's doctor husband certifies that Grandpa,
though in the early stages of senile dementia, is still competent,
and Sarah goes off to boarding school, secure in the knowledge that
Grandpa is safe--for the time being.

228.   Mathis, Sharon Bell.   THE HUNDRED PENNY BOX.   New
       York: Viking, 1975.   Illus. by Leo and Diane Dillon.
       47pp.   Grades 3-5.

Conflict is ineluctable between Michael's modern, progressive mother and his father's Great-aunt Dewbet, 100, when they
fetch her from her capacious old home in Atlanta to their cramped
apartment.   Aunt Dew lives in the past with her reminiscences and
shabby mementos, and neither she nor Michael, kindred spirits, can
understand why his insensitive mother wants to burn her meager possessions.   Chief bone of contention is the ungainly wooden box containing the collection of pennies, one for every year of her venerable
life, that was started by her late husband.   "Anybody takes my
hundred penny box takes me!" she cries in defense of her diminished
dignity and independence.   In an alliance of weakness, extreme youth
and age succeed in nettling the omnipotent and unsentimental adult
who regards the centenarian as a peevish inconvenience for childishly clinging to the past and refusing to take her nap on schedule.
Michael and Aunt Dew share their black roots in poignant intimacy.

229.   McNeill, Janet.   THE BATTLE OF ST. GEORGE WITHOUT.

Boston: Little,   Brown,   1966.   Illus. by Mary Russon.
188pp.   Grades 5-7.

The once distinguished houses of Dove Square have long
since been turned into flats and now teem with people and stray
animals.   Seeking diversion, the children of the Square, led by
Matt, 13, discover a secret entrance to the old vaulted and but-
tressed church that has been boarded up since World War II and
make it their trysting place.   They soon learn that others are interested in the edifice with the intention of stealing its valuable lead
roof, and thus is joined the battle for preservation of St. George-
Without-the-Wall.   Their only allies are two long-time parishioners,
an elderly disabled World War I veteran, who pretends he is still
in uniform, and an animated spinster who furnishes the history of the
congregation.   With ingenuity and cunning they learn the gang's
plans, and on the night of the theft, the children are on hand to try
to stop it.   The thieves lock them in the sanctuary overnight but
not before they spread the alarm and become neighborhood heroes.
They cannot save the defunct inner-city church from eventual demo-
lition, but at least the Bishop gets a crack at ringing its bell one
last triumphal time.

229a.   Mearian, Judy Frank.   SOMEONE SLIGHTLY DIFFERENT.
New York: Dial, 1980.   197pp.   Grades 5-8.

Marty Trevor, 12, is heckled by her wealthier seventh
grade classmates for being a "latchkey kid" whose mother drives a
cab for a living.   Marty's father deserted them when she was 4, and
she yearns for him to return and make them a complete family once
more.   Instead, Flossie, her paternal grandmother, comes to live
with them and contributes the warm touches of a homemaker which
Mom has never had time for.   Flossie seems antipodal to Mom, a
rigid fundamentalist.   She is pragmatic, agnostic, drinks bourbon
temperately, and bets on the horses.   Still, they blend harmonious-
ly, and Flossie informs Marty that her father is a rogue and a
charmer who is now remarried.   Mom shows her that, as the offspring of two divergent personalities, she can combine the attributes
of both Mary and Martha, the Biblical sisters for whom she was
named.   When Marty contracts a rare case of scarlet fever, Flossie
nurses her through it before succumbing to it herself.   She dies of
anginal complications, and Mom, acceding to Flossie's preference
for cremation, reveals that there will be no funeral service or in-
terment.   Mom makes a real effort to be more relaxed and sympathetic, and Marty, with the friendship of Charlie, a serious student like herself, doesn't miss the company of her snobbish acquaintances.

230.   Merrill, Jean.   THE PUSHCART WAR.   New York: Scott,
1964.   Illus. by Ronni Solbert.   223pp.   Grades 4-6.

Arrogant truckers manipulating the mayor have successfully

snarled New York City traffic in their bid to force all other vehicles off the streets, when the incident of the Daffodil Massacre, in which Morris the Florist's pushcart is run down, sparks the other street vendors to strike back. Deployed by doughty General Anna, who sells apples and pears, and inspired by the martyrdom of Frank the Flower, they begin their offensive armed with pea shooters equipped with "peapins" for "killing" the enemies' tires. They win the first skirmish, but the enraged teamsters retaliate with a sneak attack on Maxie, the Pushcart King, who cleverly deflects it and makes an ally of the Police Commissioner. An armistice is arranged which the truckers abrogate, and the pushcarts seem doomed to ignominious capitulation until Mr. Jerusalem, the junk peddler, proposes a Peace March that arouses public sentiment and turns the tide via a spontaneous newspaper campaign. The teamsters are forced to retreat under a barrage of canteloupes aimed by irate housewives supplied by the pushcart quartermasters. A Peace Conference is called in which the Flower Formula Treaty is signed, and in the postwar era, Hollywood films its version of The Pushcart War.

231.   Miles, Miska. ANNIE AND THE OLD ONE. Boston: Little, Brown, 1971. Illus. by Peter Parnall. 44pp. Grades 3-4.

Annie helps herd the sheep, irrigates the cornfield, and listens to her grandmother's stories of long ago, but she is not yet ready to learn to weave the Navajo blankets of which her people are so justly proud. When her grandmother, one of the revered Old Ones who is so mysteriously attuned to nature, announces that when the new blanket is taken from the loom she will return to Mother Earth, Annie knows that she must halt the completion of the blanket so her grandmother will not die. Being naughty at school and turning the sheep loose on the desert fail to deter her mother from the daily weaving, so in desperation Annie wakes at night to unravel the day's work. One night the Old One waylays her and explains that she cannot hold back time. As surely as the sun rises it must also set, for everything belongs to Earth and returns to Earth forever in its own unique cycle. Understanding and "breathless with the wonder of it," Annie returns to the hogan to learn to weave at last.

232.   Monjo, F. N. GRAND PAPA AND ELLEN AROON. New York: Holt, Rinehart and Winston, 1974. Illus. by Richard Cuffari. 58pp. Genealogy. Bibliography. Grades 3-5.

Nine-year-old Ellen Wayles Randolph, self-proclaimed favorite granddaughter of Thomas Jefferson, recounts intimate details of life with her scientist/statesman grandfather both in Washington City and at home at Monticello. She introduces political friends and enemies, ambassadors, Indians, and colorful personalities such as Dolley Madison and Meriweather Lewis, as well as members of the large and intellectual extended family. Ingenuously and engagingly she explains nicknames, achievements, customs and habits, anecdotes, and a dose of history in painless prose.

233.   Moray Williams, Ursula. THE CRUISE OF THE HAPPY-
        GO-GAY. New York: Meredith, 1967. Illus. by Gunvor
        Edwards. 151pp. Grades 5-6.

        Somewhat sanguinary but ever scrupulous and stalwart,
Aunt Hegarty, who detests boys, invites her five stair-step nieces,
but not their brothers, on an adventure voyage with the cryptic and
ominous admonition to bring warm underclothing designed for danger.
An intrepid explorer and lepidopterist by avocation, whose heraldry
reads "I come back alive," she provisions a South Seas expedition
and marshalls her female crew.   The cruise is replete with stow-
aways (long-lost, ill-mannered orphan cousins, one female, the other two unmentionable), dastardly pirates who take the boys hostage,
and cultured, card-carrying cannibals on a desert island, through
all of which Aunt Hegarty sails serenely and imposingly in her com-
modore's hat.   They steam home to a heroines' welcome with the
abject pirates in tow, prostrated by measles contracted from Charley-
boy and Gustus. With a stiff upper lip Aunt Hegarty adopts all
three waifs impartially.

234.   Naylor, Phyllis. WITCH'S SISTER. New York: Atheneum,
        1975. Illus. by Gail Owens. 150pp. Grades 5-7.

        Lynn Morley's sister Judith, 14, has been crooning incan-
tations since she began taking sewing lessons with mysterious Mrs.
Tuggle.   Their writer mother, who maintains her studio in the old
woman's converted henhouse next door, insists that Judith's behavior
is the result of adolescent chemistry, but Lynn and her bosom buddy Marjorie (Mouse) suspect Judith of being an apprentice to Mrs.
Tuggle who evinces all the classic symptoms of witchcraft.   When
the pale and astral boy materializes who purports to be Mrs. Tuggle's grandson but whom the girls believe is truly her long-drowned
younger brother, they prognosticate that Lynn's little brother Stevie,
5, must be the next victim to be sacrificed to complete the coven
at midnight of the next full moon.   With mounting horror, Lynn
realizes that she alone can protect Stevie on that fiendishly tempestuous night, because, in their parents' absence, they have been left in
the care of scheming Mrs. Tuggle.   When Judith and the otherworld-
ly boy try to carry the struggling toddler from the house in an ambience of tinkling bell and smoking candle, Lynn's screams seem to
break the spell.   Judith awakes in the morning with a high fever
and no recollection of the summer's mischief.   But Lynn and Mouse
have ominous premonitions of worse to come.

235.   Naylor, Phyllis Reynolds. WITCH WATER. New York:
        Atheneum, 1977. Illus. by Gail Owens. 179pp. Grades
        5-8.

Lynn and her friend Mouse are convinced that gimlet-eyed Mrs. Tuggle is a witch bent on ensnaring them for her coven (see 234), but Mouse is much more susceptible to the odious old woman's wiles than Lynn. At Mrs. Tuggle's overgrown and foreboding Victorian house, Mouse is nearly mesmerized by her powers, but avoiding the house affords no escape, for a flock of sinister crows follows her wherever she goes, and Mrs. Tuggle's enormous and malevolent cat diabolically insinuates himself everywhere, yowling like a banshee. Lynn's parents dismiss their fears as the products of overactive imaginations at best and malicious defamation of an eccentric old lady at worst. Mouse grows torpid when Mrs. Tuggle causes her immersion in the maelstrom below her house, and on a night that the two are alone, Mrs. Tuggle unleashes her full panoply of demons upon the vulnerable and terrorstruck girls. With courage and quick action, Lynn kills the leader of the crows just before it penetrates their defenses. In the morning she knows that she must dispatch the cat as well, and determinedly drowns it after a sanguinary struggle in the turbulent witchwater. She hasn't long to gloat over her new resistance; the supernatural cat returns--and Mrs. Tuggle smiles sardonically and portentously.

236.   Naylor, Phyllis Reynolds. THE WITCH HERSELF. New York: Atheneum, 1978. Illus. by Gail Owens. 164pp. Grades 5-7.

To Lynn's dismay, her mother moves her writing studio into demoniacal Mrs. Tuggle's house for the winter (see 234 & 235) and becomes increasingly irritable, distracted, and lethargic. Lynn and her friend Mouse trap Mrs. Tuggle's malicious black cat and try to hold it hostage so the witch will not harm Lynn's mother, but the beast dies supernaturally. In a daring ploy, Lynn steals Mrs. Tuggle's supply of the ennervating herb tea with which she plies her mother and destroys it, to the woman's fury. Mother tries to convince Dad that Lynn's obsession with Mrs. Tuggle is psychotic, but at last Dad senses the insidious control Mrs. Tuggle exerts over Mother, and even Lynn's sister Judith expresses her concern. In stealth, the girls gain possession of Mrs. Tuggle's mysterious box that contains nothing but a piece of chalk but which is almost powerful enough to save their souls when the execrable woman corners them. The jig is up for Mrs. Tuggle when the bones of a long-dead woman are found in her brother's grave, but Lynn is compelled to return to the menacing house once more to save her doomed mother from total subjugation and entrapment in the fire that engulfs the house, creating a fitting funeral pyre for the malignant Mrs. Tuggle.

237.   Norton, Andre. LAVENDER-GREEN MAGIC. New York: Crowell, 1974. Illus. by Judith Gwyn Brown. 241pp. Grades 5-8.

When their father is listed missing in action in Vietnam,

Mom deposits Holly and her twin brother and sister with their paternal grandparents who live in simplicity as custodians on a 300-
year-old neglected estate near Boston while she goes back to work.
Holly is defensive with her small town sixth grade classmates because she is black and lives in a junkyard, but sometimes treasure
is found among the rubbish, and both grandparents are adept at
restoring and salvaging others' discards.   The children discover an
old embroidered pillow which, when slept upon, produces premonitory dreams that lead them to an overgrown garden maze and a trip
back into time to an encounter with a benign herbalist and a malign
witch.   The children play pivotal roles in fulfilling the eternal des-
tinies of the two anomalous sisters of seventeenth century Salem.
Their interests in herbalism, shared with Grandma, and in the history of the property expand into classroom projects, and Holly's cor-
rosive defensiveness is dispelled.   The pillow also holds the key to
restoring the historic maze to its former beauty and intricacy, saving the property from development and their grandparents from
eviction.   Holly has a premonitory dream that her father will return.

238.   Norton, Mary.   BEDKNOB AND BROOMSTICK.   New York:
        Harcourt, Brace, Jovanovich, 1957.   Illus. by Erik Blegvad.
        189pp.   Grades 5-6.

        Sent to stay with an elderly aunt for the summer, Carey,
Charles, and Paul, 6, meet another aging spinster who is as warm
and fascinating as Aunt Beatrice is cold and forbidding.   Although
she appears prim and conventional, Miss Price is an apprentice
witch.   She bestows on Paul a magical brass bedknob which converts
their ordinary bedstead into a veritable flying carpet that whisks
them wherever they wish to go.   In London they are arrested for
obstructing traffic, but on a seemingly idyllic excursion to a South
Seas island, it is only Miss Price's embryonic powers that save
them from cannibals in a duel of magic with the witch doctor.
Miss Price foreswears further sorcery, but the children cajole her
into giving them a trip back into time where they meet a shy, inept necromancer.   When they return a few weeks later, they discover poor gentle Emelius about to be burned at the stake as scapegoat for the disastrous London fire of 1666.   After effecting a harrowing rescue with some very sophisticated transubstantiation, Miss
Price decides to accompany Emelius back to his own time as his
wife.   On the final one-way ride, the bed is piled precariously with
Miss Price's bathroom fittings, the only modern amenity she cannot eschew.

239.   Orgel, Doris.   A CERTAIN MAGIC.   New York: Dial,
        1976.   176pp.   Grades 5-8.

        Jenny, 11, and her swinging single aunt, 48, are kindred
spirits who even look alike except for Aunt Trudl's obvious wrinkling
and graying.   The only part of her life she will not share with

Jenny are the youthful months she spent as a Jewish refugee in England before World War II, so Jenny is naturally titillated when she discovers the dusty diary her aunt kept during that period, full of the outpourings of a lonely girl far from home, trying to adjust to an alien world and a fractious foster family.   Jenny feels guilty for having read the journal and is half-frightened by the curse young Trudl put upon anyone daring to peruse it.   When her family travels to London, Jenny feels ordained to trace the family her aunt lived with.   It is their strong physical resemblance that accomplishes that miracle, and Jenny receives the doll Trudl once coveted and even recovers her heirloom emerald, but she is increasingly fearful of having meddled in affairs beyond her sphere.   Back home in New York, Aunt Trudl reassures her by making her a gift of the old copybook.   They are more intimate than ever.

240.   Pearce, A. Philippa.   THE MINNOW LEADS TO TREASURE.
          Cleveland: World, 1955.   Illus. by Edward Ardizzone.
          253pp.   Grades 5-7.

Floodwaters bring a canoe to rest at David Moss' dock which results in his acquaintance with Adam Codling, its owner, the orphaned scion of a noble but impoverished old family who lives in the ancestral Tudor manor with his elderly aunt and senile grandfather.   The boys refurbish the canoe and explore the River Say in a summer of adventure, searching for the Codling family treasure that disappeared following the defeat of the Spanish Armada.   Using a cryptic 400-year-old clue and applying deductive reasoning, they ferret out its hiding place only to find it empty.   It seems that Grandfather unearthed it in his youth but now perversely refuses to divulge its whereabouts.   The secret dies with him, and Aunt Dinah is forced to sell the historic house to a man who intends to dismantle it stone by stone till he finds the treasure.   The boys continue to search, joined now by Aunt Dinah, in the hopes of a last-minute reprieve.   Suspensefully they relocate it, but before its final recovery, a distant cousin turns up and another mystery is solved.

241.   Peck, Robert Newton.   KING OF KAZOO.   New York:
          Knopf, 1976.   Illus. by W. B. Park.   Music and lyrics
          by the author.   81pp.   Grades 3-6.

A drollery of rollicking rhyme and purple pun in which Old Cowpuncher in quest of Cow to punch (with his red boxing glove), lachrymose lady Plumber in search of a sink to repair, and dapper but doleful Drummer sans drum are transported by a grateful ghost to the land of Kazoo where they are in danger of peremptorily being transformed into kazoos until they get their act together and mend the marriage of the local despot and his consort who then grant them three wishes.   Plumber forsakes her unpromising career to ride off into the sunet with Drummer who presumably finds it more stimulating to have a live-in Plumber than a drum, while Old Cowpuncher foreswears punching anyone, including long-suffering Cow.

242.   Pevsner, Stella. KEEP STOMPIN' TILL THE MUSIC
         STOPS. New York: Seabury, 1977. 136pp. Grades 4-6.

The family reunion called by Great-aunt Violet at Great-
grandpa Ben's home in Galena, Illinois takes on ominous overtones
when Richard's cousin Alexandra becomes convinced that Grandpa
Ben's children, led by wheeling, dealing, martini-tippling Aunt Vi,
plan to uproot him from his home of fifty years and install him in
a glorified sardine can at "Tranquility Trailerville" in Florida.
Alexandra directs all the cousins to spy on the adults for Grandpa
Ben's protection. Richard, 12, overhears several significant nug-
gets of information, but because of his dyslexia has difficulty inter-
preting the intelligence to Alexandra. When the plot is finally bared,
Grandpa Ben, 77, demonstrates his mettle by springing a counterplot.
He has rented part of his house to the local historical society in exchange for its upkeep and some personal attention from members
who are old friends. He's known about Aunt Vi's scheme right along
and feels that "A man's got a right to have a say about his own
life. " He lives up to his own motto to "keep stompin' till the music stops. "

243.   Pollowitz, Melinda. CINNAMON CANE. New York: Har-
         per, 1977. 154pp. Grades 5-7.

Cassie Bennison's parents callously move her paternal grandfather from the farm on which he has spent his life into a modern
apartment in town decorated by her modish mother. At the same
time, they try to remold Cassie herself into a social butterfly.
Cassie and Grampa are kindred spirits of simple tastes and old-
fashioned virtues who are resistant to change and progress. In
seventh grade, Cassie eagerly joins the poetry club, but reluctantly
enters the elite clique and starts dating. The more approbation
she gets from her mother on her extracurricular social activities,
the less time she has to spend with her grandfather, until one day
he suffers a stroke and Cassie sets new priorities, channeling most
of her energy into turning back the clock and making Grampa his
old self. He is uncooperative about following doctor's orders, and,
hobbling about on a cane made of cinnamon wood, wanders outside
in the snow and collapses again. Cassie is unwilling to accept that
he will never be the same again. Suddenly, surrounded by the family, the old man dies, and reality floods over Cassie. She runs
off to regain her composure before returning to say good-bye.

244.   Pomerantz, Charlotte. THE DOWNTOWN FAIRY GOD-
         MOTHER. Reading: Addison-Wesley, 1978. Illus. by
         Susanna Natti. 45pp. Grades 2-5.

A dowdy aging homemaker in curlers and slacks, bored
with housekeeping, re-enters the job market as a fairy godmother,
Grade C. She materializes to Olivia but is unable to fulfill her request for a stuffed toy. She's a whiz, however, at changing traffic

lights to green to promote Mr. Kremsky's romance and turning stairs into a wheelchair ramp for a housebound old lady. On her Public Service day, she fixes out-of-order vending machines, public telephones, and escalators. She does so nicely, in fact, that she is promoted to Grade B, and with her powers grants Olivia's wish before moving onward and upward, decorously dressed and coifed.

244a.   Potter, Marian. THE SHARED ROOM. New York: Morrow, 1979. 192pp. Grades 4-6.

As she enters fifth grade, Catherine Doyle, 10, who occupies the same bedroom in her grandparents' house that her mother grew up in, develops an obsessive curiosity about her parents whom her grandparents adamantly refuse to mention. Pleas for information only elicit tears and accusations of ingratitude from Nana, while Pop retreats behind the noise of his electric tools. A fabricated story of idyllic family life leads to the revelation by petty, gossiping small town classmates that her mother is incurably insane. Catherine's pugilistic reaction to the news earns her the sobriquet of Ali. When she learns of her grandparents' annual Christmas pilgrimage to the nearby mental hospital, she demands to be taken along, and when that ploy fails, she sends her mother a surreptitious gift. The correspondence this produces convinces Ali that her mother is normal. Intercepting a letter from the hospital director declaring that her mother is rehabilitated and can function at home precipitates Ali into bringing her home without permission. Nana is furious and almost persuades even Ali's mother that living outside the institution is hopeless. Pop explains to Ali about her mother's nervous breakdown and subsequent suicide attempts after Ali's birth and her husband's desertion, the cause of Nana's heartbreak. Ali's mother realizes that her mother will never forgive her for failing to fulfill her expectations and makes her own decision to move to a local halfway house where she can be part of Ali's life.

245.   Proysen, Alf. LITTLE OLD MRS. PEPPERPOT. New York: Obolensky, 1959. Illus. by Bjorn Berg. Trans. by Marianne Helweg. 96pp. Grades 3-5.

A collection of stories about a little old lady who, inconveniently at times, finds herself reduced to the size of a pepperpot. Resourcefully she cajoles and threatens her pets to clean house for her, the kitchen utensils to prepare a meal, and the elements to wash the clothes. In other episodes she befriends a wistful little girl, helps her forgetful husband buy macaroni, becomes queen of the crows in an aerial adventure, and acts as a mechanical doll for a bazaar prize, upstaging three very snobbish ladies.

246.   Raskin, Ellen. FIGGS AND PHANTOMS. New York: Dutton, 1974. Illus. by the author. 152pp. Grades 5-8.

The only member of her flaky, flamboyant family of retired vaudevillians that Mona Lisa Newton has real respect and affection for is her dwarfish Uncle Flo (Florence Italy Figg) with
whom, by standing on his shoulders, she forms half of the Figg-
Newton Giant, giving Uncle Flo the stature he lacks to reach high
shelves. The only true happiness he has found in life has been in
books, and when he dies suddenly but not unexpectedly, Mona, inconsolable, wants to join him in Capri, the Figg family's private
Valhalla. In one of his rare books, she finds a map which she follows in nightmare to an island of amorphous phantoms which eventually crystallize into what she recognizes as someone else's dream
where she cannot remain. She finds Uncle Flo who has found true
love and deference at last and awakes to learn that she has been
deathly ill, surrounded by the supportive, if freakish, family.
Mona decides she has a lot of remembering, living, learning, and
loving to do before she returns to Capri.

247.   Rinaldo, C. L. DARK DREAMS. New York: Harper and
         Row, 1974. 154pp. Grades 5-8.

When Carlo Santucci's widowed father leaves him in the
care of his devout, Italian-speaking grandmother while he embarks
for the Pacific in 1943, the delicate, sensitive boy, 12, experiences
terrifying nightmares impelled by fear of his weak heart and of the
brutal bullies who prowl the alley. The brain-damaged man across
the alley, whom most people ignorantly fear, protects him, and they
become companions. When Carlo's suspicious grandmother finds
out, however, she has the unfortunate Joey J committed to an institution. Carlo's fears return, and he wishes he were strong and
brave like his father, not fragile like his mother. When discon-
solate Joey J escapes, the authorities agree to let him live in peace
with his mother provided he commits no violence, but when the
hooligans attack Carlo with a knife, Joey J instinctively charges to
his friend's defense, is remanded to the asylum, and dies shortly
afterward. From his grandmother and from his father's letters,
Carlo learns revealing things about both parents' courage.

248.   Roberts, Elisabeth. JUMPING JACKDAWS! HERE COMES
         SIMON. Chicago: Rand McNally, 1973. Illus. by Pru-
         dence Seward. 192pp. Glossary. Grades 4-6.

Simon, 6, knows there will never be a dull moment when
he goes to visit his corpulent, original, and uninhibited grandmother,
77, whether she crashes through the ceiling of the apartment below
while exercising, demonstrates her proficiency on the pogo stick
that Simon gives her for her birthday, wins a prize pig in a carnival game of skill, strands them in the attic by knocking over the
ladder in heaving herself up, damages a greenhouse with a magnificent soccer punt, clears the ceiling of cobwebs by leaping at them
with a feather duster, discovers the thrills of sledding, or just
takes him on adventurous excursions to the beach, an island, and

a fireworks display.   Then enormous, ebullient Great-uncle James
arrives from Canada with the gift of a totem pole and buys them a
home in the country where more novelties await, such as the cow
that gets stuck in the kitchen, the housewarming to which the fire
department is invited when the chimney catches fire, and Grandmother's superb kite-flying exhibition. "Rain and hailstones!"
Never did grandmother and grandson find such excitement in such
homely pursuits.

249.   Rock, Gail. THE HOUSE WITHOUT A CHRISTMAS TREE.
          New York: Knopf, 1974. Illus. by Charles C. Gehm.
          87pp.   Grades 4-6.

          Strict but sympathetic Grandma acts as buffer between
Addie Mills, 10, and her dour, practical, and undemonstrative father.   Growing up in Nebraska in the late 1940's, Addie is embarrassed that their house lacks a Christmas tree, but Dad remains
adamant.   Addie wins the drawing for the classroom tree, and she
and her friend Carla Mae drag it home and set it up with Grandma's help.   Dad is furious with her for accepting charity, and she
goes to bed in tears while Dad and Grandma argue heatedly.   In
the night, Grandma confides to Addie that her father cannot bear
being reminded of her mother's death at Christmas of the year she
was born.   In contrition, Addie slips out before dawn and delivers
the offending tree to the town's poor family and experiences the true
spirit of Christmas.   After the annual Christmas pageant, Dad surprises Addie with her own Yule tree and even unpacks the precious
ornaments made by her mother.   At long last, he decides to bury
his grief, and the two of them discuss the past for the first time.

250.   Rock, Gail. THE THANKSGIVING TREASURE.   New York:
          Knopf, 1974. Illus. by Charles C. Gehm. 91pp.   Grades
          4-6.

          Addie Mills, now 11 (see 249), has a passion for art, Roy
Rogers, and horses.   Her father has had an extended feud with the
elderly misanthrope he calls old man Rehnquist, and when Addie and
her bosom buddy Carla Mae trespass on his farm to cut cattails, he
threatens them with his shotgun.   But spunky Addie is inspired by
the class Thanksgiving pageant to make friends with the old man,
and when her father vetoes her idea to have him to Thanksgiving
dinner, she boldly decides to smuggle some turkey and trimmings
to him.   Her assertiveness finally succeeds, and soon she wheedles
him into letting her exercise his horse, Treasure.   Gradually she
erodes his diffidence and irascibility, and he allows her to sketch
him.   One afternoon she finds him gravely ill and summons a doctor, but it is too late to save the old widower's life.   She confides
her furtive friendship to her grandmother who gently and wisely assuages her fear of death.   In his will, Mr. Rehnquist makes posthumous reparation for his debt to Mr. Mills and bequeaths Treasure
to Addie.   With Grandma's persuasion, her truculent father capitulates and lets her keep the horse.

251.   Rock, Gail. A DREAM FOR ADDIE. New York: Knopf,
        1975. Illus. by Charles C. Gehm. 89pp. Grades 4-6.

Constance Payne, the famous Broadway actress, is returning to Clear River, Nebraska upon her mother's death to sell the
big house in which she grew up. Addie Mills, now 13 (see 249 &
250), is determined to get her autograph and is surprised when
Constance accepts her invitation to dinner and to present the school
style show awards. She appears at the style show drunk, and Addie and her grandmother are the only two who take compassion on
her. Constance agrees to give Addie and her friends drama lessons,
but at the second one she is abusively besotted. At first Addie is
indignant and humiliated until Grandma calmly persuades her to be
forgiving. They realize that Constance is seriously ill, and Addie
has to convince her intractable father to let Constance recover with
them. Addie remains loyal even when Constance confesses that she
has never been an actress. When they attend Easter services together, Constance regains her pride and decides to begin a new
life teaching piano and drama in Clear River.

252.   Rock, Gail. ADDIE AND THE KING OF HEARTS. New
        York: Knopf, 1976. Illus. by Charles McVicker. 85pp.
        Grades 4-7.

Billy Wild is sweet on Addie Mills, 13 in 1949 (see 249,
250 & 251), but she coyly repudiates his attentions, and when the
handsome, urbane Mr. Davenport comes to teach seventh grade history, all thoughts of Billy vanish. She spends hours after school
discussing art and literature with Mr. Davenport and feeling in-
finitely more mature and sophisticated than her classmates. At
home she moons over how to project an adult image, remembering
that her father was ten years older than her mother. When she
keeps Billy dangling too long, he asks her arch rival to the Valen-
tine's Day dance, and she is faced with the dilemma of going alone
or staying home. She and Grandma discuss finding "Mr. Right"
and the many disappointments in the quest. Addie finally decides
to go, but the dance is a disaster: Billy is crowned King of Hearts
and Mr. Davenport introduces her to his gorgeous fiancée. Addie
reacts childishly, is rebuked by Mr. Davenport, and flees home.
To her surprise Billy follows her, bored with the dance, and brings
her a box of candy, and Addie even warms up to her father's ef-
fulgent new girlfriend.

253.   Rodowsky, Colby. EVY-IVY-OVER. New York: Watts,
        1978. 153pp. Grades 5-7.

Her mother named her Mary Rose--and then boarded a
Trailways bus and disappeared. Her grandmother, Gussie, re-
named her Slug-a-bed. Slug has always enjoyed their special way
of communicating, their daily forages through the community's gar-
bage cans in search of colored glass or pieces of metal, and their

impromptu dancing. She has taken for granted the castoffs they wear, their outlandishly decorated house, and Gussie's prescience. When she enters sixth grade, however, she becomes self-conscious of their eccentric lifestyle, goaded by a vicious classmate, Nelson, and a teacher who discriminates against her. Like a jump rope in one of the incessant schoolyard games, Slug's emotions flop from fierce fealty to acute embarrassment when Nelson brands Gussie a witch and a thief on cruelly contrived evidence. He also terrorizes his own senile grandmother, but it is only when Gussie is beaten senseless that Nelson's psychosis is diagnosed. A sympathetic new teacher helps Slug through the trauma of Gussie's recuperation and shows her that being different is nothing to be ashamed of.

254.   St. George, Judith. THE CHINESE PUZZLE OF SHAG
        ISLAND. New York: Putnam, 1976. 157pp. Grades 5-7.

        Kim Lauder, 13, and her mother arrive at the island bastion off the Maine coast of Kim's long-estranged maternal great-grandfather, 93, ostensibly to prepare The Anchorage for auction. But the cantankerous old man denies summoning them and has no intention of parting with the immoderate mansion built by his seafaring father. Kim makes friends with her taciturn and formidable great-grandfather, finds a secret panel containing old letters and blueprints, and begins to suspect that there is a conspiracy to commit Great-grandpa to an institution. When Mom is called away, leaving Kim and Great-grandpa alone, an apparitional parrot, blinding lights, and eerie Chinese music materialize to drive the old man insane. Kim sends for the affable realtor and grandson of the mansion's architect, Mr. Tate, the only one she trusts. Her faith is misplaced, however, when Mr. Tate reveals his duplicity, covetous of the Oriental treasure he has unearthed in the mansion's secret room. He casts girl and grandfather adrift in a leaky boat to drown on a tempestuous night. They are rescued, ironically, by one of the very persons Kim mistrusted, and Great-grandpa's remaining years are secure.

255.   Sawyer, Ruth. ROLLER SKATES. New York: Viking,
        1936, 1964. Illus. by Valenti Angelo. 186pp. Grades
        4-6.

        Mutinous at spending the Gay Nineties' year that her parents will be abroad with her snobbish, punctilious aunt and docile cousins, privileged but unspoiled Lucinda is sent instead to the small apartment of the Misses Peters. The elder Miss Peters, a teacher at Lucinda's exclusive Manhattan school, is proper and sedate but capable of great understanding, flexibility, and tolerance. Miss Nettie, a seamstress, is timid and indulgent. Lucinda, buoyant, uninhibited, gregarious, and ingenuous, is free to roam the city on her roller skates like a "Winged Victory on wheels," making friends democratically with Irish cops and cabbies, an Italian street vendor's son, a starving musician's family, a newspaper

reporter, and an Oriental princess. She is introduced to the joys
of Shakespeare, borne by elephant in a circus parade, suspended
from school, and touched by natural and unnatural death. With her
intense elan, she spreads delight wherever she spins that insouciant
year and wishes always to remain 10.

255a.   Schaefer, Jack. OLD RAMON. Boston: Houghton Mifflin,
         1960. Illus. by Harold West. 102pp. Grades 4-6.

The son of the patrón, the Mexican-American sheep rancher,
has been entrusted to the gnarled hands of the venerable sheep herder to learn the practical side of the business in the school of experience. Unlettered but wise in the ways of sheep, nature, and
the elements from long observation and practice, Old Ramon firmly
but kindly instructs the boy in signs of trouble to be alert for and
demonstrates the kind of swift but never foolhardy judgments that
must be made to avert disaster. The flock must ford a river and
cross a desert to reach summer pastures, and along the way encounters rattlesnakes, sandstorms, coyotes and wolves. Under Ramon's tutelage the boy learns to overcome fear, ease tension, and
face responsibility and reality when he loves and loses his first dog,
a sheep herder's trusted partner and companion in his isolated oc-
cupation. Ramon knows how to be alone without being lonely and
communicates it memorably.

256.   Seredy, Kate. A BRAND-NEW UNCLE. New York: Viking,
         1961. Illus. by the author. 143pp. Grades 5-6.

On their thirty-fifth wedding anniversary, Mr. and Mrs.
Bardow Smith, pillars of the community and grandparents extra-
ordinaire, declare their independence of responsibility and the brood
of clinging children and grandchildren they have overindulged, and
leave town surreptitiously. Their resolve to travel incommunicado
and remain unencumbered is short-lived when they learn of the plight
of a 10-year-old orphan boy who has been institutionalized with older
incorrigibles. Papa wins the confidence of the frightened and defiant
boy and battles hostile authorities on his behalf. Bombastically
chauvinistic Papa and passively catalytic Mama return to their commodious home with a newly adopted uncle for their fourteen ram-
bunctious young grandchildren.

257.   Seredy, Kate. PHILOMENA. New York: Viking, 1955.
         Illus. by the author. 93pp. Grades 3-6.

Before she dies, Philomena's grandmother instructs the
orphan, 12, to go to Prague, find her aunt, learn domestic skills,
and then come home to the village where she belongs. She adds
that if there are any difficulties in following these instructions, she
has only to ask for further directions because Babushka will be
watching and listening from Heaven. Philomena dutifully goes to

Prague but cannot locate her aunt, so she entreats Babushka for
help in implementing the rest of the plan. Twice Babushka sends
her signs leading to employment, but because both prove so incompatible with her ebullient nature, she is worried that Babushka is
playing games with her. The third sign is charmed, and Philomena
finds a luxurious berth with a loving, caring family, but she is still
unfulfilled in finding her kin. Babushka sends yet another sign, and
in giving succor to a disease-ravaged woman and starving child,
Philomena is at last united with her aunt. The three of them return home under Babushka's providential good offices.

258.   Sewell, Hope. THE LITTLE OLD WOMAN WHO USED
          HER HEAD. Nashville: Nelson, 1935. Illus. by Margaret
          Ruse and Ann Merriman Peck. 127pp. Grades 4-5.

          Because this Little Old Woman is so poor, she must be
practical and inventive. She uses her head by tying a wet towel
around it, placing her forefinger along her nose, and shutting her
eyes till she thinks of solutions to such problems as how to keep
the geese warm after plucking them to make a featherbed for herself. (She makes jackets for them out of her old motheaten blanket
and lets them roost by the fire, while she curls up in the featherbed in the barn.) To keep rats from eating her out of house and
home and nesting in her drawers, she makes pets of them and
keeps them in their own cozy box. When her Christmas tree is
too tall to fit in her house, she chops holes in floor and roof to
accommodate it, reasoning cleverly that later she can sweep the
dirt down the one hole and collect rainwater from the other so she
won't have to go to the well in inclement weather. For all her ingenuity, however, she is frequently diddled, reinforcing the stereotype of the foolish, gullible old woman.

258a.   Shecter, Ben. THE RIVER WITCHES. New York: Harper
          and Row, 1979. 180pp. Grades 4-7.

          Andrew VanAken is apprehensive about spending the summer
with the ancient crone, proprietress of a Hudson Valley apothecary
shop, whom he and his sisters call Auntie Lizard. Mysterious and
alarming occurrences begin even as he approaches her town. Pooter, his dog, also has misgivings about his master's absence, especially when he discovers that Andrew has forgotten to pack his prayer book, and he sets forth to find the boy and deliver it to him.
Auntie Lizard is gleefully preparing for "the night of the Crescent
Moon." Also scheming is the nefarious confectionery shop owner,
Miss Celestial Grace, who is seeking the formula for hexing everyone out of the ability to read, thus making them her gulls. She
has also managed to capture poor Pooter in his parallel adventure.
Andrew learns that appearances are deceiving when Auntie Lizard
reveals that she is a good witch trying to forestall Grace's machina-
tions. In the anticlimactic ending of this eerie and droll farce,
Grace outwits herself; Pooter finds his way home without meeting

his master; Andrew, who has been initiated into the company of warlocks in a midnight rite, is reunited with his prayer book; and Auntie Lizard, whom Andrew levitated before he lost his new powers, comes to earth abruptly.

259.   Shecter, Ben. THE WHISTLING WHIRLIGIG. New York:
        Harper and Row, 1974. Illus. by the author. 143pp.
        Grades 5-6.

Sent to a rigid New York military academy by his divorced parents, lonely, artistic Josh Newman is disappointed when neither his mother nor father includes him in their respective vacation plans. His kindly history teacher with the prosthetic hand invites him to spend the holidays with him, and at first Josh is nervous with Otis Wicker. Gradually he relaxes and enjoys the sprightly sage's gourmet cooking. The day after Christmas, a black boy of his own age appears out of nowhere, and Josh learns that Matthew is the ghost of a slave boy who died in the house when it was a station in the Underground Railroad, a soul in limbo whose immediate concern is what will become of him if the historic house is condemned to make way for a road. Discussing life and death with his new friends helps Josh resolve to make the most of each day and stop pitying himself. He, in turn, helps Matthew cross over. Mr. Wicker retires to Florida, and Josh comes to terms with his overbearing roommate and decides to make his own plans and not rely on those of his parents.

260.   Shotwell, Louisa R. MAGDALENA. New York: Viking,
        1971. Illus. by Lilian Obligado. 124pp. Grades 5-6.

When shy Magdalena Mendez, 11, is transferred to the intellectually gifted sixth grade classroom, some of her classmates deride the long, thick braids her old-fashioned, Spanish-speaking grandmother coerces her to wear, and when odd old Miss Lilley provides the opportunity, she wastes no time in having her hair cropped, causing her horrified grandmother to think she has been bewitched by American frippery. In the meantime, the principal has assigned her the hopeless task of befriending another new Puerto Rican girl whom everyone calls Spook, the victim of a wretched homelife and an atrocious behavior problem. The girls' mutual respect for wispy Miss Lilley and Magdalena's grandmother, Nani, eventually draws them together and tames Spook's behavior, but Nani remains intractably suspicious of Miss Lilley and her American influence. Miss Lilley's collapse from malnutrition reconciles the two women, and Magdalena and Spook write the two best stories for the class literary magazine.

261.   Shura, Mary Francis. THE GRAY GHOSTS OF TAYLOR
        RIDGE. New York: Dodd, Mead, 1978. Illus. by Michael
        Hampshire. 128pp. Grades 4-7.

In quest of a misplaced compass, Nat, 13, and his sister
Nan, 10, are frightened off by an old man with a gun.   On further
acquaintance, old Boomer proves to be friendly, though unwilling
to admit to his obvious blindness.   He tells them wild tales of Civil
War treasure and of the ghosts who return even now after dark to
hunt for it, for they can plainly be heard on still nights.   In searching on the ridge, the children make some mysterious and frightening
discoveries, and one dark, snowy night Nat is called upon to rescue
a man from an abandoned well and thus solves the mystery of the
ghost and of the treasure.   The man in the well is Boomer's foster
son who quarreled years ago with the old man over his failing eyesight, but who in the meantime has been searching surreptitiously
for the treasure so that Boomer can afford cataract surgery to cor-
rect the blindness he so stubbornly denies, fearing loss of independence.   The two are reconciled, and Boomer's fears are laid to
rest.

261a.   Skolsky, Mindy Warshaw.   CARNIVAL AND KOPECK AND
         MORE ABOUT HANNAH.   New York: Harper and Row,
         1979.   Illus. by Karen Ann Weinhaus.   74pp.   Grades 3-5.

Life is exciting in the Depression-era melting pot of Nyack,
New York for exuberant Hannah, especially because her grandparents,
Polish Jews, live just down the street.   Grandmother, particularly,
is a good sport, patiently acting the pupil when Hannah plays school
and telling her intriguing tales of her own childhood.   The story of
the temper tantrum and the kopeck proves that she and Hannah are
not so different, even though reared half a world and two generations
apart.   Tonight Grandmother has promised to take her to the street
carnival, and Hannah can scarcely wait till dinner is over and chores
are done.   But Hannah fails to keep her end of the bargain, protecting Grandmother, who speaks little English, from garrulous
neighbors, and Grandmother carries her home in humiliation.   They
cannot remain angry with one another for long, however, and Grandmother pledges to take her to the carnival the following night instead.

262.   Snyder, Zilpha Keatley.   THE EGYPT GAME.   New York:
         Atheneum, 1968.   Illus. by Alton Raible.   215pp.   Grades
         5-6.

April Hall, 11, is resentful when her ambitious show business mother, awaiting her big break, sends her to live with her
patient paternal grandmother who works in a university library and
whom she condescendingly calls by her first name.   In spite of her
Hollywood affectations, she makes friends with Melanie because both
are imaginative and like to read.   Finding a plaster bust of Nefer-
titi in the cluttered yard of an antique dealer, they conceive their
Egypt Game, recruiting Melanie's little brother Marshall as boy
pharoah Marshamosis and a new girl, Elizabeth, as Neferbeth.
When a child in the neighborhood is foully murdered, everyone sus-

pects the gruff old proprietor of the shop in whose yard they play.
Two boys, erstwhile bullies, join the Egyptians at Halloween, and
the game gets eerier as the Oracle of Thoth begins speaking mysteriously.   April almost becomes the murderer's victim, and the
Egypt Game terminates suddenly.   When April's mother marries
her agent, April finally realizes that she never intended to send
for her and accepts with dignity her new life with "Grandma."

263.   Spyri, Johanna.   HEIDI.   Philadelphia: McKay, 1880, 1923.
        Illus. by Anne Alexander.   356pp.   Grades 5-6.

        The enduring classic in which Heidi, 5, comes to live with
her grandfather, the truculent Alm-Uncle, endears herself to him
and to Peter the goatherd and his grandmother, only to be carried
off again to the city to be companion to the wealthy invalid, Clara.
Her homesickness is physically and emotionally debilitating in spite
of her love for Clara, and the discerning doctor prescribes a return to her natural habitat.   There she repatriates her grandfather
into human society and brings light into Peter's grandmother's darkness.   When Clara pays a visit to the Alm, Peter's jealousy precipitates a crisis, but he atones by assisting Heidi and Grandfather in
restoring the stricken girl to health.   Clara's grateful father bestows beneficences on all.

264.   Stockton, Frank R.   THE BEE-MAN OF ORN.   New York:
        Holt, Rinehart and Winston, 1964.   Illus. by Maurice Sen-
        dak.   46pp.   Grades 3-5.

        A cocky Junior Sorcerer stirs a hornet's nest by informing
a gentle and contented old apiarist that he has been metamorphosed
into his present lowly status from a higher order and that he should
strive to restore himself to his true destiny.   Greatly disturbed,
the poor old man embarks on a journey of self-discovery.   He falls
in with a Languid Youth in quest of revitalization, and they are led
by a Very Imp into the abysmal abode of monsters and evil spirits
to seek their identities.   An encounter with the Ghastly Griffin in-
vigorates the L. Y., but the Bee-man, horrified to see a dragon
about to devour an infant, valiantly saves the baby from the jaws
of death.   Captivated by its innocence, he decides to become a
babe himself and is transmogrified by the Masters to an infantile
state.   Years later when the Junior Sorcerer has become a Senior
and ventures through Orn again, he sees the same old Bee-man living happily in his humble hut and exclaims, "Upon my word!...
He has grown up into the same thing again!"

265.   Stockton, Frank R.   OLD PIPES AND THE DRYAD.   New
        York: Watts, 1969.   Illus. by Catherine Hanley.   48pp.
        Grades 3-5.

        Old Pipes, 70, whose lifelong job has been to pipe the

livestock down from the mountain every evening for his Scottish village, has grown short of wind and hard of hearing, and the towns-people have retired him on a generous pension. He is too proud to accept their charity, however, even though he and his mother, 90, have no other means. In this plight, he happens upon a Dryad tree and frees the elven creature within. In gratitude she kisses him on both cheeks, a magical gesture that makes him twenty years younger. He is able to resume his duties, and everyone is happy but the Echo-dwarf who is forced to come out of retirement to mirror the sound of the pipes again. Old Pipes now seeks a new lease on life for his failing mother, and at last the Dryad finds the opportunity to kiss her on both cheeks, then kisses them both once again for good measure, reducing their ages to 40 and 60, respectively. She asks Old Pipes to seal her up in her tree for the winter, but when he goes to release her in the spring, he finds that the tree has been uprooted in winter storms and the Dryad is nowhere to be found.

265a.   Strete, Craig Kee. WHEN GRANDFATHER JOURNEYS
          INTO WINTER. New York: Greenwillow, 1979. Illus. by
          Hal Frenck. 86pp. Grades 3-5.

          Grandfather Tayhua illustrates in the dust the Indian peo-
ple's sacred symbols--the eagle, the bear, the deer, and the turtle.
Then he contrasts them with the white man's sacred idols--the dollar sign, the automobile, the TV antenna, and the F for Failing,
which, he chides, seems to be his fifth grade grandson Little
Thunder's favorite mark in school. In spite of his age and apparent frailty, Tayhua insists upon trying to break a wild but magnificent stallion at the rodeo after stronger, younger men have failed.
With sheer determination, raw nerve, contempt for pain, and superb
horsemanship he succeeds and secures the gentled horse for Little
Thunder, but the effort costs him his life. As he lies dying with
his distraught grandson in attendance, he sees the wild geese over-
head and tells the grieving boy that the birds know when the seasons change and fly south as a reminder to all creation that they
have been given the gift of a journey through life--a journey into
winter.

266.   Sunderlin, Sylvia. ANTRIM'S ORANGE. New York: Scrib-
          ner, 1976. Illus. by Diane deGroat. 57pp. Grades 3-5.

          Antrim's grandmother brings him a single, precious navel
orange from war-ravaged London. It would be sacrilege to eat such
a rare treasure without savoring its possession, so he shows it to
all the envious neighbors, takes it to bed with him, and brings it
to school to show the teacher. To his horror, she thinks it is a
present for her, but he is overjoyed when she returns it the following day. In his exuberance, the orange falls on a rock, is rup-
tured, and must be eaten at once. Generously he apportions each
segment to a neighbor, reserving the last crescent for himself. In
a fateful split second, it flies from his hand and is trampled under-

foot. The stricken boy resigns himself to martyrdom until his mother remembers the discarded microcosmic orange under the navel.
Though tiny, every fragrant, succulent morsel is just as he imag-
ined it would be.

267.   Talbot, Charlene Joy.   A HOME WITH AUNT FLORRY.
         New York: Atheneum, 1974.   200pp.   Grades 5-7.

         Accustomed to the accoutrements of wealth and ease, twins
Jason and Wendy, 12, orphaned by a plane crash, are appalled
when they come to live in New York with their bohemian, iconoclastic Aunt Florry in a derelict newspaper plant.   She is an inveterate
junk collector who never cleans house and keeps common pigeons in
the loft.   Robbed of the security of order and regulation in their
lives, they are first frightened and then resentful at having to help
with chores which consist of opening cans or heating TV dinners,
hanging the laundry on the roof, feeding and exercising the pigeons,
and scavenging in trash bins for wood to stoke the stove.   When
Aunt Florry is hospitalized for a fractured hip, the two must practice self-reliance, and they begin to appreciate their independent and
unorthodox lifestyle.   But the day of their eviction to make way for
urban renewal quickly approaches.   Resourceful Aunt Florry, however, has already a relocation which satisfies both the children's
bourgeois attorney and her own idiosyncrasies.

268.   Taylor, Mildred D.   SONG OF THE TREES.   New York:
         Dial, 1975.   Illus. by Jerry Pinkney.   48pp.   Grades 3-5.

         The Depression years in rural Mississippi are lean for
Cassie, 8, her brothers, parents and grandmother.   Papa is laying
railroad tracks in Louisiana, but the family is justly proud of the
stand of timber that is part of Big Ma's property.   To Cassie the
trees murmur a song of security, but to Mr. Andersen, their white
neighbor who regards black property rights casually, they mean
money, and he has marked the best of them for felling with neither
rightful remuneration nor even consent from Big Ma.   The two wom-
en are helpless against the arrogant and peremptory redneck, so
Stacey, 11, is dispatched to summon Papa.   In the meantime work
proceeds, and Cassie is sickened by the devastation of her forest
friends.   The younger children instigate guerilla action but are apprehended and about to be thrashed when Papa appears.   He and
Stacey have spent the night wiring the woods with dynamite which he
threatens to detonate if Mr. Andersen does not vacate the matriarchal property.   He is prepared to sacrifice his life and the remaining trees for principle and self-respect if his bluff is called.
Mr. Andersen capitulates, but the forest does not resume its song.

269.   Taylor, Theodore.   THE CAY.   Garden City: Doubleday,
         1969.   137pp.   Grades 4-6.

The gnarled black septuagenarian, Timothy, plucks Phillip Enright, 11, from the sea into an unprovisioned life raft when their ship is torpedoed in the Caribbean during World War II.   When they make landfall on an uninhabited, waterless cay, the boy is blind from a blow to the head incurred when the ship went down, and Timothy knows he must teach the pampered boy self-sufficiency if they are to survive.   Taught racial prejudice by his Virginian mother, Phillip at first stubbornly resists the black man's tutelage, but Timothy is patient and persistent.   With incredible ingenuity he fashions catch basins for rain, a signal pyre, and a shelter, and teaches Phillip, in pidgin English and by feel, to fish and climb trees for coconuts.   When a monumental hurricane approaches, they lash themselves to palm trees, and Timothy heroically shields Phillip's body with his own which is already weakened from malaria. The strain is too great and the old man succumbs, leaving the boy to test his survival skills alone.   Despair descends when a plane passes near and doesn't spot him, but the day arrives when he is able to light his signal fire as his friend Timothy instructed him and attract attention.   Reunited with his parents, he undergoes surgery to restore partial eyesight.

270.   Terris, Susan. PICKLE. New York: Four Winds, 1973.
           Illus. by Ted CoConis.   154pp.   Grades 4-6.

Adjustment from farm life to urban life in San Francisco is difficult enough for Sarah Barnes, 10, a diffident and imaginative bookworm, but there is no arrow in her quiver for handling the contentious city kids who quickly brand her hyperbole lies and tease her unmercifully about smelling of the pickles she helps her mother make and market.   Her chief tormentor defies her to confront the neighborhood "witch" who is reputed to eat stray cats.   More fearful of the children than of the witch, she boldly rings the bell and is invited into an enchanting world of beautiful treasures and exotic teas with a warm and gracious old lady who was a sophisticated world traveler before losing her eyesight.   The children are even more skeptical of Pickle's veracity when she reports such opulence and hospitality.   They insist that she steal a music box to prove it. Sarah does so, intending to return it, but before the opportunity arises, she learns that Madame Cassani, who is partially sighted, knows of the theft and is greatly disappointed in her.   They agree to begin their friendship with a clean slate, and Madame Cassani provides Sarah with a formula for ridding her hands of the pickle stench.

271.   Theroux, Paul. A CHRISTMAS CARD.   Boston: Houghton
           Mifflin, 1978.   Illus. by John Lawrence.   84pp.   Grades
           4-6.

Lost in the snow as darkness falls on the way to their isolated new beach house in New England, Marcel and his family are grateful to accept the hospitality of an odd but accommodating old

man who calls himself Pappy, their host in a deserted old mansion
with very lifelike paintings.   Pappy fails to appear in the morning
but leaves what appears to be a Christmas card whose scene is like
a map of the neighborhood, indicating the directions to their own
house.   Further examination of the card reveals that it is a magical
miniature window on their world, showing not only the location of
inanimate objects but also people and their movements.   The living
picture leads them on an adventure of discovery to a ghost cabin
with a blazing fire.   In the dead of the night on Christmas Eve,
the mysterious old man, now revealed to Marcel as the Torchbearer,
brings the cabin's radiance to their own cold, dark hearts through
the boy's faith, then steps back into the empty canvas of the self-
portrait from whence he came.

272.   Thiele, Colin. THE HAMMERHEAD LIGHT. New York:
        Harper and Row, 1976. 109pp. Grades 5-8.

        The hamlet of Snapper Bay in Southern Australia is proud
of its historic lighthouse, but none is so possessive of it as Tessa
Noble, 12, and Axel Jorgensen, 72, its keeper until the automatic
light was installed and who wonders why Adelaide bureaucrats are
so intent upon demolishing it.   The structure is still sound, though
tide and tempest have taken their toll of the headland, and when
Axel, now a naturalist, loses his shack, he moves into the lighthouse.   One day as a storm brews, local vandals shoot out the automatic light, leaving Tessa's fisherman father stranded at sea.   Axel
and Tessa heroically fire up the old beam one last time to guide
the Cuttlefish to port, but the storm's vicious buffeting delivers the
coup de grace to the old lighthouse.   Tessa and Axel are rescued,
but Axel is injured as he pitches into the chasm between the mainland and the promontory.   The broken old man, now 74, must be
institutionalized against his will.   Tessa is distraught at her inability
to control the march of time or to heal the wounds of parting.

273.   Thiele, Colin. THE SHADOW ON THE HILLS. New York:
        Harper and Row, 1977. 216pp. Grades 5-8.

        Roaming the fog-shrouded hills near his family's South
Australian farm, waggish Bodo Schneider meets the wild old hermit,
Ebenezer Blitz, who resembles a stern Old Testament prophet, and
his half-dingo dog, Elijah.   Thus begins an odd alliance that he can't
share even with his boon companion, Ossie, with whom he enjoys
numerous humorous high adventures.   Bodo learns firsthand of the
feud between Ebenezer and Moses Mibus, the baron of their bucolic
fiefdom, who cheated Ebenezer of his property years earlier.   Then
the Depression grips their community, exacerbated by the decima-
tion of their livestock by wild animals.   Moses, the heaviest loser,
traces the depredations to Ebenezer's faithful Elijah and kills the
dog, and Ebenezer invokes the wrath of the Lord upon Moses.
When Moses' enterprises are torched and Ebenezer is found on the
scene with incriminating evidence, he goes to trial.   Bodo, who

knows that Moses set the fire himself to collect the insurance, testifies courageously, even though his own family will suffer from the insurance loss.   Ebenezer is acquitted but remanded to an old folks' home.   Bodo knows he will be comfortable but wonders if he will be happy.

273a.   Thomas, Ianthe.   HI, MRS. MALLORY!   New York: Harper and Row, 1979.   Illus. by Ann Toulmin-Rothe. 48pp.   Grades 3-5.

Every afternoon when she steps off the school bus, the young rural black girl goes to visit old Mrs. Mallory, whose parents were poor itinerant farm laborers.   The girl's mother aloofly disapproves of the white woman's drafty, ramshackle cabin with cardboard for windowpanes, but the girl finds it exotic, as she does the meager fare that Mrs. Mallory so generously provides for snacks.   The girl helps Mrs. Mallory bring in wood from the woodpile and transcribes letters to her military son when her hand cramps with arthritis.   The two dance barefoot together while Mrs. Mallory's dog joins in, and the old woman regales her young friend with fanciful tales.   One day Mrs. Mallory does not greet her from her porch when the bus stops, and the girl's mother tells her that Mrs. Mallory has died.   When her grief is spent, she adopts Mrs. Mallory's dog to supply the missing warmth and companionship.

274.   Tolan, Stephanie S.   GRANDPA--AND ME.   New York: Scribner, 1978.   120pp.   Grades 4-6.

The dynamic 80-year-old grandfather who is Kerry's swimming coach and jogging companion suddenly and unpredictably begins acting "crazy" and childish.   Kerry, 11, is worried for his safety when he stumbles into the pool and flounders helplessly, but she is mortified among her friends when he appears with his trousers on wrong side out.   Her best friend acquaints her with Shakespeare's Seven Ages of Man, and she reasons that if Grandpa had to take care of Mom when she was a baby, then by rights the family should care for him in his dotage.   The doctor, however, explains the irreversible deterioration of encroaching senile dementia, and after Grandpa makes a mess in the kitchen, the family holds a lachrymose counsel on what to do with him.   Because he is still lucid most of the time, and because it is his own life, Kerry and her brother think Grandpa should have some choice in his fate.   Grandpa has the same thought.   After sorting and labeling his personal possessions, without ceremony, he deliberately drowns himself.

274a.   Turner, Ann.   A HUNTER COMES HOME.   New York: Crown, 1980.   118pp.   Grades 5-8.

After his father and brother froze to death while seal hunting, Jonas' Inuit Eskimo mother becomes overprotective of her last

son and exacts a promise from his grandfather, a dauntless and proficient hunter who wants to teach the boy the timeless skills of survival, to let him finish school and then decide his future for himself. In the meantime, the old man, 70, becomes the family pro-
vider. Jonas later discovers that the BIA boarding school is con-
descending, mongrelizing, and humiliating, and he endures the year
stoically. Back at home, he finds that Grandfather is just as uncompromising as his teachers and is contemptuous of the boy's inexperienced attempts to master the traditional ways. Smarting from
Grandfather's criticism of his clumsy seal hunting technique, he
vents his frustration by wantonly slaughtering a herd of caribou and
feeling great remorse. In his third endeavor to earn the old one's
respect, the two depart on a comradely fishing expedition, but in
trying to recover the turgid nets, Grandfather is swept away in the
spring freshet. At first Jonas panics but later collects himself
and recovers the valiant warrior's body. He decides that the finest
tribute he can offer to Grandfather's spirit is to bear the body home
with dignity and responsibility, along with their bountiful catch, as
a true hunter would do.

275.   Unnerstad, Edith. THE JOURNEY WITH GRANDMOTHER.
         New York: Macmillan, 1960. Illus. by Claes Backstrom.
         197pp. Grades 5-6.

         In 1908 when the Kers homestead is beset with misfortunes,
indomitable Grandmother rallies the family and takes her youngest
daughter abroad with her to ply their art of haircrafting to save the
croft, as the women of their Swedish village have done for generations. Anders, 12, begs to go along to earn enough to recover his
mare and foal who have been sold to pay debts. They travel first
to Stockholm where Anders learns his first lessons in the ways of
the world. His first sea journey takes them to Finland where they
meet with their first good fortune, and Anders makes friends with
a defiant street urchin. A herring boat takes them to St. Petersburg and true providence. A flood cements their friendship with
dissident student Volodya, and their intricate haircrafting wins the
good will and patronage of an enlightened patrician family. When
Volodya is sought by gendarmes for his underground activities,
Grandmother gives the finest performance of her life to save
Volodya's. When they return home, Anders has mastered three
new languages and earned more than enough to redeem his horses.

276.   Waldron, Ann. THE HOUSE ON PENDLETON BLOCK.
         New York: Hastings House, 1975. Illus. by Sonia O.
         Lisker. 151pp. Grades 5-6.

         Mrs. Hamilton, deceased for two years, was a philanthropist
and patron of the arts, loved antiques, grew herbs, and was adored
by all except her avaricious daughter. Chrissie Ransom, 12, fer-
rets these facts about the former owner of the mansion she and her
family are renting on a once-elegant block in Dallas. Homesick for

Georgia and bored at being the only girl on a street of eccentric
and enigmatic elderly neighbors, Chrissie, with the eye of an artist,
explores the fabulous but eerie showplace that was leased furnished
from Mrs. Hamilton's son.   She recognizes that the tacky prints on
the walls are incompatible with the tasteful furnishings and finds
records in the attic indicating Mrs. Hamilton had purchased some
choice paintings.   Together with the granddaughter of an art gallery
owner, her first friend, Chrissie attempts to solve the mystery of
the missing oils.   On the evening Chrissie is left to babysit her
brothers, someone furtively enters the house, and in the ensuing
denouement an unlikely culprit is bared.   The affair is settled
satisfactorily for all, and Chrissie settles back to enjoy summer
vacation at Alberta Hamilton's stately manor.

277.   Warner, Gertrude Chandler.   THE BOXCAR CHILDREN.
          Chicago: Whitman, 1942, 1950.   Illus. by L. Kate Deal.
          154pp.   Grades 4-6.

          Four orphaned children fear going to live with the paternal
grandfather they have never met but who disliked their mother, and
so disappear en route to his home.   They set up housekeeping in an
old boxcar on an abandoned railroad siding, and Henry, the eldest,
does odd jobs in the nearby town for a friendly doctor, while Jessie
cares for Violet, 10, and Benny, 5.   When Henry wins the annual
marathon, neither he nor the race's sponsor, his grandfather, is
aware of the other's identity when the prize is awarded, but when
the whole family turns out to pick cherries, the observant doctor
sums up the situation and bides his time.   All is idyllic in the boxcar until Violet falls seriously ill and the good doctor evacuates
them to his house where he gradually and tactfully acquaints them
with their altruistic grandfather who whisks them off to his mansion
to live happily ever after.

278.   Warner, Gertrude Chandler.   SURPRISE ISLAND.   Chicago:
          Scott, Foresman, 1949.   Illus. by Mary Gehr.   182pp.
          Grades 4-6.

          In which the Boxcar Children (see 277) are presented with
a vacation island on the Maine coast by their magnanimous Grandfather Alden where they spend the summer living cozily in the old
barn.   Their companions are old Captain Daniel, who provides supplies and communication with the mainland, and the mysterious
"handyman, " Joe, who incongruously identifies flora and fauna,
searches for buried Indian treasure, and teaches Violet the violin.
When Joe proves to be their cousin and missing museum director
who has been recovering from an unspecified illness, care must be
exercised in breaking the news to Grandfather or the old man's
heart and veins may not endure the strain.   The reunion is un-
eventful.

279.   Warner, Gertrude Chandler. THE YELLOW HOUSE MYS-
        TERY. Chicago: Whitman, 1953. Illus. by Mary Gehr.
        191pp.   Grades 4-6.

        The Alden children, now 16, 14, 12 and 7, ask their grand-
father about the deserted house on Surprise Island (see 277 & 278)
and hear an enigmatic tale of a man missing for forty years and the
money he absconded with.   Scrutinizing the house, they find a clue
that leads them to an exciting canoe trip in the Maine wilderness
with Cousin Joe and his new bride, a junket which is too strenuous
for Grandfather.   At the end of Bear Trail lie the pieces of the
puzzle which, when assembled, bring about the recovery of the
money and the reunion between Mr. Alden's housekeeper and her
long-lost husband.

280.   Whitehead, Ruth. THE MOTHER TREE.   New York: Sea-
        bury Press, 1971. Illus. by Charles Robinson.   149pp.
        Grades 5-7.

        Tempe's mother's death changes her life radically, com-
pelling her at 10 to be housekeeper for her father and brother Phil,
14, and nursemaid for her sister Laurie, 4, on their Texas farm
at the turn of the century.   The burden of responsibility, crowned
by Phil's needling and jocular superiority, frays her young nerves.
When Father and Phil depart to follow the harvest across the South-
west, she leaps at the opportunity to stay with her grandparents
which will enable her to be a little girl again.   Under their gentle
guidance and direction she still has chores and the care of Laurie,
but it is not worrisome, and there is time for carefree fun with
her best chum.   The three construct a playhouse in a lofty old
mesquite which she calls the Mother Tree because its branches en-
fold her like a surrogate mother.   When Father and Phil return at
the end of the summer, she is reluctant to leave the comfort and
security of Grandma's house and the sanctuary of her tree, but
through Laurie's dependence on her, she realizes that she has
more strength than she supposed.

281.   Wier, Ester. THE BARREL.   New York: McKay, 1966.
        Illus. by Carl Kidwell.   136pp.   Grades 5-7.

        For years Chance has been shunted from one foster home
to another after his father abandoned him.   Now at 12, he is being
sent to family he didn't know existed, his maternal grandmother
and brother Turpem, 15, in the Florida Everglades.   He has immediate affinity for his homely Granny, but Turpem, whom their
father, a braggart, drilled to be brave and daring, swaggers and
boasts before Chance who inherited his dead mother's gentle disposition and slight build and who, as a city boy, nurtures a healthy
respect for the alligators, wild boars, and poisonous snakes that
infest the swamp.   Chance soon realizes that Turpem's bravery is
nothing but bravado, and later proves that he and his doughty runt

pup are no cowards when a hurricane blocks their normal egress
to civilization and they must detour through dreaded Doomsday
Slough, Turpem's nemesis.   Resentment is forgotten as the boys
finally make peace, to the delight of their wise but simple Granny.

282.   Wier, Ester. THE LONER. New York: McKay, 1963.
         Illus. by Christine Price. 153pp.   Grades 5-7.

The boy has known no life but that of itinerant crop picker,
has had no friend but the golden-haired girl whose family he has
been traveling with.   When she is killed, the grieving boy strikes
out blindly on his own and is found starving and exhausted in open
sheep range in the Montana foothills by Boss, the Amazonian owner
of the ranch who has brought her flock to winter pasture personally
in order to track the grizzly that killed her beloved grown son Ben.
The boy selects the name David at random from Boss' Bible, and
she starts teaching him the intricacies and rigors of shepherding,
subconsciously comparing him to her flawless Ben.   The strong,
laconic woman and the willful loner misunderstand one another's
motives, but David quietly learns.   When Ben's widow, Angie, tells
him to use his own good judgment, he summons the confidence to
save a ranch hand from the bear trap and kill the behemoth, his
personal Goliath, to win his own place in the family and his first
home.

283.   Willard, Barbara. THE MILLER'S BOY. New York:
         Dutton, 1976. Illus. by Gareth Floyd. 143pp. Grades
         5-6.

In fifteenth century England, Thomas Welfare, 12, works
as miller's boy to his grandfather, but prays for a day when he can
own any old nag and ride to his married sister Betsy's farm.   He
also dreams of having a friend, a wish that is fulfilled when lonely
and unhappy Lewis comes to be ward of Squire Orlebar.   The two
vow to be brothers, spending all their free time together.   A bigger and better mill is built in the district which will soon put Gaffer out of business, and the brusque old man becomes obsessed with
the quixotic task of upgrading his mill with his attenuating strength
and skill.   When a tumultuous storm arises, he battles it insanely
to save his doomed livelihood but dies inevitably in its destruction.
Thomas is taken under Squire Orlebar's wing and shares lessons
with Lewis, but while the boys consider themselves equals, the
squire means for Thomas to be whipping boy and lackey to Lewis.
When the squire gives his ward a spirited horse, Lewis makes a
handsome sacrifice to his blood brother by presenting the prized
palfry to him.   Thomas accepts gravely, knowing that they will
never meet again, and rides off to Betsy.

283a.   Williams, Jay. THE MAGIC GRANDFATHER. New York:
         Four Winds, 1979. Illus. by Gail Owens. 149pp.   Grades
         4-6.

Sam Limner's mother believes that his paternal grandfather, 60, is not quite respectable because he drinks beer, smokes cigarettes, plays cards, wears no tie, seldom attends church, and has been unemployed since he transferred his hardware business to Sam's father, in general betraying the family's proud colonial ancestry. Sam, 11, loves to visit his flamboyant grandfather whose basement apartment is filled with fascinating gadgets and gimmicks from the world over. Grandpa is a bona fide sorcerer with the inherited gifts of enchantment--transformation, transportation, and the conjuration of beings from another sphere. With Sam to help him, Grandpa gives a demonstration of the latter art, but because of Sam's inattention, Grandpa is accidentally sucked through the portal into the alien universe. Only Sam, whose powers of concentration have atrophied because of his addiction to television, can bring him back. With the help of his cousin, he doggedly learns the ancient incantations from his grandfather's books while deceiving the suspicious adults around them, and eventually, after some amusing and suspenseful false starts, manages to materialize Grandpa who proudly accepts them as pupils.

284.   Windsor, Patricia. MAD MARTIN. New York: Harper and Row, 1976. 119pp. Grades 5-8.

Martin Drivic shares the squalid London bachelor diggings of his grandfather in mutual respect but emotionless silence and sameness. At school when the other boys bully him, he hasn't the ire to fight back. His complacency is marred only by occasional recurrent waking dreams that inexplicably frighten him. One day his grandfather is hospitalized with a fractured hip, and Martin is placed in a foster home with six gregarious and loquacious children who are prepared to be friendly but are annoyed by Martin's gaminess and unsmiling taciturnity. A bath and laundering solve the first problem, but the contemplative introvert is physically incapable of feeling or expressing emotion and is repelled by garrulity. Though he mistrusts the other Crimp children, he likes Charlie, his roommate, and asks him to educate him about hate and love. When the time approaches to go home, Martin grows morose and even more introspective. He suddenly realizes that his waking dreams are actually memories of a remote time when he as an angry and selfish child spoiled his grandfather's chance for remarriage. As Charlie rushes to his rescue when he is accosted by bullies, his passivity vanishes. Both he and Grandpa return home with bright eyes and expansive spirits, the better for their apocalyptic contact with people.

285.   Winthrop, Elizabeth. WALKING AWAY. New York: Harper and Row, 1973. Illus. by Noelle Massena. 219pp. Grades 5-8.

Emily eagerly anticipates returning every summer to her grandparents' small farm where she helps her energetic and enthusi-

astic grandfather with his endless chores.   She and Grandfather enjoy an easy rapport and are inseparable at work or play.   This
summer promises to be extra special because Emily's best friend,
Nina, is coming to spend two weeks.   But to bright, bold, impetu-
ous Nina, fun on the farm does not consist of following Emily's
grandfather about his work, and Emily cravenly but uneasily deserts
him, knowing that Grandfather would disapprove of Nina's attitudes
and behavior.   Because Grandfather will not pace himself in accord with his diminishing vigor, and because Emily is not on hand
to help him, he hurts himself and Emily is remorseful. Then Nina
breaks her leg in defying Grandfather's orders, and Emily has the
few remaining days of summer to try to atone to Grandfather for
her disloyalty.   That winter he dies suddenly in his sleep and walks
away from her life forever.   It comforts Emily in her grief to
think that Grandfather understood her contrition.

286.   York, Carol Beach.   BEWARE OF THIS SHOP.   Nashville:
         Nelson, 1977.   127pp.   Grades 5-8.

         Life with frugal, waspish, and regimented Aunt Sophie in
1892 Massachusetts is arduous and dreary for shy Hester, her grown
orphaned niece, but for the companionship of her frivolous and impulsive friend, Isabel, who one day coaxes her into a queer new
shop with a gnomish proprietor and buys her a figurine.   In the
night she has grotesque nightmares and forebodings linked to the
shepherdess, and in the morning she smashes it.   The more she
learns of the strange shop, the more she realizes that every item
from it causes grief for its owner, though she cannot communicate
her suspicions to anyone who will believe her.   When her aunt ap-
prentices her, because she has no prospect of marriage, to the
shop's repugnant proprietor, Mr. Mordrian, she is appalled.   The
source of his powers is the strangely animate brass toad he keeps
in a locked cage, and when he reveals to Hester his sadistic plans
to expand his operations and control an ever-increasing sphere, she
knows that she alone must break the spell and destroy the repulsive
toad.   With heavy suspense and grim fortitude she exorcises the
evil and witnesses Mr. Mordrian's demise.   The parsimonious life
at Aunt Sophie's seems suddenly less dismal by comparison.

287.   Young, Miriam.   NO PLACE FOR MITTY.   New York:
         Four Winds, 1976.   123pp.   Grades 4-6.

         In 1896 when Mitty is 10, her religious fanatic father over-
taxes Mama's pontifical patience, and she bundles Mitty and the
boys off to her parents' farm near San Francisco.   A tomboy, Mitty
loves the harum-scarum life at Emeryville, already teeming with
relatives.   Grandpa races horses for a haphazard living, and Grandma, who crossed the country by covered wagon alone with two small
children, contributes to the commotion and conviviality by clanging
on a dishpan to waken them, playing practical jokes on Grandpa, and
faking punishment for infractions by thwacking a trunk and telling

them to yell. At the divorce proceedings, Papa's wealthy sister offers Mitty a home and education. Mama sees it as the opportunity of a lifetime, and Mitty trades her life of abandon for an oppressive one of rigid decorum and stifling supervision. She lives only for vacation visits to the farm. One day Grandma pays an impulsive call on Mitty at Aunty Bowman's house, and discovers that she is being transformed into a mincing prig. Instantly, she packs her back to Emeryville.

287a.   Zhitkov, Boris. HOW I HUNTED THE LITTLE FELLOWS.
         New York: Dodd, Mead, 1979. Illus. by Paul O. Zelinsky.
         Trans. by Djemma Bider. Unpaged. Grades 4- 5.

The joy of vivid imagination and exquisite artwork is canceled by the horror of stark reality and strong emotions in this true story of the author's childhood, originally published in the 1920's. A small Russian boy visiting his beloved Granny discovers a miniature steamship on a shelf, intriguing in its verisimilitude. It is precious to his grandmother's memory, and she offers to hide it so he won't be tempted to play with it. He solemnly promises, however, never to touch it. Alone with the model at night, he imagines that it is manned by a Lilliputian crew, all waiting to go about their duties when he is not watching. All of his schemes and ruses fail to flush the elusive little fellows. Frustrated, he purposely dismantles the superstructure and pries open the deck--to find absolutely nothing. Belatedly he realizes that the ship is a total wreck and flings himself into bed, sobbing in remorse. His grandmother, believing him ill, comes in and comforts him with endearments. Ominously, the author adds, "She hadn't seen the little steamer yet. "

288.   Ziner, Feenie. THE DUCK OF BILLINGSGATE MARKET.
        New York: Four Winds, 1974. Illus. by Robin Jacques.
        53pp. Grades 3- 5.

A fisherman in his youth, Tom Codley never got around to marrying. In his middle years he began packing fish at London's Billingsgate Market, a job he took pride in and that masked his loneliness. Now in his later years, he is provided with a young, strong, unsentimental assistant, leaving Tom hurt and frightened. One evening as he is brooding by the Thames, he sees a family of ducks swimming directly into an oil slick. He is able to save one duckling from drowning, takes it home, and suddenly there is meaning to his life. His pet makes a conversation piece with Whippersnapper Smith and inaugurates friendship with Mrs. Primrose in the flat below his. Then an accident leads to Ducky Dear's escape, and for a while he is inconsolable, but with his new skills at social intercourse, he has the courage to propose matrimony to Mrs. Primrose, and Whippersnapper Smith is best man.

289.   Barnwell, Robinson. SHADOW ON THE WATER. New
         York: McKay, 1967. 216pp. Grades 6-8.

         Romantic, cultured, city-bred Mama and pragmatic, un-
demonstrative, country-bred Papa are bickering more and more
acrimoniously over the disposition of money and other amenities,
and communicating less and less, as the lingering Great Depression
continues its siege of their South Carolina truck farm. Imperious
and intrusive maternal grandmother Talbot prevails upon Mama to
file for legal separation and move into her gracious Virginia mansion with the two younger children, Camden, 13, and Talbot, 6,
much to the youngsters' dismay. One-time tomboy Cammie ad-
justs to society life and the prospect of a new boyfriend better than
Tal, but both miss home, father, old friends, and beloved and zest-
ful paternal grandfather Rutledge. It is his death that reunites the
family, but a reconciliation between their parents seems hopeless
until a posthumous letter is found from Grandpa to Mama telling her
of the profound love that Papa is too proud to articulate.

290.   Bauer, Marion Dane. FOSTER CHILD. New York: Sea-
         bury, 1977. 155pp. Grades 6-8.

         Great-grandmother has been a friend, mother, and grand-
mother to Renny since her mother deposited her there as an il-
legitimate infant, and Gram has promised to live to see her grown.
Now, at 79, she has been hospitalized with a stroke, and Renny,
12, has been placed in Mom and Pop Beck's foster home, temporar-
ily, she believes, until she and Gram can take care of one another
again. Her roommates are a toughened runaway, 15, and the vulnerable Karen, 6, who is there until her parents can make a home
for her. Renny soon learns to her horror that Pop Beck is a religious fanatic who practices child molestation on the side, and to
protect little Karen, she runs away with her to Gram's home. It
comes as a great shock to learn that the house is being sold, the
furniture disposed of, and that Gram is a terminal patient in a
nursing home. Only seeing Gram's comatose body and articulating
her distressing experience with Pop Beck to Karen's mother bring
her to the verge of reality and catharsis. Karen's parents recon-
cile their differences and make a home for the two of them who
have become as close as sisters.

291.   Bauer, Marion Dane. SHELTER FROM THE WIND. New
         York: Seabury, 1976. 108pp. Grades 6-8.

Fulminating with fury at her pregnant stepmother's intruding presence between her and her father and revolted by the reproductive process, Stacy, 12, runs away from her Oklahoma panhandle home to try to find her mother. Almost overcome by exposure and dehydration on the desert, she is led by pet dogs to the primitive abode of reclusive Old Ella who takes her in until she is ready to go on, instilling in her self-reliance and responsibility. Through encounters with unsentimental Ella and Mr. Henderson who brings her supplies once a month, she vaguely recalls that her mother was an alcoholic who probably wouldn't want her even if she found her. The bittersweet whelping of Nimue's pups and its tragic aftermath teach her the miracle of birth and the futility of hating. She decides to return to her father and stepmother but to visit Ella often.

292.   Blume, Judy. THEN AGAIN, MAYBE I WON'T. Scarsdale: Bradbury, 1971. 164pp. Grades 7-9.

Tony Miglione is 13 when his father, who has always been a blue collar worker in Jersey City, strikes it rich on a new patent and becomes a sycophantic stooge to his new boss. He moves the family from penury to the posh suburbs of Long Island where Tony makes friends with his next-door neighbor, Joel. Tony deplores it when his devout Italian grandmother, who lost her larynx to cancer and who has always done the family cooking, is relegated to her room and placated with a new color TV set when his mother hires a cook. He is also disturbed when he learns that Joel is an accomplished shoplifter. But it is his own sexuality, erections at embarrassing moments, nocturnal emissions, and his habit of watching Joel's older sister undress through binoculars, that worries him that he is abnormal. His anxieties manifest themselves in attacks of "nervous stomach," and a psychiatrist is called in. Tony improves, but he can't amend his grandmother's situation. They comfort one another silently.

292a.   Bosse, Malcolm J. THE 79 SQUARES. New York: Crowell, 1979. 185pp. Grades 7-9.

Eric Fischer, 14, is gratified to be accepted into the gang of toughs with whom he is serving probation for breaking school windows. Trespassing as usual across a neighboring garden, they are riveted by the sudden appearance of a wizened old man in a wheelchair, who transfixes them with blazing eyes and bellowing voice. He dismisses the other punks but orders Eric to remain. Unaccountably mesmerized, Eric does, and mysterious Mr. Beck assigns him the task of measuring the garden, dividing it into equal blocks of six square feet, and, over the course of the summer, spending an hour of isolation in each of those squares, examining it in minute detail. The boy warms to the exacting daily duty and to the odd old man, 82, but can't disclose their relationship to the gang because he can't explain it. Then it is revealed that Mr. Beck is a wife-murderer who, terminally ill with cancer, has been released to his daughter. Eric's parents forbid him from associating with the ex-jailbird and urge him to rejoin his old pals whom they believe, ironically, to be a favorable influence on him because of their impeccable family credentials. Eric defies them and learns that intense scrutiny of a microcosmic world, his prison cell, was the technique that saved Mr. Beck's sanity in his forty-year incarceration. The vindictive town ostracizes the Becks, and Eric's old ring of drug-emboldened bullies mounts a physical assault on the old man with only Eric to defend him. Both are seriously injured, and on the day Eric is released from the hospital Mr. Beck dies. The stricken boy knows that he will carry both the garden and the man in his heart forever.

293.   Bradbury, Ray. DANDELION WINE. New York: Knopf,
        1957, 1975. 269pp. Grades 10-12.

A modern classic novel limning vignettes of 12-year-old Douglas Spaulding's significant summer of 1928. It begins with his grandfather making the dandelion wine that Grandma will mete out medicinally the following winter; hanging the porch swing; and refusing to have his lawn sodded with grass that never needs mowing, simply because the sound of a lawn mower epitomizes summer to him. It continues with impressions of Mother, Grandma, and Great-grandma beating carpets as if venting their spleen over the events that caused the spots; with his aunt's disastrous attempt at modernizing Grandma's cooking habits; with Mrs. Bentley, 72, whom the small, heedless children won't believe was ever a child named Helen; with old Colonel Freeleigh who lives in the past and commits suicide; with the elderly spinsters who are beguiled by a glib salesman into buying an electric runabout; and with the 95-year-old sage who charms a young man who is devastated at her death. It ends with the intimate deathwatch for Great-grandma and Douglas' own near-death and mystical, miraculous salvation by old Mr. Jones, the junkman. It is a vintage season.

293a.   Bridgers, Sue Ellen. ALL TOGETHER NOW. New York:
        Knopf, 1979. 238pp. Grades 7-12.

Reticent Casey Flanagan, 12, comes to spend the summer of 1951 with her paternal grandparents in their small town in North Carolina while her father is fighting in Korea and her mother is singing in a nightclub. She soon becomes a companion to the insouciant but lonely mentally retarded man across the street, Dwayne, whose obsession is baseball and who mistakes her for a boy because of her short hair and jeans. She is also quickly assimilated into her grandmother's relaxed and hospitable household which includes her grandfather Ben, who operates a lumber yard; her extroverted uncle Taylor, a stock-car racing enthusiast; her grandmother's lifelong friend Pansy, a settled spinster; and the aging, unemployed but buoyant Hazard, whose late-blooming, on-again-off-again romance with Pansy unfolds frustratingly before their eyes. When Dwayne's

self-serving brother tries to have Dwayne institutionalized, Casey
and Taylor spearhead a community-wide drive to help him remain
at liberty.   And when Casey herself falls desperately ill and polio
is suspected, her anxious friends and family keep unstinting vigil,
willing her to live.   Secure in their love and with fond memories
to bolster her, she returns home.

293b.   Butterworth, William E.   LeRoy and the Old Man.   New
          York: Four Winds, 1980.   154pp.   Grades 7-9.

          Inadvertent witness to the brutal slaying of an elderly wom-
an by teenage toughs in his Chicago housing project, LeRoy Cham-
bers, 18, ambitious black high school graduate, is threatened with
agonizing death if he squeals on the punks.   Terror-stricken, his
mother buses him off to Mississippi to stay with his paternal grandfather, an undemonstrative but industrious and widely respected
shrimp fisherman.   LeRoy regards his sojourn in Southern back-
waters as an irritating but practical hiatus in his life, but the stal-
wart old man views it as an opportunity to proselytize for his salubrious rural lifestyle.   He makes the youth a partner in his enterprise of selling seafood to New Orleans' Cajun restaurants and
builds a substantial home for the two of them.   When the murderers
are apprehended and LeRoy is subpoenaed to testify against them,
he is appalled that his uncompromising grandfather expects him to
return to Chicago and naively rely on apathetic police protection
against the avowed vengeance of the hooligans.   Suddenly, the father
who deserted him and his mother when he was a boy appears to
dangle before him an attractive alternative: to jump bond and live
anonymously in New York with him and his paramour, sharing the
spoils of his lucrative book making racket.   Weighing his father's
facile turpitude against his grandfather's immutable rectitude, Le-
Roy finds that he is unwilling to incur the latter's denunciation.
He swallows his apprehensions and heeds the old man's advice to
remove his mother from her inimical environment and bring her
South to live with them after the trial.

294.   Carter, Forrest.   THE EDUCATION OF LITTLE TREE.
          New York: Delacorte, 1976.   216pp.   Grades 10-12.

          Little Tree is 5 when he is orphaned and goes to live with
his Cherokee grandparents in the mountains of Tennessee.   His
Granma supervises his education by having him memorize the dic-
tionary by day and reading to him from Shakespeare by night, while
his unschooled, half-Scottish Granpa teaches him the time-honored
trade of moonshining, pride in his Indian ancestry, and the Indian
way of replenishing natural resources.   They are content and self-
sufficient on their isolated mountain, and, except for the time
Granpa intercepts a rattlesnake bite meant for Little Tree, all of
their troubles are created by intruders motivated by greed, mistrust, or convention.   Their darkest hour comes when Little Tree
is forced to attend a sanctimonious and stigmatizing church-oriented

boarding school as a charity student where he is mistreated until his grandfather comes to deliver him.   When Little Tree is 9, Granpa dies without commotion or sentimentality, and his devoted wife follows within months.   They promise to wait for him in the next life, and he helps bury them in their secret place from which Granpa watched each day dawn, saying, "She's coming alive!"

295.   Cawley, Winifred. GRAN AT COALGATE.   New York: Holt, Rinehart and Winston, 1974.   Illus. by Fermin Rocker. 211pp.   Glossary.   Grades 6-8.

Jinnie, 11, is so anxious and tense over upcoming scholarship exams that the doctor prescribes a rest-cure.   Dogmatic Dad suggests a week with his dour Methodist mother who preaches fire and brimstone, speaks in Initial Capitals, and serves slimy suet pudding.   Moderate Mam counters with a week at her mother's at Coalgate which Dad considers a Den of Iniquity and an enclave of dangerous liberality in the 1920's.   With filial fealty, Jinnie is prepared to be as condemnatory as her sanctimonious and parsimonious father, but finds that her "Common" maternal relatives are warm and unstinting in spite of poverty and the imminence of a crippling strike.   She discovers to her guilt and discomfiture that Sin is mystical and marvelous.   Her cousin, 14, introduces her to the forbidden fruits of motion pictures and decadent dances.   Worse yet, her uncle's wife is brazenly cuckolding him, and he has turned to Drink.   The adventurous and revelatory week is abruptly curtailed when Dad sees the headlines that licentious Aunt Polly has almost been murdered and both her husband and son are suspected. Through the scandal Gran acts with strength, serenity, and devotion to maintain family solidarity.   Jinnie, sadder but wiser, returns home to qualify for her scholarship.

296.   Clifford, Eth. THE ROCKING CHAIR REBELLION.   Boston: Houghton Mifflin, 1978.   147pp.   Grades 6-9.

Opie Cross, 14, whose mother wants her to be an English teacher and whose father prefers her to be a social worker, visits her former neighbor, Mr. Pepper, who has been dumped unceremoniously in the Maple Ridge Home for the Aged.   She leaves the institution as a volunteer, though she hasn't planned to get involved with those pathetic, prating, palsied, querulous, rocking, staring, senile, antediluvian fossils.   Several of the residents also find the atmosphere demoralizing in spite of enlightened, sympathetic management.   Opie organizes a raffle for Mrs. Sherman's fancywork, refers Mrs. Longwood to her attorney father to have her penurious guardian changed, and lobbies to have the annual guild benefit altered to a block party so the residents of the home can mingle with the community and participate.   When vigorous Mr. Pepper and his four cohorts decide to buy a house to maintain communally, Mr. Cross goes to court for them against neighbors' objections that they plan to run a boarding house for immoral purposes.   Mr. Pepper and Mrs.

Sherman, intimates, marry to allay gossip, even though they will
lose some Social Security benefits.   Opie rejects both parents' as-
pirations for her and decides to be a lawyer specializing in advocacy
of senior citizens' rights.

297.   Colman, Hila.   THE AMAZING MISS LAURA.   New York:
         Morrow, 1976.   192pp.   Grades 6-10.

     Josie's only ambition on high school graduation is to leave
her annoying and autocratic grandfather's farmhouse, but he refuses
to sell any of his valuable Connecticut land to enable her to go to
art school.   She takes a job as companion to the town's eccentric
doyenne but expects her to be as boring and senile as everyone
over 60.   Miss Laura is vain and meticulous, and Josie wonders
how insignificant details can matter to an octogenarian.   Like her
grandfather, Miss Laura wants control over her affairs instead of
letting the younger generation make more practical and sensible de-
cisions.   Then Miss Laura's brother-in-law, a crass businessman,
tries to have her declared incompetent to gain possession of her
art collection.   While the vibrant lady has occasional memory lapses,
it is only when she is agitated that she loses her regal bearing and
sense of humor.   Josie gravitates to her defense with the aid of
Miss Laura's nephew.   Following a successful showing of her husband's paintings, Miss Laura suffers a heart attack, and her avaricious brother-in-law prevails.   She resigns herself to the nursing
home with the knowledge that no one can take away her memories.
Josie's grandfather relents.

297a.   Cookson, Catherine.   MRS. FLANNAGAN'S TRUMPET.
         New York: Lothrop, Lee and Shepard, 1980.   192pp.
         Grades 6-8.

     Eddie Morley, 15, bears a grudge against the grandmother
who disowned his mother when she married beneath her station and
whom he had never met until his father's untimely death.   Now that
his mother is entering a sanitarium for her asthma in the year
1890, she has arranged for him and his sister Penny, 12, to live
with his grandparents for the duration at their remote house on a
promontory on the Northumberland coast, and he is rebellious.
Not only does Gran Flannagan have a shrewish tongue that constantly carps at him, his grandfather (a retired sea captain), and
the hired girl Daisy, but she is also deaf and hears selectively with
the aid of a speaking trumpet.   Eddie is also at odds with his
grandmother's nephew Hal.   It is only when Eddie overhears a plot
between Hal and a Belgian gentleman, and it becomes clear that the
lives of his grandfather, Penny and Daisy are at stake at the hands
of white slavers, that Gran reveals her true mettle--the agility,
tenacity, indefatigability, shrewdness and decisiveness that belie
her 66 years.   To his consternation, he learns that her deafness is
a sham and that the house conceals the entrance to a treacherous
subterraneous passageway that they must negotiate to redeem their

loved ones and bring Hal to justice.   At last Eddie and his grandmother are able to express their mutual affection.

298.   Corcoran, Barbara.   THE FARAWAY ISLAND.   New York:
         Atheneum, 1977.   158pp.   Grades 6-10.

         Lynn, 14, is shy and inarticulate and refuses to go to Bel-
gium when Dad is appointed a Fulbright lecturer, preferring to stay
with her grandmother on Nantucket.   The island off-season offers
her a wild, isolated freedom she has never known.   Her grandmother is different, also, sometimes forgetful, occasionally calling
Lynn by her mother's name, and losing track of days.   The discovery that the local girls are not friendly to off-islanders prompts
the insecure adolescent not to enroll in school but to pretend to
Grandmother that she has.   Each morning she sets off with bike
and lunch to explore remote reaches.   Evenings and weekends with
Grandmother are pleasant, too, for she is competent and companionable, alert and effervescent most of the time.   When Grandmother
develops one of her infrequent migraines and needs medication at
the height of a severe storm, Lynn fears exposure of her truancy,
but the danger passes.   A minor fender bender triggers a crusading
couple to blow Lynn's cover and suggest institutionalizing her grandmother.   Lynn is contrite for compromising Grandmother, but
Grandmother is unruffled and understanding.   A sensible young doctor rises to their defense, and Lynn enrolls herself in school.

299.   Corcoran, Barbara.   HEY, THAT'S MY SOUL YOU'RE
         STOMPING ON.   New York: Atheneum, 1978.   122pp.
         Grades 6-10.

         Because her parents are quarreling and her possessive
mother is distraught, Rachel, 16, is sent for a vacation to her retired maternal grandparents in Palm Springs.   At their apartment
hotel she meets an assortment of Jewish senior citizens, all couples
who appear to love each other after all these years.   The only
young people nearby are the pampered but neglected children of a
sybaritic ex-starlet who slept her way into the movies.   Their life
seems very glamorous until Rachel realizes how debilitatingly neu-
rotic they are because of their unstable homelife.   When her parents
divorce, she decides that a broken home with two loving parents is
preferable to an uncaring one.   And when the lady with "heartburn"
dies of angina, shocking the close little retirement community into
a realization of its own mortality, she becomes aware of the dependency of humankind on one another, especially when partnerships
are wrenched asunder.   She rescinds her decision not to return to
her querulous mother.

300.   Corcoran, Barbara.   THIS IS A RECORDING.   New York:
         Atheneum, 1971.   Illus. by Richard Cuffari.   168pp.
         Grades 6-9.

Marianne Temple is an immature sophomore who resorts to
hyperbole and occasional prevarication for effect when her parents
send her to her grandmother in Montana while they try to mend an
impaired marriage.   Never having been west of the Hudson, Marianne is expecting Wild West.   Instead she finds an urbane grandmother with a commodious Victorian mansion, educated Indians,
hostile classmates reacting to her loftiness, and a bigoted deputy
sheriff with a carbon copy son.   Grandmother Katherine, who gave
up an illustrious stage career to marry a rancher, comes out of
retirement to give a vibrant performance that wins the respect of
Marianne's classmates who then make friendly overtures to her.
Marianne herself earns the respect of Katherine and her young Indian friend by saving his little brother's life.   When her parents'
marriage fails, Marianne is resentfully reluctant to return to Boston
with her mother who seems so unfeeling, but she has acquired the
maturity to cope with it.   She confides events and emotions to her
tape recorder.

301.   Corcoran, Barbara.   THE WINDS OF TIME.   New York:
        Atheneum, 1974.   Illus. by Gail Owens.   164pp.   Grades
        6-9.

Teenage Gail becomes the ward of her disarmingly solicitous
but rapacious uncle when her mother returns to a mental hospital,
and she seeks the first opportunity for escape.   It comes when Uncle
Chad's car crashes on a snowy mountain road in Colorado and he
is pinned in the wreckage.   Gail, unharmed, follows her cat down
an overgrown lane straight into the forgotten splendor of the nineteenth century, the munificent estate of the pioneering, financiering
Partridge dynasty.   Diminutive Mrs. Partridge, 90, and her stroke-
disfigured son, now recluses, graciously take her in without question, yet her grandson, a serious naturalist, is suspicious of her
until he is convinced her story is true.   While awaiting word from
her father whose last known address was Hawaii, Mrs. Partridge
predicts Gail's checkered future in Tarot cards, and they all con-
nive to keep her out of the clutches of the underhanded sheriff and
wily Uncle Chad.   When her affable father finally appears, the
Partridges offer him a job and a place in the family for the summer.

302.   Cresswell, Helen.   ORDINARY JACK.   New York: Macmil-
        lan, 1977.   195pp.   Grades 6-8.

Jack Bagthorpe grieves and grouses at being the only ordinary individual in his whole phrenetic, over-achieving, egomaniacal
family.   Father is a histrionic, bombastic BBC scriptwriter, Mother
does Yoga and Brisk Conversations, and each of his sisters and
brothers has numerous academic, artistic, and athletic "strings to
their bows. " His 4-year-old cousin is a subtle and accomplished
pyromaniac, his grandmother at 75 is an egocentric matriarch who
loquaciously laments her long-departed pet, while Grandfather at 85

is "selectively deaf" and as slavishly devoted to wolfing stuffed eggs as he is to exterminating wasps.   Jack himself is inept at everything except training his doltish dog until Uncle Parker, iconoclast and ebullient hedonist, decides that Jack can rivet the others' attention by becoming a Prophet.   He directs Jack to effect Mysterious Impressions and intone Messages, leading to a spectacular culmination at sister Rosie's birthday extravaganza.   Jack succeeds in unnerving the rest, and when the conspirators are finally unmasked, their triumph is only slightly dented.   Jack reverts to normality with new respect from the family.

303.   Cunningham, Julia.   COME TO THE EDGE.   New York: Pantheon, 1977.   79pp.   Grades 6-9.

Gravel Winter, 14, tolerates Dickensian orphanage life because of the anticipation of reunion with his father, but when his father abruptly rejects him, Gravel crashes out of solitary confinement and flees.   His first benefactor is an aging sign painter, Mr. Paynter, who is companionable and incurious.   Gravel seems to have found an ideal niche until Mr. Paynter casually mentions that he loves him like a son.   A gray curtain of remembered hurt and fear envelops him and he flees again.   Fate decrees that his next benefactors are an irascible and penurious aged blind man who gives him a bed for the use of his eyes; a kind old lame woman who mothers him and offers him meals for the use of his legs; and a poor but trusting old deaf woman who asks for the use of his ears for nothing because she cannot hear him grumble.   He gives of his services but not of himself, because he feels empty and worthless, but the two sympathetic women mistake his attention for love.   He feels guilty for misleading them and knows he must extricate himself again, galvanized by the avaricious, malevolent, and tyrannical blind man who is the antithesis of love and trust.   He returns inexorably to Mr. Paynter whose parting words he remembers: "Don't go so far you lose the way ... I trust you to come back."   The faith becomes mutual.

304.   Degens, T.   TRANSPORT 7-41-R.   New York: Viking, 1974.   171pp.   Grades 6-9.

Cast out of her home in Russian-occupied East Germany to attend boarding school in Cologne, a 13-year-old abused girl is compelled to cross the 1946 Cold War border alone.   Bitter experience and false allegiances to the Nazis, the Communists, and finally to God have encrusted her emotions until she is cynical, calculating, aloof, and inured to the degredations of cattle car transportation, DP barracks, soup lines, and contemptuous, patronizing, and menacing officials, not to mention the bestiality of her crisis-crazed compatriots.   Envied by the children and resented by the adults of her Transport, she perversely defends the elderly couple excoriated by the others because the wheelchair of the gravely ill wife takes up coveted space.   When his wife dies en route, the girl, who has vowed

never to make another promise, surprises herself by agreeing to
help Mr. Lauritzen smuggle her corpse through the herds of refugees and past the armed borders for five harrowing days and nights
of stealing, lying, bribing, cajoling, and finagling so that Mrs.
Lauritzen can be buried in Cologne, her dying wish.   The more involved the resilient girl becomes with the faltering old man's desperate and quixotic mission, the more protective layers of callus
peel from her seared soul, and she realizes that a commitment
freely given, not forced, is worthy of keeping.

304a.   Denker, Henry.   HOROWITZ AND MRS. WASHINGTON.
         New York: Putnam, 1979.   409pp.   Grades 9-12.

    Mugged by black youths on the streets of New York City,
Sam Horowitz, 68, proud, self-reliant Jewish immigrant and widower,
mistrustful now of all blacks, finds himself partially paralyzed by a
stroke and ironically dependent on a black physical therapy nurse,
Mrs. Harriet Washington, 61, equally dignified and spirited.   Instantly defensive, the old man is deliberately obstinate, truculent
and sarcastic.   But Mrs. Washington, with monumental patience,
tact and pertinacity, slowly erodes his resistance and hostility.
Horowitz' overbearing daughter is the catalyst that galvanizes them
into declaring a truce in their war of wills while they both battle to
save Horowitz from being institutionalized.   Mrs. Washington becomes a tyrannical taskmaster in assigning him exercises to regain
his dexterity and independence, and as his trust and self-confidence
return, he begins to reveal the gentler and more benevolent side of
his nature that has been eclipsed by the awful loneliness of his
widowhood.   After many demoralizing reverses, they manage to convince the medical review board of Horowitz' competence, but the
victory is bittersweet when he realizes that Mrs. Washington, the
professional, will not remain as his companion and pinochle partner.

305.   Donovan, John.   REMOVE PROTECTIVE COATING A LIT-
        TLE AT A TIME.   New York: Harper and Row, 1973.
        91pp.   Grades 7-9.

    Product of a shotgun wedding between high school prom king
and queen, Harry reaches puberty before his parents turn 30.   The
summer that he is 14, he is sent to camp where he experiments unsuccessfully with heterosexuality, contemplates homosexuality, and
settles for self-gratification.   He returns home to find that his father, a Madison Avenue mogul, is absent on business most of the
time, and his mother, idle and rudderless, is airing her neuroses
and frustrations on a psychiatrist's couch.   Harry has no one with
whom to discuss his problems until he meets the 72-year-old female vagrant, Amelia Myers, who resides in a vacant, condemned
tenement and lives by panhandling, scavenging, and snaring pigeons.
The two loners form an odd alliance of mutual acceptance and trust.
When cold weather comes, Harry tries to provide Amelia with warm
clothing and sustenance from home, but one day he arrives to find

her weak and bruised, and the next day the tenement has been razed.
He never sees her again nor learns her fate, but visits to the Metropolitan Museum with his father improve their relationship, and his
mother announces her intention of enrolling in college.

306.   Gauch, Patricia Lee.   THE GREEN OF ME.   New York:
         Putnam, 1978.   156pp.   Grades 7-12.

Recent high school graduate, Jennifer Lynn Cooper, in
search of self, entrains for Virginia from her home in Ohio, and
whiles away the monotonous miles by recalling significant episodes
in her life.   Dreamy and diffident as a child, she is pierced deeply
when her aggressive cousin cajoles Grandma Stokes into giving her
the garnet ring Jennie covets, when her strict father will not allow
her to keep her adorable Christmas puppy, and when her only close
friend moves away.   In her adolescence, when the pressure of
making new friends with the sophisticated crowd becomes too intense, she finds relaxation with Grandma and Grandpa Cooper, the
latter a jovial raconteur, who lack material wealth but abound with
love and spiritual riches.   Then she meets charismatic Chris Coch-
ran and goes into orbit around him, even though she knows he lies
to and about her.   On the night of graduation she goes to visit
Grandpa Cooper, just home from the hospital after a stroke, and
is shocked to see what she has refused to believe, that he is a
helpless, mindless invalid.   After a year of separation from Chris,
Jenny, knowing she must make her own mistakes in life, answers
Chris' summons from Charlottesville as a moth goes to the flame.

307.   Gray, Elizabeth Janet.   JANE HOPE.   New York: Viking,
         1933.   276pp.   Grades 7-9.

Widowed Southern gentlewoman, Mollie Lou Kennard, takes
her children, Mary Louise, 16, Jane Hope, 12, and Pierce, 9, to
the convivial gentility of her parents' home in the stately antebellum
college town of Chapel Hill, North Carolina.   Mary Louise is a natural belle like her mother, but Jane Hope is an unabashed tomboy
who seeks adventure and considers it a vexation to behave like the
lady her refined grandmother and warm grandfather, a retired
clergyman and benevolent slave owner, expect her to be.   She defends a beleaguered freshman, and she and Stephen become firm
friends.   Left at home as punishment for cropping her hair short,
she rises to the occasion as hostess when handsome Cousin Flavel-
lus comes to call, but when her mother wants to marry her girlhood beau, Jane Hope obstinately withholds her approval.   Later,
Stephen persuades her to reconsider.   Suddenly he recognizes in his
old chum a mature poise and beauty at 16 and asks her to wear his
fraternity pin as he goes whirling off to war.

308.   Greaves, Margaret.   STONE OF TERROR.   New York:
         Harper and Row, 1972.   215pp.   Grades 6-10.

Sent by his dying mother in Cromwellian England to live
with his grandfather on an isolated channel island with links to its
Breton past, Philip Hoskyn, 15, learns that his grandfather and the
zealot minister, Mr. Noel, are the only educated persons among the
native fisher folk and are engaged in a war of wills with the self-
proclaimed sorceress and priestess of the primitive heathen mono-
lith known as the Grandmother Stone who hold the island in their
terrible thrall.   Enlightened Grandfather, alone, believes that the
execrable woman, Annette Perchon, is more the victim of circum-
stances than the agent of Beelzebub.   Philip befriends Annette's wild
and alienated niece, Marie, but makes enemies among the brutal
and ignorant islanders.   On the night of a pagan festival, Mr. Noel
rallies his small force of church officials to destroy the Grandmother Stone and thus break Annette's stranglehold of superstition.
The tormented woman, robbed of her cult and her sanity, leads the
vengeful villagers against Philip.   The mob then turns on Annette,
bent on burning her for witchcraft, but she flings herself to her own
destruction, and Philip comforts the girl he has tamed and fallen
in love with.

309.   Hoban, Lillian.   I MET A TRAVELER.   New York:
        Harper and Row, 1977.   182pp.   Grades 6-9.

The only Jew in her Christian missionary school in Jerusalem, Josie Hayden, 11, is lonely and obsessed with adolescent
woes, while her mother, a breezy and charismatic artist, is absorbed in the exciting, exotic Israeli life and her new love affair.
An aging Russian immigrant couple moves to a nearby apartment,
and when the husband dies, Josie fills the gap in his 58-year-old
widow's existence, even though Mira speaks no Hebrew or English.
The grandmotherly woman becomes a surrogate mother to the unhappy girl in her mother's frequent absences.   Josie sees the pos-
sibility of returning to her old home in Connecticut given the adult
companionship of Mira, since her mother has no intention of returning to suburbia.   She quietly sets about fundraising, telling no
one of her scheme.   Her disillusionment is unbounded when she
learns that her beloved Mira and a male Russian immigrant, Grisha,
are having an affair of their own, and Mira has no desire to emi-
grate to America.   Her mother provides her with a book on sex
after 60 and concedes that she is a poor parent but a loving one
and not about to change to suit Josie.   At the end of the school
term her mother ends her affair and begins a new one as the two
depart Israel for parts unknown, and Josie glosses her lips and decides to take a grownup interest in boys herself.

310.   Johnston, Norma.   THE SWALLOW'S SONG.   New York:
        Atheneum, 1978.   192pp.   Grades 7-10.

Alerted that Gran is mentally and physically incapable of
caring for herself any longer in her home on the Jersey Shore,
Allison Standish, 16, and her family hurry there to spend the sum-

mer of 1920 putting Gran's affairs in order. Surveillance of Gran,
who is usually vague and tractible, or girlish, but who sometimes
wanders off and acts unreasonable, is shared three ways, and Allison and her brother Jerry have ample free time to be drawn into
the heady, sybaritic world of the wealthy Farraday family. Allison
is madly infatuated with magnetic but degenerate Dirk Farraday who
takes her soaring like a swallow at licentious dances and beach
parties. But Dirk expects repayment of the sort she is unwilling
to give, and she finally comes to earth with a jolt when Jerry and
Dirk are arrested for possession of the bootleg gin and cocaine
which Dirk supplies. She breaks permanently with impenitent Dirk
while retaining the friendship of his sister, Lisa, and the troubled
family whose glamorous existence is hollow and brittle. She appreciates anew her more pedestrian parents. Gran's effects are sold
at a rummage sale, and she goes to live with the Standishes (see
311).

311.   Johnston, Norma. IF YOU LOVE ME, LET ME GO. New
        York: Atheneum, 1978. 162pp. Grades 7-10.

        Gran has four different personalities. Occasionally she is
her old, proud self, but most frequently she is coquettish Sara Dale,
herself as a debutante, balky at being moved from her own home to
live with Allison, 16, and her family (see 310). Sometimes she regresses to a petulant preschooler, and at her most frightened and
bewildered times, she lashes out like a demented old witch. At
one of these times she falls down the stairs, breaking her hip and
becoming a permanent invalid. In addition to coping with Gran,
Allison is also burdened with her own social adjustment with her
Roaring Twenties New Jersey high school crowd, her best friend
and alter ego Lisa's family trauma, her mother's physical and emotional exhaustion, her father's impending bankruptcy, and her brother's failing grades at Harvard. Then Lisa abruptly draws away,
leaving Allison hurt and confused. A sensitive and enlightened
Italian medical student, Mario, helps her see her problems in perspective. She is romantically attracted to him, though his national-
ity is a detriment in her social circle. She is alone with her grandmother when she dies and sees at firsthand her willing release into
death. Only then does she understand that she need not fear death,
change, nor her own independent judgment. Her relationships with
Lisa and Mario evolve naturally.

312.   Kerr, M. E. GENTLEHANDS. New York: Harper and
        Row, 1978. 183pp. Grades 7-10.

        The fateful summer preceding his senior year, attractive
Buddy Boyle, son of a plodding, narrow-minded resort town cop and
déclassé mother, is enamored of a summering debutante and becomes acquainted with his urbane and aristocratic grandfather, long
estranged from Buddy's mother. Skye Pennington at first regards
Buddy as a decoration and diversion, but puts him at ease among

her sophisticated family and friends and develops a stronger attachment to him as their mutual friendship with Grandpa Trenker grows. Buddy comes to revere his grandfather as a model of courtesy, culture, and compassion, but has to sever relations with his hostile, bourgeois family.   An investigative reporter who is a frequent guest at Skye's estate finally discloses his mission and brands Mr. Trenker as a Nazi war criminal, code-named "Gentlehands, " who was guilty of unspeakable atrocities at Auschwitz.   The peace of the Long Island summer colony is shattered, and Buddy is incredulous and outraged that others believe so willingly in the culpability of his exemplary grandfather.   Dawning realization when his grandfather flees brings disillusionment before Buddy can face the desertion of Skye and reconciliation with his family.

313.   Krumgold, Joseph. ONION JOHN. New York: Crowell, 1959. Illus. by Symeon Shimin. 248pp. Grades 6-8.

Andy Rusch, Jr. is content to be a normal junior high boy in the community of Serenity, New Jersey, playing Little League ball, helping after school in his father's hardware emporium, and especially being Onion John's best friend.   John is an aging Eastern European immigrant whose broken English only Andy can understand. He dresses eccentrically, munches onions like apples, does odd jobs, scavenges in the dump, and practices the superstitious lifestyle of the Middle Ages.   Andy's logical, scientific father scoffs at Onion John's spells and incantations and has plans for Andy to go to MIT and become the astronaut he would have liked to be.   Misguidedly trying to boost Onion John into the twentieth century, he organizes the town into constructing a modern house for John.   The scheme backfires when the unhappy John accidentally burns down the house the day he moves in and hurts himself in trying to rescue his most prized possession, a fading icon.   John flees the overzealous townspeople, and Andy plans to join him to thwart his father's interference in his life, but John suddenly realizes that the boy's childish faith in his magic has evaporated and betrays him.   His father agrees at last to let Andy select his own career or even to follow in his footsteps as a tradesman, and Onion John returns to Serenity on his own terms.

314.   LeRoy, Gen. HOTHEADS. New York: Harper and Row, 1977. 249pp. Grades 7-9.

When Geneva Michellini, 12, starts classes at her new school, she is shamed by poverty, a poor address, plebeian parents, and especially the stigma of Babu, her volatile, violent, alcoholic, Italian-speaking grandfather.   She and her moody, vacillating sister Jo, 15, each find a secret friend at school and life seems tenable until the construction of a new road and shopping center adjacent to their property, and the ensuing vandalism on the construction site brings harassment to the family.   Her parents' passivity in the presence of a penetrating searchlight and prowling guards irks her, and she joins her grandfather in retaliating against insolent workmen, earning them ribald notoriety.   Her despondency and disillusionment reach a nadir when she and Jo learn that Jo's perfidious friend's father is actually working covertly to evict them.   Geneva discovers that it is Babu who is sabotaging the construction in an attempt to salvage his property.   The old man suffers a stroke, and in saving his honor she is arrested.   A new pride is born of comprehension, and she heroically and steadfastly inculpates herself until a discerning attorney redresses injustices.   She returns to Babu, now an incontinent, bedridden shell, and renews her pledge to defend and protect his interests where her undemonstrative, equivocal, and fatalistic family fails.

315.   Lingard, Joan.   THE CLEARANCE.   Nashville: Nelson, 1974. 160pp.   Grades 6-10.

Maggie McKinley, 16, resents being sent to her grandmother's primitive house in the Highlands, but someone must pay a duty visit and it is Maggie's turn.   She hates mountains and midges and the lack of plumbing and electricity.   Moreover, their nearest neighbors, the Frasers, are snobs from Edinburgh whose summer home has all the amenities.   Then Granny tells her of a bloody episode in Scottish history when poor crofters were violently evicted by avaricious lairds in a "Clearance" and of how her own family came to the glen.   Maggie begins to appreciate Granny's staunch pride in her roots and traditions, and she is flattered when James Fraser, 17, takes a romantic interest in her.   One evening while Maggie is out, Granny accidentally burns the house down about her.   She is saved by the Frasers who make a home for Maggie while Granny is hospitalized.   It falls to Maggie and Mrs. Fraser to decide where Granny, 83, will be when she is released.   Living with Maggie's family or being institutionalized would demoralize her.   An alternative is found in subsidized retirement apartments on the edge of town with a view of her beloved hills and someone to look in on her regularly.   Granny is not displeased with the compromise and sets Maggie an example for making the most of change.   (THE RE-SETTLING, THE PILGRIMAGE, and THE REUNION recount Maggie's further romantic adventures and include her reaction to her Granny's death.)

315a.   Lingard, Joan.   ODD GIRL OUT.   New York: Elsevier/ Nelson, 1979. 187pp.   Grades 7-10.

Fiery-tressed Ellen Ferguson, 14, feels awkward enough at being a head taller than her friend Davie and at not yet sharing her girlfriend Isadora's interest in boys.   Then her mother decides to remarry and sell their light and airy flat in the heart of Edinburgh and move to her husband's cramped bungalow in the sleepy suburbs. Ellen stubbornly rebels.   Her happiest moments are snatched with Nicolas, 70, a cultured Czechoslovakian who was a concert pianist before cataracts took his eyesight.   Nicolas gives her confidential

daily piano lessons in exchange for the evening meals she prepares
for him.   When Nicolas is hospitalized for sight-restoring surgery
and life becomes untenable in her new household, Ellen runs away
and hides in Nicolas' apartment.   When she is found, her mother
delivers a bitter diatribe against the old gentleman whom she has
never met for the wedge she imagines he has driven between Ellen
and her stepfather.   It is only when Nicolas confronts Ellen's mother
and convinces her that she must speak forthrightly to Ellen about her
musical endowment, and of the father from whom she inherited it,
that mother, daughter, and stepfather can purge themselves of preju-
dicial influences and learn to compromise.   While Ellen has been
preoccupied with domestic strife, Davie has grown appreciably taller.

315b.   Maguire, Gregory.   THE LIGHTNING TIME.   New York:
         Farrar, Straus and Giroux, 1978.   247pp.   Grades 6-8.

         Daniel Rider, 12, imagines that the paternal grandmother
he seldom sees is a robot, programmed to emerge from her closet
periodically to phone or send cards and gifts on holidays.   Now his
mother is to be hospitalized and he is being sent from his Manhattan
apartment to his grandmother's secluded home on an Adirondack lake
where he has never visited because his father never takes vacations.
Daniel is pleased that Grandma does not fit his stereotype, and
Grandma, a woman of many parts, is gratified that Daniel does not
seem like an arrogant city boy.   They have a mutual friend in the
girl Carrie, a distant cousin who lives with Grandma and who introduces Daniel to the grandeur and mysticism of Saltbook Mountain,
to which Grandma holds title.   Soon they discover that they also
have an avaricious and formidable enemy, Stephen Spurr, who is
diabolically intent on desecrating the mountain and lake with a taste-
less resort complex crowned by an egregiously monstrous monument
to the triumph of technology over Mother Nature.   The three cohorts
cannot battle the crass and cunning Spurr alone, because he has ap-
pealed to the greed of the town's leading businessmen, but a supernatural convocation of creatures and elements, of which Daniel and
Carrie are the catalysts, coalesce to spare the mountain.   Grandma
almost capitulates when the children's lives are in mortal danger,
but right prevails over might, and Carrie is revealed to be one
facet of Grandma's heterogeneous personality.   The valiant old lady
dies after passing her baton to Daniel.

315c.   Mayne, William.   THE JERSEY SHORE.   New York: Dut-
         ton, 1973.   159pp.   Grades 6-8.

         When Arthur and his mother come to spend their summer
vacation with his paternal aunt and grandfather in a small New Jersey coastal town, they find that the two live in separate dwellings
divided by a stretch of beach and have grown alienated and reclusive.
While his mother tries to revivify his maiden aunt, Arthur attempts
to get acquainted with his grandfather.   Unaccustomed to human intercourse, the old man at first speaks tersely and haltingly.   Later,

as he becomes used to the boy's pensive presence, he grows increasingly communicative, expatiating soberly on his boyhood and young adulthood in a Dickensian English village.   Arthur is absorbed into his grandfather's memories of the hell-raising preacher, the penurious landlord, the unrequited love, the exigency of menial labor, and especially of the pestilential miasma that claimed the lives of his grandfather's first two wives and all of their children before he emigrated to America and started the family that would eventually produce Arthur.   At the end of the visit Grandfather and Aunt Deborah still agree to disagree, but many years later, when Arthur is a World War II aviator, he has the opportunity to fulfill his grandfather's single but urgent request of him and erect memorials to those who so tragically preceded him in death.

316.   Mazer, Norma Fox. A FIGURE OF SPEECH.   New York:
          Delacorte, 1973.   197pp.   Grades 7-9.

Jenny, an unplanned baby, was reared by her paternal grandfather who has occupied the family's basement apartment since the death of his wife.   The two are inseparable, but now that Grandpa is 83, he has outlived his usefulness to all the family but Jenny, 13.   Her big brother Vince and his presumptuous wife Valerie evict Grandpa from his basement, and he is forced to bunk in with another grandson.   The deprivation of his independence and privacy is physically and mentally debilitating, and the family complains. Jenny's horrifying revelation of her parents' plans to put Grandpa in a home where the immured sit in numbered rocking chairs and are treated like naughty children arrests his decline and galvanizes his actions.   He runs away to his ancestral farm with Jenny's company.   The farm is derelict, and after several days of toil, discomfort, hunger, and fatigue, Jenny realizes they cannot manage alone through the approaching winter.   She awakens one night after a severe thunderstorm to find Grandpa missing, and in the morning she finds his body in his prided apple orchard where he voluntarily went to die, not "pass away," one of the euphemistic figures of speech Jenny's mother uses.   She returns to her hypocritical family but remains detached.

317.   Means, Florence Crannell. SHUTTERED WINDOWS.   Boston: Houghton Mifflin, 1938.   Illus. by Armstrong Sperry.
          206pp.   Grades 7-10.

Orphaned Harriet Freeman, 16, is offered a home with her kindly minister and his wife where she can pursue her music career, but she has a strong compulsion to find her only living relative, the great-grandmother she has never seen.   An honor student from a middle class Minneapolis milieu, she is appalled and ashamed of the poverty, segregation, illiteracy, and superstition of Granny and her black neighbors in rural, insular South Carolina.   But she is also entranced by her stately Granny, the loud and easy laughter shared by her race, the spirit of unity in the local church, and a handsome

boy with musical talent of his own with a desire to help his people
at grass roots level. She decides to stay for a semester. At
boarding school nearby, she remains aloof from the local girls and
makes friends with another cosmopolite. The two are only accepted
into school life as they become more tolerant and find they have
something to contribute. At semester's end, she elects to remain
and cast her lot with Granny and Richard in the place of her ancestry.

318.   Montgomery, L. M. ANNE OF GREEN GABLES. New
         York: Farrar, Straus and Giroux, 1908, 1935. 319pp.
         Grades 6-9.

The beloved classic in which the spirited and engaging
Titian-tressed orphan, Anne Shirley, 11, is sent in place of the expected boy to the Prince Edward Island farm of severe Marilla Cuthbert and her more malleable brother, Matthew, and of how the
imaginative, exuberant, and loquacious girl wins the elderly couple's
affection and that of the entire hamlet of Avonlea, including bosom
friend, Diana, and teasing archenemy, Gilbert. It concludes with
Matthew's death, Marilla's failing eyesight, and a teaching position
and romance for Anne who is now 16. (Anne's chronicles are continued in ANNE OF AVONLEA and ANNE OF THE ISLAND.)

319.   Newton, Suzanne. REUBELLA AND THE OLD FOCUS
         HOME. Philadelphia: Westminster, 1978. 197pp. Grades
         7-10.

Three vivacious, aging individualists descend upon the coastal North Carolina town of Shad in search of a place to spend the
remainder of their lives. There they establish an "unrest" or "nurturing" home in the tourist home run by Reubella Foster and her
father where they will have latitude to find focus for their considerable interests and abilities: Ms. Cromwell is a retired college
athletic coach, Ms. Nesselrode a composer and concert pianist,
and Ms. Smithers a noted painter. They contract to lease the
house from Mr. Foster, investing him as general manager, re-
model it to suit their dichotomous personalities, and plunge into
community involvement. Ms. Cromwell goes to bat with principal
and school board to reinstate Reubella's high school girls' basketball team and then to coach it to victory. Then Ms. Nesselrode's
glaucoma is diagnosed, and she is forced to curtail her composing
and concert appearances. The three, in gloom, almost lose sight
of their motto that "old is not dead," and Mr. Foster loses faith
in the project. It is almost terminated until Reubella forces them
to face their fears, explore other options, and acknowledge that the
opposite of composing is not decomposing. They induct a younger
retiree to balance their group and plan a "commencement" with their
old aplomb.

319a.   Oliphant, Robert.   A PIANO FOR MRS. CIMINO.   Englewood Cliffs, N. J. :   Prentice-Hall, 1980.   366pp.   Grades
9-12.

The sudden onset of mental confusion, diagnosed as irreversible senile dementia, after a fall resulting from double cataract surgery induces 76-year-old Esther Cimino's mercenary sons to
have her declared legally incompetent and committed permanently to
a Minneapolis nursing home, sell her home and auction her personal
possessions, and place in trust the music store she operated with
her late husband.   Only her granddaughter Karen, 19, is truly concerned for her grandmother's welfare.   Seeking an alternative to the
custodial institution her father chose, obsequious to families but
patronizing to patients, she scouts a reputable rehabilitative one.
St. Hild's approach is not to coddle or commiserate with Mrs.
Cimino who takes refuge in passive withdrawal, turns off her hearing aid, shuffles along cautiously, and doesn't like to bother dressing.
Goaded into participating in group discussions and activities, she
makes rapid progress and regains her old poise, spunk and acuity.
Learning of the loss of her personal effects is a demoralizing blow,
but she wins her competency battle in spite of it, graduates from
St. Hild's, and retires to Florida where she encounters an old
friend, Barney Feldman, who reawakens her need to give and receive affection.   Her final victory on the road to total independence,
reclaiming control of her remaining financial assets and the music
store, is won after a stiff legal fray.   Secure and content at last,
Esther Cimino moves in with Barney, acquires a new piano, prepares to give music lessons, and plays the first of many projected
duets with Barney.

320.   Peck, Richard.   FATHER FIGURE.   New York: Viking,
1978.   192pp.   Grades 7-12.

Jim Atwater, 17, has been very conscious of his role as
father figure to his kid brother Byron since their father's defection
nine years earlier when their mother brought them to live with their
imperial, patrician, impersonal, and resolute grandmother in Brooklyn Heights.   Now his mother has taken her own life in the face of
terminal cancer, and Jim shoulders Byron's emotional burdens as
he continues to run physical interference for him.   But Grandmother has an emotional crisis of her own, and dealing with an outspoken teenager and a broken-armed adolescent only aggravates it.
She arranges to send the boys to their father in Florida, a stranger
to both of them, for the summer.   Jim is resentful when his dad
makes fatherly overtures to Byron who seems receptive to them.
He also develops a sexual rivalry with his father.   These feelings
erupt into open warfare, then lapse into uneasy armistice before
open dialogue and catharsis can erase the tension.   Jim returns to
Grandmother's to make college plans, but Byron remains behind to
spend the school year with his father.

321.   Peck, Richard. THE GHOST BELONGED TO ME. New
         York: Viking, 1975. 183pp. Grades 6-8.

         In the year 1913, Alexander Armsworth, 13, is confronted
with conflicting behavioral expectations: the need to be the model
of decorum so he won't disgrace his sycophantic family, and his
need to pursue the prescience that classmate Blossom Culp's mother
assures him he has. Temperamentally he is a throwback to his
great-uncle Miles who is often profanely outspoken, peripatetic, and
does sporadic carpentry around the family's Victorian mansion in
southwestern Illinois. Of the other facet of his personality he is
highly skeptical, but he has no other explanation for the glowing
emanation from the barnloft, the damp dog that disappears into thin
air, and the sepulchral smell he alone perceives. On the evening
following his sister's disastrous coming out party, the specter of a
young girl appears to him in the loft and warns him of impending
danger to the late trolley. Alex dashes out in his nightshirt, saves
the passengers, and becomes a celebrity to his staid mother's horror. When he reveals the source of his information, his mother is
mortified until the small town's leading citizen extols him for relieving her ennui. Uncle Miles identifies the ghost and relates her
tragic history, the body is exhumed, and Alex, Blossom and Uncle
Miles play cat and mouse with publicity mongers until her spirit
can be laid to rest.

322.   Pope, Elizabeth Marie. THE SHERWOOD RING. Boston:
         Houghton Mifflin, 1958. Illus. by Evaline Ness. 266pp.
         Grades 6-9.

         On her father's death, Peggy Grahame, 17, goes to live
with her irascible elderly uncle on the family's ancestral estate in
upstate New York where she encounters a young British historian,
Pat Thorne, skulking about the property researching Revolutionary
history. Her uncle is hostile to Pat and peremptorily loath to share
old family secrets, but the lively shades who seem to step right out
of their somber portraits are not, and appear frequently to unfold
to Peggy a fascinating tale of wartime romance and intrigue that
draws a prophetic parallel to Peggy's budding, clandestine romance
with Pat. Uncle Enos' sudden illness galvanizes the search for the
missing chapter of the story that brings history full circle, links
the Grahame and Thorne families, and closes the schism between
them.

323.   Richards, Judith. SUMMER LIGHTNING. New York: St.
         Martin's, 1978. 271pp. Grades 10-12.

         Branded a recalcitrant and a truant, Terry has good re-
solves but lacks the self-discipline for attending his structured first
grade class. Worldly wise and adventuresome for his 6 years, he
barters his school lunch for more attractive victuals and heads for
Mr. McCree's camp in the Everglades where the old man subsists

off the swamp.   McCree calls him Little Hawk and teaches him to
catch fish bare-handed and other survival skills, to work arithmetic
problems, and even to drive his old truck.   The boy eventually
leaves home altogether to live with Mr. McCree, calling himself an
orphan.   When McCree sustains a compound fracture in harvesting
orchids, the plucky boy saves his life by evacuating him from the
swamp and driving him to the hospital.   But McCree is charged
with contributing to Terry's delinquency, and Terry is in danger of
being sent to the reformatory.   Acting as his own defense, McCree
interrogates the little hawk to whom he gave flight in a moving
courtroom scene, winning freedom for them both.   But World War
II erupts and Terry's dad goes off to war, leaving him with responsibility to his mother and baby sister.   His carefree "Seminole
summer" is over.

324.   Schellie, Don. KIDNAPPING MR. TUBBS.   New York:
         Four Winds, 1978.   182pp.   Grades 6-10.

         A. J. Zander, 16, is the nervous and reluctant partner in
the conspiracy to spirit nonagenarian cowboy, Mr. Tubbs, from his
rest home for an overnight pilgrimage to the ranch where he lived
for half a century as a birthday present for the old man.   A. J.
hasn't liked old people since he was a toddler when an elderly neighbor died and betrayed his affection for her.   In a comical getaway,
Eloise Spencer, 17, volunteer at the home and plot engineer, maneuvers Mr. Tubbs, A. J. , her obese bassett, and Mr. Tubbs' saddle
and bedroll into an ancient VW to negotiate the trip from Tucson to
Flagstaff.   When a motorcycle gang accosts them, and later when
they develop carburetor problems, Mr. Tubbs produces, respectively,
a gun and a length of bailing wire from his trusty bedroll to save
the day.   But at their destination, the mettlesome old man is dis-
illusioned to find that the ranch has become a subdivision and that
his old friend has been dead for decades.   On the return home that
night, he disappears into the desert like an old Apache going off to
die.   A. J. blunders after him, realizing that he has become fond
of Mr. Tubbs, but sprains his ankle in the dark.   Determined to
die with his boots on, Mr. Tubbs recognizes that the boy can't survive without his help and changes his mind.

325.   Shannon, Monica. DOBRY.   New York: Viking, 1934.
         Illus. by Atanas Katchamakoff.   176pp.   Grades 6-9.

         Young Dobry dreams of being a great artist and spends all
his spare time drawing pictures.   His hearty grandfather encourages
his ambition, declaring that it has been prophesied that he will grow
up to have the fire of God in him, but his pragmatic mother thinks
he should take his dead peasant father's place in the fields.   She
changes her mind when the boy sculpts an inspirational nativity scene
in the snow by the stable, and he is given the job of herding cows
to free him from fieldwork so he can practice his art.   Over the
years as he hones his talent, the three of them partake with gusto

of the seasonal events of their Bulgarian village: the annual journey
to the milltown at harvest, the coming of the Gypsy Bear, Grandfather's victory in the Snow-Melting Game, and his anecdotal
prowess.   To earn money for his formal training, Dobry proves his
physical endurance by diving in icy water for the golden crucifix in
the traditional February ceremony before his departure for Sofia,
but he promises his childhood sweetheart that he will return to her.

326.   Smith, Doris Buchanan. TOUGH CHAUNCEY. New York:
         Morrow, 1974. Illus. by Michael Eagle. 222pp. Grades
         7-8.

         Chauncey, 13, couldn't hurt animals, only people, because
people hurt him.   His thrice-divorced mother whom he adores can't
make a home for him because of her succession of boyfriends, so
he lives with his grandparents who inflict brutality under the aegis
of moral rectitude.   His grandfather believes it is sinful to attend
movies but barbarously shoots kittens, beats the boy, and locks him
in the closet when he is ten minutes late from school.   Calculatedly,
Chauncey has become the toughest, meanest kid in his Georgia
town, cutting a swath of malicious mischief and destruction.   In a
last ditch effort to live with his mother, he is badly hurt jumping
from a train and returned to his grandparents on crutches.   When
his grandfather tries to shoot his last defenseless kitten, he has no
recourse but to run away, despite his incapacitation.   He is aided
by his erstwhile archenemy and fellow scapegrace, a black, who
tells him of his own intolerable homelife and suggests a foster home
as an alternative in Chauncey's bid to make good.

327.   Stephens, C. A. GRANDFATHER'S BROADAXE. New
         York: Scott, 1967. Illus. by Jerome B. Moriarty. 224pp.
         Grades 6-8.

         Originally penned for THE YOUTH'S COMPANION, these
eighteen stories are excerpted from experiences collected by the author when he and his cousins, Addison, Halstead, Theodora, Ellen,
and Wealthy, all orphaned in the Civil War, came to live on the
old homestead in Maine of the Old Squire and Grandmother Ruth.
There they find piety and impiety, labor and mirth, wisdom and
justice, generosity and sacrifice, patriotism and adventure, and of
course, love and understanding, whether haying, hoarding apples,
smoking out bees, hunting bears, entertaining unexpected distinguished
visitors, or listening to the Old Gentleman's tales of the pioneering
past.   The incomparable Sheffield broadaxe the Old Squire's father
brought to America before the Revolution and used to clear the farm
was still in use in a World War I shipyard in 1916 in defense of the
country the Old Gentleman loved so greatly.

328.   Stephens, Mary Jo. WITCH OF THE CUMBERLANDS.
         Boston: Houghton Mifflin, 1974. Illus. by Arvis Stewart.
         243pp.   Grades 6-9.

Dr. McGregor, a recent widower, brings his children, cautious Susan, 17, impulsive Betsy, 15, and inscrutable Robin, 4, to the peace and beauty of the Cumberland Mountains of Kentucky. Immediately, they are embroiled in a 40-year-old mystery in which they are the catalysts to a suspenseful denouement along with gentle, sensitive Miss Birdie, the elderly herbalist and fortune teller; Broughton, the foreboding figure in black; and the spirit of the dead coal miner who rises from his dank grave to exact retribution and bare the culpability for the mine disaster that killed 49 men during the Depression. In the meantime they learn to accept and be accepted by "holler" folk and townfolk alike; understand the alliance of magic, superstition, simple faith, and inspired evangelical oratory that comprises religion in the hills; deplore the exploitation of the mountain region and people; and develop an appreciation for the uncanny gifts of compelling Miss Birdie and clairvoyant Robin.

328a.   Strang, Celia.   FOSTER MARY.   New York: McGraw-Hill, 1979.   162pp.   Grades 6-9.

Aunt Foster Mary and Uncle Alonzo Meekins are itinerant fruit pickers following the harvests from Missouri to California to the Northwest and back again. They are also pushovers for orphaned, abandoned, and mistreated children. Their family now numbers four from Bud, 15, to Amiella, 5. Hard-working, God-fearing, optimistic, and deeply caring, they have set an example that even belligerent Lonnie, 7, tries to emulate. But the years of heavy labor have taken their toll of Alonzo, who is crippled with arthritis, and Foster Mary is determined to find a permanent home after the apple harvest near Yakima. Somewhat apprehensively she convinces Alonzo, who is handy with tools and takes the initiative but is short on salesmanship, to apply as winter caretaker to the apple rancher. He secures the job, however, and energetically he and Foster Mary start to make their shack cozy. The children begin school, and there is even money for early but practical Christmas gifts. Then disaster strikes in the form of a compound fracture that immobilizes Alonzo. Mary draws on her well of faith, hope and good cheer, new friends rally round, and Bud decides that he can tackle Alonzo's tasks with the old man's supervision. Alonzo is released from the hospital in time to see the children perform in the Sunday School Christmas play, and the children exult over their first pets.

329.   Stuart, Colin.   WALKS FAR WOMAN.   New York: Dial, 1976.   342pp.   Grades 10-12.

In 1946 when Dewey Elk Hollering returns from overseas and brings home a white girl, his wise matriarchal grandmother, 79, sees in Janet Sinclair a fine wife for her favorite grandson, and confides in the two of them her life story. Born a Blackfoot, she was named Walks Far Away for her peregrinations as a toddler, but as a teen she is truly forced to flee on foot for killing the murderers of her sister and husband. Her escape is aided by Janet's grandfather, Jack Sinclair, and she finds refuge with her mother's tribe of Sioux. She wins their respect both as a medicine woman and for her valor and stamina in masculine pursuits. Eventually she marries the tribe's noblest specimen. They prosper as nomadic buffalo hunters, living by barbaric but comprehensible tribal justice, until their victory over Custer leads to persecution, starvation, and finally capitulation. Her baby is killed in the wars, and she is forced to kill her husband when he insults her. She marries a half-breed who teaches her white man's ways but who is killed by thieves, and finally settles down for life with Elk Hollering. Unable to endure reservation life, they turn to Jack Sinclair whose life she saved at Little Big Horn, and he helps establish them as ranchers. Walks Far Away dies at 102 in communion with the spirits.

330.   Walsh, Jill Paton.   UNLEAVING.   New York: Farrar,
        Straus and Giroux, 1976.   145pp.   Grades 8-12.

        Teen Madge Fielding has inherited her kindred-spirited grandmother's gracious seaside home in Cornwall, and one summer is persuaded to open it to a group of Oxford philosophers, their families and students. The return induces frequent flashback memories of the gregarious, spirited, and indulgent old gentlewoman. Paralleling the events of the summer, these reminiscences exert a profound influence on Madge's goals in life. Patrick, Professor Tregeagle's mercurial teenage son, is an emotional square peg in a coldly intellectual round hole. Together the two tramp the beaches and cliffs, cogitating the meaning of life and death and the existence of God and afterlife. Patrick is particularly sardonic about the nature of the cruel Fate that created his severely retarded sister, and one day in despair and outrage he ends her life because he can't protect her from torment forever. In recovering the body, an old friend, Jeremy, is killed, and Patrick, who suffers no remorse for his act of euthanasia, wallows in guilt over the loss of Jeremy. Madge, an optimist like Gran, decides to devote her life toward lifting Patrick from despondency, equating love with compassion.

331.   Wellman, Alice.   THE WILDERNESS HAS EARS.   New York:
        Harcourt, Brace, Jovanovich, 1975.   140pp.   Grades 7-9.

        Luti, 14, has grown up in the bush of Angola where her father, an American geologist, is employed. Because he is often on field trips, she is left in the care of the native Nduku who taught her to speak his dialect before she could speak English. When Nduku is mauled by a leopard, he insists on returning to the healer and diviner in his Kimbutu village instead of to a modern hospital. She accompanies him but is reviled and stoned for her sunburned white skin. Only the wise old diviner, Onavita, welcomes her and tends her burns after treating Nduku with her ancient remedies. When a sacred chameleon takes refuge in Luti's hair, Onavita reveals

her to be the embodiment of an Old Soul, and the villagers accord
her reverence and respect.   Marooned in the bush till her father
comes for her, she shares the deprivation of the Long Dry that
brings hunger-crazed hyenas to the very gates of the stockade, and
participates in rites so old and sacred that sacrificial goats may
not be eaten in the teeth of starvation.   Ironically, the rain that
ends the drought brings flash floods that threaten their holiest relics
which Luti valiantly saves when Onavita is swept away.

332.   Wersba, Barbara.   THE DREAM WATCHER.   New York:
          Atheneum, 1968.   171pp.   Grades 7-9.

          Product of an alcoholic gray-flannel father and an ambitious,
harping mother, Albert Scully is bright but failing his freshman
classes.   He is a suicidal loner who prefers the effeminate pursuits
of literature, cooking, gardening, and fantasy.   Then he meets the
diminutive doyenne who has eschewed fame, fortune, and material-
ism to live shabbily but happily with the silent but eloquent companionship of the world's greatest literature.   Mrs. Woodfin, 80,
tells him of her privileged childhood, her illustrious career as an
actress, her fated but idyllic marriage, and her subsequent retirement to anonymity and seclusion in suburban New Jersey.   Then
she bolsters his self-esteem and encourages his individuality within
the framework of acceptable standards by showing him that history's
greatest achievers were also individualists, and gradually she ele-
vates him from despair.   Suddenly she succumbs to a heart attack,
and Albert learns that the exciting life she spun for him was a web
of lies, that in fact she was an unemployable, alcoholic spinster
school teacher from a poor family.   At first he feels betrayed until he realizes that far from being insignificant, Mrs. Woodfin had
something of great substance to offer him: his present and his future.

333.   Wiggin, Kate Douglas.   REBECCA OF SUNNYBROOK FARM.
          New York: Macmillan, 1903, 1962.   Illus. by Lawrence
          Beall Smith.   301pp.   Grades 6-8.

          Elderly aunts Mirandy and Jane offer a home and education
to their plodding eldest niece, but in her place, effervescent, imaginative, sensitive, idealistic, intelligent, and emotional Rebecca,
10, is sent to the "brick house" in Maine.   Irascible, penurious,
and sanctimonious Aunt Mirandy immediately tries hammering her
into her own rigid puritanical mold.   Of course Rebecca does not
fit, though she strives valiantly, and the spots where the spirit pops
out come into bruising conflict with the punitive, punctilious spinster.
Affectionate Aunt Jane tries to palliate her older sister's intractible
devotion to duty but has lived too long in her shadow to be effectual.
Saintly Rebecca suffers silently and wins the adulation of adults, the
adoration of her lesser peers, the envy of her rivals, and the accolades of academia over the ensuing seven years.   She even wins
the grudging approval of Aunt Mirandy who only posthumously makes
amends for her acerbity in life.

334.   Wilkinson, Brenda.   LUDELL.   New York: Harper and
        Row, 1975.   170pp.   Grades 6-8.

Growing up poor in the segregated South holds its share of
rewards for Ludell who has lived with the warm but strict grandmother she calls Mama since birth when her unwed mother ran off
to New York.   Mama does day work to support them, and there
isn't much left over for frills, but Ludell and her irrepressible
friends manage to share lighthearted fun, endure embarrassing moments, make occasional mischief, and take adversity in stride.
The narrative follows her from the fifth grade, with boys teasing
girls, through the seventh grade, with boys getting serious about
girls, under the watchful eye of Mama.   It describes her personal
nadirs and zeniths at school, on Sunday School picnics, picking cot-
ton, celebrating Christmas, hoping for a TV set, washing the laundry,
and just fooling around.   An encomium to the dignity and reality of
the life of blacks in the South at mid-century told in lyrical patois.

335.   Wilkinson, Brenda.   LUDELL AND WILLIE.   New York:
        Harper and Row, 1977.   181pp.   Grades 8-12.

To Ludell and her sweetheart, Willie, both 17, it is a fore-
gone conclusion that they will marry following high school graduation
when Willie will join the army to support them, but Mama, Ludell's
grandmother/guardian, is overprotective, belaboring her with her
mother's past transgressions (see 334) and men's age-old design on
women.   It is increasingly difficult to snatch time alone together or
even to attend school functions when Mama retires from her housekeeping job because of failing health and becomes a tenacious watchdog, growing increasingly querulous and punitive as senility en-
croaches.   Sometimes Ludell thinks aloud in the black idiom of the
South that she hates Mama, but eventually, when the deteriorating
old lady takes to her bed, opportunity to sneak trysts becomes more
abundant.   Suddenly Mama dies and Ludell's biological mother arrives to take her back to New York with her, even though neighbors
offer to make a home for her for the last few months of school.
Ludell rails against such injustice to no avail and transfers her resentment to Dessa whom she refuses to call Mother.   While she
mourns Mama, her grief in parting with Willie overshadows it.
They exchange poignant letters declaring their undying affection.

336.   Yep, Lawrence.   CHILD OF THE OWL.   New York:
        Harper and Row, 1977.   217pp.   Grades 7-9.

Casey, 12, has learned to be tough, streetwise, and brash-
ly American from following her father, Barney, a compulsive, debt-
ridden gambler, the length and breadth of California.   When he is
hospitalized as the result of a mugging, she is farmed out to her
maternal grandmother, Paw-Paw, who lives in penury in San Francisco's Chinatown.   The ambience is alien to her, and she is
scorned because she doesn't speak the language.   Gradually Paw-Paw

steeps the lonely outcast in the lore and traditions of her Chinese heritage, particularly of the valuable old owl charm she wears about her neck.   Barney continually promises her by postcard that he will come and deliver her from her purgatory but just as regularly reneges.   His sudden reappearance coupled with the theft of the owl charm and Paw-Paw's injury in the robbery injects an aura of mystery and intrigue followed by bitter disillusionment.   In the end, the owl charm must be sold to a museum to pay Paw-Paw's hospital bills and to rehabilitate Barney through Gamblers Anonymous, but Casey elects to stay with proud Paw-Paw and her newly won friends in Chinatown.

337.   Zindel, Paul.   THE PIGMAN.   New York: Harper and Row, 1968.   182pp.   Grades 7-10.

Alienated New Yorkers Lorraine Jensen and John Conlan, both 15, join in perpetrating malicious mischief in retaliation for their repressive home lives.   A prank telephone call to a lonely widower, Mr. Pignati, backfires when they discover he is tolerant, indulgent, trusting, and convivial, not at all the sort of adult against whom they are rebelling.   John and Lorraine take turns chronicling their ensuing friendship: the zoo excursions, the exotic refreshments, even the roller skate tag that leads to Mr. Pignati's heart attack.   While he is hospitalized, the two continue to meet at his home and one night throw a party for all their acquaintances.   It turns into a drunken brawl in which the house is nearly wrecked and Mr. Pignati's sentimental collection of piggy banks is smashed. The police and the broken old man, his trust betrayed, arrive simultaneously.   Mr. Pignati forgives them but dies before they can make restitution.   The contrite youths, sobered by the ungovernable turn of events, resolve to quit blaming their parents for their own escalating truancy and delinquency and to make something of their lives.

Note: Author and annotation number appear parenthetically following each profile. Numbers from 1 through 137 indicate preschool/primary level, 138 through 288 denote intermediate level, and 289 through 337 signify middle and high school level.

ADDIE AND THE KING OF HEARTS: Pragmatic grandmother explains to young teen some of the pitfalls on the road to romance from her own experience (Rock - 252).

ADOPTED JANE: Orphan girl chooses adoption by sedate widow over a home with ebullient farm family (Daringer - 192).

AFTER THE GOAT MAN: Children help defend friend's reclusive grandfather in his bid to fight eviction by progress and bureaucracy (Byars - 168).

ALL TOGETHER NOW: Shy girl blossoms in the love she both gives and receives from her grandparents and their small town neighbors (Bridgers - 293a).

AMAZING MEMORY OF HARVEY BEAN, THE: Thrifty and outgoing older couple teach lonely and distracted lad some amusing ways of keeping busy and happy (Cone - 185a).

AMAZING MISS LAURA, THE: To escape vexatious grandfather, teen becomes companion to capricious, tyrannical but dynamic old gentlewoman (Colman - 297).

ANASTASIA KRUPNIK: Bright, introspective only child feels ambivalent about a baby brother and a grandmother who lives entirely in the past (Lowry - 224a).

ANN AURELIA AND DOROTHY: Girl's loyalties are divided between her biological mother and her aging, caring foster mother (Carlson - 173).

ANNE OF GREEN GABLES: Effervescent orphan charms obdurate old spinster and her bachelor brother (Montgomery - 318).

ANNERTON PIT: Blind boy's supersensory gifts save grandfather from grim death at the hands of revolutionaries in abandoned mine (Dickinson - 193).

ANNIE AND THE OLD ONE: Dying Navajo grandmother sagaciously assuages granddaughter's anxiety over her impending death (Miles - 231).

ANTRIM'S ORANGE: Grandmother's wartime gift of scarce orange makes celebrity of boy and occasions nearly disastrous ceremony (Sunderlin - 266).

AT GRANDMOTHER'S HOUSE: Evocation in vivid color and text of pre-war Malayan life at grandmother's plantation (Lim - 77).

AUNT VINNIE'S INVASION: Elderly aunt, unaccustomed to children, improvises quickly and successfully when six nieces and nephews come to stay (Anckarsvard - 142).

AUNT VINNIE'S VICTORIOUS SIX: Beloved aging aunt rises to every occasion instigated by lively and unpredictable charges and hits the jackpot (Anckarsvard - 143).

BABOUSHKA AND THE THREE KINGS: In perennial pursuit of Wise Men and Christ Child, compassionate Russian peasant becomes harbinger of Christmas (Robbins - 96).

BABUSHKA AND THE PIG: Needing "something to do and someone to do it for, " Russian peasant adopts voracious porker (Trofimuk - 125).

BAG FULL OF NOTHING, A: Boy's imagination turns paper bag into escape device from patronizing dowager's cheek chucking (Williams - 132).

BAGEL BAKER OF MULLINER LANE, THE: Vivacious old baker and his enchanted bagels create a bagel-happy holiday (Blau - 21).

BARREL, THE: Orphan boy makes peace with contentious brother when he comes to live with swamp-wise granny (Wier - 281).

BATTLE OF ST. GEORGE WITHOUT, THE: Elderly characters play minor roles in helping children save historic church from vandalism (McNeill - 229).

BECKY AND THE BEAR: Plucky young Colonial feminist proves her valor when grandmother and menfolk are gone for the day (Van Woerkom - 127).

BEDKNOB AND BROOMSTICK: Prim English spinster's appearance is deceiving; she is a practicing and adventurous witch (Norton - 238).

BEE-MAN OF ORN, THE: Grizzled old apiarist metamorphoses into an eminently suitable entity (Stockton - 264).

BEFANA: Lonely old woman becomes spirit of Christmas to children as she makes eternal pilgrimage to Bethlehem (Rockwell - 98).

BENJIE: Bashful black boy finds his tongue when he goes in search of grandmother/guardian's lost earring (Lexau - 75).

BENJIE ON HIS OWN: When his grandmother is suddenly stricken ill, small, shy black boy reacts resolutely and resourcefully (Lexau - 76).

BEWARE OF THIS SHOP: Life with priggish, penurious old aunt is far more tolerable to teen than evil, insidious alternative (York - 286).

BIG ANTHONY AND THE MAGIC RING: Wistful dolt tampers with "Grandma Witch's" magic and attracts more infatuated females than he can handle (dePaola - 34d).

BIG BLUE ISLAND: Sullen city boy and cantankerous great-uncle/guardian are at loggerheads in confines of small island (Gage - 202).

BIG SNOW, THE: A bucolic bestiary of woodland animals sustained through severe winter by considerate elderly neighbors (Hader - 57).

BILLY BEDAMNED, LONG GONE BY: Is grandmother's colorful but crude ex-cowboy brother an inveterate liar or a gifted raconteur? (Beatty - 151).

BOBO, THE TROUBLEMAKER: Old man's wild predictions of natural disaster bring him the attention he craves but upset his neighbors (Schlein - 106).

BOXCAR CHILDREN, THE: Runaway orphans discover belatedly that grandfather is not the ogre they feared him to be (Warner - 277).

BOY OF TACHE, A: Indian boy takes on adult responsibility when grandfather is stricken with pneumonia in Canadian wilderness (Blades - 20).

BOY WHO WANTED A FAMILY, THE: Insecure orphan boy is adopted by an original, reassuring, single, aging author (Gordon - 205a).

BRAND-NEW UNCLE, A: Older couple comes out of retirement to adopt and rear yet another grandchild (Seredy - 256).

BROWNIES--HUSH!:   Timid elves befriend enfeebled old couple but are better at giving than receiving kindnesses (Adshead - 4).

BROWNIES--IT'S CHRISTMAS!:   Winsome sylphs trim tree for oldsters and get a surprise in return (Adshead - 5).

BROWNIES--THEY'RE MOVING!:   Old folks opt for labor saving new home and loyal sprites furnish service contract (Adshead - 6).

BUCKETFUL OF MOON, A: Elusive moon leads old woman a merry chase till she recaptures it in a bucket of water (Talbot - 117).

BURT DOW, DEEP-WATER MAN: Doughty old sea dog has a whale of an adventure a la Jonah (McCloskey - 83).

BUS RIDE: Girl strikes up friendship with elderly seat companion on night bus journey to grandfather's home (Jewell - 68).

BUTTERFLY CHASE, THE: Boy and grandfather are eminent, intrepid French huntsmen on butterfly safari (Trez - 123).

CARNIVAL AND KOPECK AND MORE ABOUT HANNAH: Immigrant grandparents contribute immeasurably to young Depression girl's zest for life (Skolsky - 261a).

CARRIE HEPPLE'S GARDEN: Bashful British children learn that eccentric old woman is not as forbidding as they suppose (Craft - 34a).

CARRIE'S GIFT: Young girl's guileless gift of implicit trust plucks at brusque old recluse's heartstrings (Holmes - 61a).

CARTOONIST, THE: Victim of strife among mother, grandfather and sister finds release in private retreat (Byars - 169).

CAY, THE: Elderly black man and blind boy surmount handicap and prejudice to survive at sea (Taylor - 269).

CERTAIN MAGIC, A: Determined girl unearths intimate details of beloved Jewish bachelor aunt's pre-war refugee period (Orgel - 239).

CHARLIE AND THE CHOCOLATE FACTORY: Eccentric old man devises retribution for intemperate children and recompense for deserving, virtuous boy (Dahl - 189).

CHARLIE AND THE GREAT GLASS ELEVATOR: Boy and languishing grandparents share spacy adventure and oldsters sample fountain of youth (Dahl - 190).

EDUCATION OF LITTLE TREE, THE: Orphan boy learns love and
respect for nature from proud, independent and nurturing
Cherokee grandparents (Carter - 294).

EGG TREE, THE: Grandmother's vivid traditional Easter egg designs inspire children to create old-fashioned egg tree (Milhous - 86).

EGYPT GAME, THE: Girl condescends to patient grandmother until she finds adventure and involvement in her new environment (Snyder - 262).

EMMA'S DILEMMA: Allergic grandmother upsets equability of girl
and her dog on moving into family apartment (LeRoy - 224).

ENEMY AT GREEN KNOWE, AN: Staunch English great-grandmother
and boys defend their bastion against malevolent and diabolical
enchantress (Boston - 159).

EUPHONIA AND THE FLOOD: Old extrovert collects foundering
animal friends and follows floodwaters to impromptu picnic
(Calhoun - 30).

EVY-IVY-OVER: Her grandmother's poverty, eccentricity and ESP
embarrass girl when classmate heckles her (Rodowsky - 253).

EYES OF THE AMARYLLIS, THE: Power and romance of the sea
are revealed to girl by her proud, loyal and independent
grandmother (Babbitt - 145).

FAMILY UNDER THE BRIDGE, THE: Debonair old French vagabond becomes protesting protector to respectable but destitute
family (Carlson - 174).

FARAWAY ISLAND, THE: Shy teen comes to stay with her charming, intelligent, independent, but occasionally forgetful grandmother (Corcoran - 298).

FATHER FIGURE: Imperial but permissive grandmother sends resentful teen and his kid brother to their estranged father
(Peck - 320).

FEMI AND OLD GRANDADDIE: In this African version of Rumpel-
stiltskin, old beggar helps peasant boy win hand of dusky
maiden (Robinson - 97).

FIGGS AND PHANTOMS: Surrealistic phantoms appear to reassure
grieving girl of her favorite uncle's happiness in the here-
after (Raskin - 246).

FIGURE OF SPEECH, A: Extraneous octogenarian chooses dignity
of death over institutionalization while granddaughter grieves
(Mazer - 316).

GIFT FOR A GIFT: Simple old man spends savings to honor beauty and initiates intricate chain of Oriental etiquette and romance (Rockwell - 99).

GIRL CALLED AL, A: Unique retiree reverses adolescent's negative image of herself (Greene - 209).

GLAD MAN, THE: Sister and brother learn that old people are not necessarily dull, irritable or vacillating (Gonzalez - 205).

GONE-AWAY LAKE: Cousins discover a forgotten summer colony and the insouciant, anachronistic old pair who inhabit it (Enright - 194).

GRAN AT COALGATE: Strait-laced English schoolgirl gets liberal education on vacation at grandmother's in Roaring Twenties (Cawley - 295).

GRAND PAPA AND ELLEN AROON: An encomium to Thomas Jefferson delivered animatedly by his favorite granddaughter (Monjo - 232).

GRANDFATHER AND I: Small boy and grandfather appreciate nature at leisure, oblivious to workaday hustle-bustle (Buckley - 26).

GRANDFATHER'S BROADAXE: Evocation of life on grandparents' nineteenth century farm, ordained by divinity, duty, devotion, and irrepressible humanity (Stephens - 327).

GRANDFATHER'S CAKE: Brace of boys and their pony run a gauntlet of gluttonous gothic villains to deliver cake to grandfather (McPhail - 83a).

GRANDMA DIDN'T WAVE BACK: Girl faces effects of senility in her beloved grandmother and accepts her eventual institutionalization (Blue - 154).

GRANDMA IS SOMEBODY SPECIAL: Preschool girl visits her employed, part-time student grandmother who also has traditional attributes (Goldman - 56).

GRANDMOTHER: Enchanting picture story of girl's visit to her grandmother's Victorian house and verdant garden (Baker - 12a).

GRANDMOTHER AND I: A study in laps (and grandmotherly intimacy) for the very young through small girl's eyes (Buckley - 27).

GRANDMOTHER CAT AND THE HERMIT: Old recluse teaches boy pacifism with nature and acceptance of change and impermanence (Coatsworth - 183).

GRANDMOTHER FOR THE ORPHELINES, A: French orphans' yearning for grandmotherly love is fulfilled in Christmas Eve miracle (Carlson - 174a).

GRANDMOTHER LUCY GOES ON A PICNIC: Girl and grandmother spend an idyllic summer day by the river (Wood - 133).

GRANDMOTHER LUCY IN HER GARDEN: Little girl and grandmother take springtime stroll through English garden (Wood - 134).

GRANDMOTHER OMA: Quintessential granny orchestrates large German household tactfully, prudently, energetically and humorously (Kleberger - 218).

GRANDMOTHER TOLD ME: Roles are reversed when granny imagines magical monsters lurking in odd places that small boy can't see (Wahl - 130).

GRANDMOTHER'S PICTURES: Lovingly drawn verbal and visual images of black boy's grandmother (Cornish - 34).

GRANDPA: Grandpa is clearly the more sympathetic and entertaining grandparent to this preschool girl (Borack - 22).

GRANDPA AND FRANK: Valiant girl "kidnaps" grandfather to spare his commitment to County Farm by disaffected uncle (Majerus - 227).

GRANDPA AND ME: Boy and grandfather spend idyllic summer at the lake (Gauch - 50).

GRANDPA--AND ME: Wishing to spare his own dignity and his family anguish, incipiently senile grandfather takes his own life (Tolan - 274).

GRANDPA AND ME TOGETHER: Little girl enthusiastically accompanies retired grandfather to his former place of business and to a baseball game (Goldman - 56a).

GRANDPA HAD A WINDMILL, GRANDMA HAD A CHURN: There is art and beauty in the simple appurtenances of girl's grandparents' 1940's Texas farm (Jackson - 64).

GRANDPA, ME AND OUR HOUSE IN THE TREE: Stroke curtails physical activity of erstwhile active grandfather but not his spirit of comradeship (Kirk - 70a).

GRANDPA'S FARM: Fantasy turns adversity to advantage in grandpa's tall tales of his 1930's farm (Flora - 46).

GRANDPA'S GHOST STORIES: Creepy creatures abound in adventuresome outing with grandfather as a boy on spooky inclement night (Flora - 47).

GRANDPA'S MARIA: Observant grandfather's hobby of candid pho-
tography captures girl's perplexing and amusing introduction
to life (Hellberg - 212a).

GRANNY AND THE DESPERADOES: Deceptively ingenuous granny
turns tables on bumbling ruffians (Parish - 90).

GRANNY AND THE INDIANS: Granny practices frontier diplomacy
on hostile Indians without ruffling her poke bonnet (Parish -
91).

GRANNY REARDUN: British boy, reared by grandparents, decides
not to follow his grandfather, a stonemason, in trade (Garner -
202a).

GRANNY, THE BABY AND THE BIG GRAY THING: Gullible granny
adopts an Indian papoose and a wolf to be its watchdog (Parish - 91a).

GRAY GHOSTS OF TAYLOR RIDGE, THE: Fearing loss of independence, old recluse denies blindness while haunted by
audible but unseen ghosts (Shura - 261).

GREAT-GRANDFATHER IN THE HONEY TREE: Divine Providence
humorously stocks the larder of pioneer couple (Swayne -
114).

GREAT-GRANDFATHER, THE BABY AND ME: Great-grandfather assuages preschooler's fears of the stranger who is his new
baby sister (Knotts - 71).

GREEN OF ME, THE: Young woman recalls influencing events and
people in her life, including grandparents and testing of first
love (Gauch - 306).

GROWING UP, GROWING OLDER: Depicts the developmental stages
of upper middle class male from birth to retirement (North
Shore Committee on the Older Adult - 89).

HALFWAY UP THE MOUNTAIN: Old blind woman monotonously
follows only recipe she knows but finds it effective for dressing out bandit (Gilchrist - 52).

HAMMERHEAD LIGHT, THE: Man and lighthouse grow old together
while their young friend learns bitterly the inevitability of
change (Thiele - 272).

HAPPY BIRTHDAY SAM: Grandpa's wonderful gift gives toddler boy
a big boost in life (Hutchins - 63).

HEIDI: Winsome Swiss miss tames curmudgeon (Spyri - 263).

HEY, THAT'S MY SOUL YOU'RE STOMPING ON: A variety of
aging couples and two young people help teen view her broken
home in perspective (Corcoran - 299).

HI, MRS. MALLORY!: Friendship of rural black girl and elderly
poor white woman transcends barrier of poverty until death
parts them (Thomas - 273a).

HILDILID'S NIGHT: Old woman is never awake to enjoy the day because of her exhausting battle with the night (Ryan - 101).

HOME WITH AUNT FLORRY, A: Dubious children learn to relax
and enjoy the unconventional lifestyle of their iconoclastic
aging aunt (Talbot - 267).

HOROWITZ AND MRS. WASHINGTON: With dogged determination,
aging black nurse rehabilitates and gentles antagonistic Jewish
stroke patient (Denker - 304a).

HOTHEADS: Stigmatized pre-teen comes to appreciate her immigrant, alcoholic grandfather (LeRoy - 314).

HOUSE OF DIES DREAR, THE: Family moves into historic house
of mystery and terror presided over by elderly black "demon"
(Hamilton - 211).

HOUSE OF WINGS, THE: Embittered, egocentric boy learns compassion from his eccentric, reclusive grandfather (Byars -
170).

HOUSE ON PENDLETON BLOCK, THE: Cultured woman plays
posthumous role in old mansion mystery (Waldron - 276).

HOUSE ON THE ROOF, THE: Inspired judge spares grandfather's
commemoration of Sukkoth for his grandchildren (Adler - 2).

HOUSE THAT SAILED AWAY, THE: Madcap family and fatuous
grandmother take unexpected South Seas cruise that literally
and gratuitously includes kitchen sink (Hutchins - 216).

HOUSE WITHOUT A CHRISTMAS TREE, THE: Sensible grandmother is arbiter between girl and intransigent father over
a Christmas symbol (Rock - 249).

HOW I HUNTED THE LITTLE FELLOWS: Fantasy leads boy to
succumb to the temptation of breaking a promise to his
grandmother (Zhitkov - 287a).

HUNDRED PENNY BOX, THE: Black centenarian and her great-
nephew share common empathetic bond against boy's unsentimental mother (Mathis - 228).

HUNTER COMES HOME, A: Alaskan Eskimo boy, seeking his own

identity, discovers compelling medicine in his grandfather's traditional ways (Turner - 274a).

I DON'T BELONG HERE: Her grandmother's unexpected symptoms of senility shock and dismay the teen who has come to live with her (French -201a).

I HATE RED ROVER: Girl and grandfather bolster one another's self-confidence over a playground game and false teeth, respectively (Lexau - 76a).

I HAVE FOUR NAMES FOR MY GRANDFATHER: Photographic portfolio of small boy's special relationship with his busy and active grandfather (Lasky - 72).

I LOVE GRAM: Black inner-city girl finds life empty when her beloved grandmother is hospitalized and welcomes her home exuberantly (Sonneborn - 112a).

I LOVE MY GRANDMA: Photo story recounts the after school activities of live-in grandmother and young girl of working parents (Palay - 89a).

I MET A TRAVELER: In contemporary Jerusalem, lonely product of jet-set divorce finds surrogate mother in aging Russian immigrant (Hoban - 309).

IF YOU LOVE ME, LET ME GO: Grandmother's senility and infirmity agonizingly exacerbates teen's family's personal emotional crises (Johnston - 311).

IN SEARCH OF COFFEE MOUNTAINS: Crisis-drilled resiliency enables girl and grandmother to become survivors of postwar German DP camps (Gottschalk - 206).

IN THE MORNING MIST: Boy and grandfather embark on a fishing expedition in the muted intimacy of a foggy farm morning (Lapp -71b).

IT COULD ALWAYS BE WORSE: Venerated rabbi demonstrates amusingly to large, indigent family that peace and comfort are relative (Zemach - 135).

IT'S SO NICE TO HAVE A WOLF AROUND THE HOUSE: Miscast wolf reforms when he becomes companion to old man and his pets (Allard - 10).

JANE HOPE: Yankee tomboy finds adventure and romance in grandparents' gracious ante-bellum Southern home (Gray - 307).

JERSEY SHORE, THE: Immigrant grandfather relates the hardships that caused him to leave England and the memories that make him retrospective (Mayne - 315c).

JOHN AND HIS THUMBS: Patient grandfather teaches maladroit boy to become a good gardener (Shortall - 109).

JOHNNY MAY: Unabashed pubescent tomboy makes adventure of living and maturing in grandparents' earthy Ozark home (Branscum - 162).

JOLLY WITCH, THE: Happy young witch, ostracized in her coven, trades places with cross old woman (Burch - 29).

JOURNEY CAKE, HO!: Corn meal cake escapes fate of The Gingerbread Man to bring good fortune to elderly couple and boy (Sawyer - 102).

JOURNEY WITH GRANDMOTHER, THE: Journey abroad with enterprising grandmother proves lucrative, exciting and enlightening for Swedish boy (Unnerstad - 275).

JULIA AND THE HAND OF GOD: Imaginative girl and pious, pragmatic grandmother are temperamentally unsuited to living under one roof (Cameron - 172).

JUMPING JACKDAWS! HERE COMES SIMON: Energetic English granny serves banquet of fun and excitement concocted from mundane ingredients (Roberts - 248).

KEEP STOMPIN' TILL THE MUSIC STOPS: Cousins plot to foil overbearing great-aunt's plan to transplant independent great-grandpa into alien environment (Pevsner - 242).

KEVIN'S GRANDMA: Contrasts lifestyles of two preschoolers' respectively orthodox and progressive contemporary grandmothers (Williams - 131).

KIDNAPPING MR. TUBBS: Teens taking AWOL nonagenarian on nostalgia trip develop empathy and appreciation for the aged (Schellie - 324).

KING OF KAZOO: A caprice of outrageous rhyme and egregious pun starring Plumber, Drummer and Old Cowpuncher (Peck - 241).

KNEE-BABY, THE: A knee-baby who still likes to be a lap-baby dreams of visiting with his grandmother (Jarrell - 65).

LADY WHO SAW THE GOOD SIDE OF EVERYTHING, THE: Optimistic old woman philosophically lands on her feet through chain of flood-fostered catastrophes (Tapio - 118).

LAVENDER-GREEN MAGIC: Historic fantasy embroils black children in seventeenth century witch hunt at site of grandparents' junkyard (Norton - 237).

LEROY AND THE OLD MAN: Black refugee from urban violence absorbs competent fisherman grandfather's integrity and fortitude (Butterworth - 293b).

LIGHTNING TIME, THE: Potent parable on wilderness preservation featuring a redoubtable grandmother, grandson and magical consortium (Maguire - 315b).

LIKELY PLACE, A: Deprecatory parents erode boy's self-confidence until old immigrant and new baby sitter bolster it (Fox - 201).

LILITH SUMMER, THE: Competent elderly baby sitter and callow youthful "lady-sitter" both benefit from sharing in one another's care (Irwin - 216a).

LINNETS AND VALERIANS: Edwardian children choose rigorous life with great-uncle over suppressive existence with grandmother (Goudge - 207).

LITTLE AT A TIME, A: Impatient, inquisitive boy and dignified, erudite grandfather derive enjoyment and edification from leisurely walk to museum (Adler - 3).

LITTLE OLD MAN WHO COOKED AND CLEANED, THE: Old man gets crash course in housekeeping when his wife goes out for the day (Black - 19).

LITTLE OLD MRS. PEPPERPOT: Old woman finds herself in variety of predicaments when she shrinks to minuscule size (Proysen - 245).

LITTLE OLD WOMAN WHO USED HER HEAD AND OTHER STORIES, THE: Foolish old woman provides amusement at the expense of the aging (Sewell - 258).

LITTLE TIM AND THE BRAVE SEA CAPTAIN: Boy realizes dream of going to sea, but he and captain almost go down with the ship (Ardizzone - 12).

LITTLE WOMAN WANTED NOISE, THE: Country proves too quiet for aging city woman who seeks to enliven her new farm (Teal - 120).

LONER, THE: Orphan boy meets exacting standards to win approbation of resolute, autocratic old ranch woman (Wier - 282).

LONG JOURNEY, THE: Sheltered teen confronts terrors of wilderness and civilization to summon aid for her blind grandfather (Corcoran - 187).

LONG SECRET, THE: Sheltered girl living with patrician grandmother learns to become more assertive with help of friend
(Fitzhugh - 200).

LOST FARM, THE: Granny and boy rely on ingenuity when they
and their farm are reduced to Lilliputian proportions (Curry - 188).

LUCKY STONE, THE: Young black girl delights in listening to her
great-grandmother's stories of the Old South (Clifton - 180a).

LUDELL: Pert, Southern black girl has known no other mother but
her industrious, devout grandmother/guardian (Wilkinson -
334).

LUDELL AND WILLIE: Teenage romance meets impediments as
black grandmother/guardian loses rationality and eventually
dies (Wilkinson - 335).

MAD MARTIN: Boy and grandfather exist in companionable taciturnity till fractured hip separates and changes them (Windsor - 284).

MAGDALENA: Puerto Rican grandmother mistrusts frail, eccentric
old lady who exerts "American influence" over her granddaughter (Shotwell - 260).

MAGIC AND THE NIGHT RIVER: Chinese grandfather's wisdom
and experience outweigh mere brawn and dexterity in catching
fish (Bunting - 28).

MAGIC GRANDFATHER, THE: Only passive TV addict, whose
negligence caused the predicament, can rescue his necro-
mantic grandfather (Williams - 283a).

MANDY'S GRANDMOTHER: Girl and grandmother learn to respect
one another for what each is, not for what the other expects
her to be (Skorpen - 110).

MARCO MOONLIGHT: Boy leads privileged life with grandparents
till stranger and long-lost twin surface to threaten his very
being (Bulla - 166).

MARRA'S WORLD: When a new friend draws her out of her shell
of neglect, girl's grandmother loses her hatred and contempt
of her (Coatsworth - 184).

MARY JO'S GRANDMOTHER: Cool-headed black kindergartener
braves deep rural snow to get help when grandmother suffers
fracture (Udry - 126).

MATT'S GRANDFATHER: Grandfather in nursing home convinces

grandson that the middle-aged are too self-serious and patronizing (Lundgren - 80).

MIA, GRANDMA AND THE GENIE: Grandmother's courtesy to inanimate objects pays off when thieves try to steal her personal genie (Jeschke - 67).

MIDDLE MOFFAT, THE: Young girl is self-appointed guardian
angel of town's celebrated centenarian (Estes - 196).

MILDRED MURPHY, HOW DOES YOUR GARDEN GROW?: In her
desperation, cast-off grandmother receives support and sympathy of a lonesome girl (Green - 208).

MILLER'S BOY, THE: Unhappy at being apprenticed to grandfather,
boy is torn between friendship and family fealty when old
man dies (Willard - 283).

MILLIONS OF CATS: A lonely old couple's search for a pet cat is
prodigally rewarded (Ga'g - 49).

MINNOW LEADS TO TREASURE, THE: Boys spend adventurous
summer hoping to restore family fortune to elderly aunt and
afflicted grandfather (Pearce - 240).

MISS PICKERELL GOES TO MARS: Sporting spinster accidentally
becomes first woman to explore Mars (MacGregor - 226).

MISS TESSIE TATE: Rugged Medieval individualist skates her way
anachronistically to home economic fame and fortune (Berg -
17).

MR. MCFADDEN'S HALLOWE'EN: Determined girl doggedly tames
dour old Scot who surprises himself and others by embracing
altruism (Godden - 203).

MISTER PENNY: Indolent, egocentric animals cause humble, industrious old man grief until they redeem themselves (Ets -
41).

MISTER PENNY'S CIRCUS: Old man assimilates pair of runaway
circus animals into his "family" to their mutual benefit (Ets -
43).

MISTER PENNY'S RACE HORSE: Lame horse saves old man and
his recalcitrant menagerie from disgrace at the fair (Ets -
42).

MR. PLUM AND THE LITTLE GREEN TREE: Humble old cobbler
fights city hall to save a tree (Gilbert - 51).

MR. SIMKIN'S GRANDMA: Comedy of chairs makes sport of the
elderly in general and of stereotypical grandparents in particular (Allen - 10a).

MISTY AND ME: Pre-teen sacrifices her dream of having a puppy because lonely incapacitated elderly lady needs its companionship more (Girion - 202e).

MITTEN, THE: Grandfather's lost mitten becomes refuge to absurd agglomeration of animals (Tresselt - 121).

MITZVAH IS SOMETHING SPECIAL, A: Two Jewish grandmothers of polaric personality have one thing in common: their adoring granddaughter (Eisenberg - 40).

MONSTER NIGHT AT GRANDMA'S HOUSE: Boy's imagination runs wild on a night in his grandmother's Victorian house (Peck - 92).

MORGAN FOR MELINDA, A: Aging author bequeathes to timid girl her enthusiasm for horses and the encouragement to write (Gates - 202c).

MOTHER RASPBERRY: Resourceful French peasant woman barters her special jam for a favor from furry friends (Careme - 32).

MOTHER TREE, THE: Summer's interlude at grandparents' 1900's farm gives young girl respite from drudgery and anxiety of being homemaker (Whitehead - 280).

MRS. BEGGS AND THE WIZARD: Nightmare creatures stalk the boarding house when the widowed landlady rents to a necromancer (Mayer - 82).

MRS. FLANNAGAN'S TRUMPET: British boy's formidable deaf grandmother reveals a startling depth of character and spirit in mystery adventure (Cookson - 297a).

MRS. PIGGLE-WIGGLE: This sprightly and original widow has a cure for every behavioral aberration known to childhood (MacDonald - 225).

MY AUNT ROSIE: Boy comes to appreciate smarmy old aunt when he contemplates life without her (Hoff - 60).

MY BROTHER STEVIE: Vituperative grandmother cannot control unruly inner-city boy until his sister gets outside help (Clymer - 182).

MY GRANDPA DIED TODAY: Boy doesn't understand grandfather's explanation of his impending death till he experiences the loss (Fassler - 45).

MY GRANDPA IS A PIRATE: Boy and grandfather embark on fantasy adventure against Arabian corsairs (Loof - 78).

MY GRANDSON LEW: Small boy suddenly articulates recollections of his very memorable and long-deceased grandfather (Zolotow - 136).

MY GREAT-GRANDFATHER AND I: A literary confection of rhyme, reason, and story concocted by German great-grandfather and grandson (Kruss - 221).

MY ISLAND GRANDMA: Rugged, resourceful and versatile grandmother shares the wonders of nature with granddaughter on their vacation island (Lasky - 72a).

MY NOAH'S ARK: Nonagenarian reminisces over hand-crafted toy ark from her childhood (Goffstein - 55).

MYSTERY OF SEBASTIAN ISLAND: Teenage boy and girl help solve harrowing harassment of old lobsterman (Clark - 179).

NANA UPSTAIRS AND NANA DOWNSTAIRS: Preschooler loves both grandmother and bedridden great-grandmother and experiences loss when latter dies (dePaola - 35).

NAVAHO SISTER: Timid Indian girl leaves grandmother's reservation for boarding school and fortuitously finds ready-made family for both of them (Lampman - 222).

NEVER IS A LONG, LONG TIME: Close-knit family is saddened by dog's death and worried by grandmother's sudden illness (Cate - 176).

NINE HUNDRED BUCKETS OF PAINT: Old woman and her animal family play musical houses until they find a model that suits them all (Becker - 16).

NINO: His grandfather is the loom for Italian boy's life tapestry while waiting to join his father in America (Angelo - 144).

NO PLACE FOR MITTY: Girl loves life with convivial grandparents, and when forced to live elsewhere, longs to return (Young - 287).

NO TRESPASSING: Boys outwit hostile black neighborhood crone to retrieve their ball from her yard (Prather - 95).

NONNA: Boy relates events following grandmother's death and how grief is assuaged by keeping her memory alive (Bartoli - 15).

NOW IS NOT TOO LATE: Tempestuous girl learns to exercise discretion and handle conflicting emotions through grandmother's calming guidance (Holland - 214a).

ODD GIRL OUT: Gawky Scottish teen finds refuge in her friendship with an elderly blind musician when her mother remarries (Lingard - 315a).

OLD MAN AND THE ASTRONAUTS, THE: Old Oceanian fears space-age tampering will destroy the age-old balance of nature (Tabrah - 115).

OLD MAN AND THE MULE, THE: Disaffected old codger and ornery mule gratify themselves by tormenting one another (Snyder - 112).

OLD MAN AND THE TIGER, THE: Old Bengalese befriends tiger and is almost devoured for his beneficence (Tresselt - 122).

OLD MAN ON OUR BLOCK, THE: Lonely retiree is befriended by neighborhood children in wordless picture story (Snyder - 111).

OLD MAN RIDDLE: Sprightly mountain man whimsically leads neighbors to impromptu barn dance (Memling - 84).

OLD MAN UP A TREE: A disparate agglomeration of individuals gathers to guess why old man is climbing a tree (Adamson - 1).

OLD MAN WHICKUTT'S DONKEY: When no one can agree on how to load a donkey, old man employs his singular ingenuity (Calhoun - 31).

OLD NURSE'S STOCKING BASKET, THE: Perennial nanny regales charges with tales of a demographic distribution of former wards right back to the Flood (Farjeon - 198).

OLD ONE-TOE: French children defend valiant fox from human predator while retaining the aging Nimrod's amity (Stockton - 265).

OLD PIPES AND THE DRYAD: Mythical creature graces worthy old man and his failing mother with partial immortality (Stockton - 265).

OLD RAMON: Wise old Mexican-American shepherd, intimate with animals and nature, steeps boy in the practice and lore of sheep ranching (Schaefer - 255a).

OLD WITCH'S PARTY, THE: Children mistake wicked witch for benevolent grandmother and learn to associate "old" with "mean" (DeLage - 34c).

OLD WOMAN AND THE PEDLAR, THE: Cavalier male chauvinist peddler shamelessly dupes magnanimous and guileless spinster into marriage (Taylor - 119).

PICKLE CREATURE: Grandmother is unshaken when boy brings home a warty green creature instead of the pickle she sent him for (Pinkwater - 92a).

PIGMAN, THE: Rebellious teens' practical joke on lonely widower leads to friendship, tragedy and sudden maturity (Zindel - 337).

PLEASE DON'T EAT MY CABIN: Boy solves problem of voracious porcupines at artist grandmother's camp compound (Merrill - 85).

PRISONERS IN THE SNOW: Austrian children and grandfather save livestock and injured aviator in appalling avalanche (Catherall - 177).

PRIVATE MATTER, A: Affable retiree becomes surrogate father to lonely girl of divorced parents until his wife's sudden death (Ewing - 197).

PUSHCART WAR, THE: Tough teamsters are toppled by ragtag cadre of aging hucksters over control of city streets (Merrill - 230).

QUEEN OF HEARTS: Girl becomes lackey to blunt and truculent grandmother who refuses to modify her lifestyle after disabling stroke (Cleaver - 180).

QUESTION OF TIME, A: Elderly apparition gives girl entree to and involvement in life and history of her new hometown (Anastasio - 141).

RABBI AND THE TWENTY-NINE WITCHES, THE: Venerable and resourceful rabbi cleverly exorcises bewitchers of the full moon (Hirsh - 59).

RACCOONS ARE FOR LOVING: Inner city black girl duplicates rural grandmother's girlhood experience (Bourne - 23).

REBECCA OF SUNNYBROOK FARM: Saintly turn-of-century girl rises above well-meaning elderly aunt's caustic character-building regimen (Wiggin - 333).

REMOVE PROTECTIVE COATING A LITTLE AT A TIME: Troubled male teen and aging female vagrant derive reciprocal security from unlikely comradeship (Donovan - 305).

RETURN TO GONE-AWAY: Congenial elderly recluses get new neighbors when young family restores old summer residence (Enright - 195).

REUBELLA AND THE OLD FOCUS HOME: Innovative elders establish bold new alternative to conventional retirement home to enhance their active lives (Newton - 319).

REX: Squat but sympathetic retiree befriends runaway preschooler and accompanies him back home (Sharmat - 108).

RIVER WITCHES, THE: Nineteenth century boy is apprenticed to deceptively sinister old witch in this allegorical farce (Shecter - 258a).

ROBBERS, THE: His father's remarriage disrupts British boy's happy and serene life with his grandmother (Bawden - 148a).

ROCKING CHAIR REBELLION, THE: Teen becomes involved in improving life of institutionalized elderly and exploring desegregation of the active aging (Clifford - 296).

ROLLER SKATES: Enlightened spinsters give untrammeled Gay Nineties girl latitude to expand her experiences and acquaintances (Sawyer - 255).

RUNNING WILD: Heedless of grandfather's warning, Spanish boy allows pups to go wild and be mistaken for marauding wolves (Griffiths - 210).

SECRET OF THE ANDES: Incan boy chooses life of asceticism, following in the footsteps of his wise and sacred old mentor and guardian (Clark - 178).

79 SQUARES, THE: Aged, dying ex-felon teaches delinquent boy to value the quest for truth and cognizance above immediate gratification (Bosse - 292a).

SHADOW ON THE HILLS, THE: Humorous and bittersweet story of boy growing up in Depression Australia and his friendship with disenfranchised old man (Thiele - 273).

SHADOW ON THE WATER: Overbearing, aristocratic grandmother persuades children's mother to leave her husband during the Depression (Barnwell - 289).

SHAMAN'S LAST RAID, THE: Modern Apache twins learn that Indians can grow up to be anything they wish to be when their anachronistic ancestor visits (Baker - 146).

SHARED ROOM, THE: Misguided grandmother attempts to shield girl from her mother's psychosis and refuses to acknowledge her recovery (Potter - 244a).

SHELTER FROM THE WIND: Runaway girl finds shelter with elderly female recluse who inculcates in her independence and maturity (Bauer - 291).

SHEPHERD, THE: Humble, aging shepherd follows star to the scene of the Nativity in this picture book (Aichinger - 7).

SHERWOOD RING, THE: Fantasy, romance, intrigue, and history envelop young woman who comes to live with cantankerous great-uncle (Pope - 322).

SHUTTERED WINDOWS: Orphaned Northern black teen finds life with great-grandmother in the segregated South both compelling and repugnant (Means - 317).

SHY STEGOSAURUS OF INDIAN SPRINGS, THE: Atavistic animal restores honor to Indian boy's proud and independent medicine man grandfather (Lampman - 223).

SILVER COACH, THE: Grandmother's guidance transforms self-pitying child of broken home into responsible big sister and cooperative daughter (Adler - 137a).

SIR TOBY JINGLE'S BEASTLY JOURNEY: Aging knight single-mindedly outwits whole bestiary of mythical monsters infesting Medieval forest (Tripp - 124).

SOMEONE SLIGHTLY DIFFERENT: Adolescent's nonconformist grandmother demonstrates that it is not a handicap to be slightly idiosyncratic (Mearian - 229a).

SONG OF THE TREES: Black grandmother and courageous family win skirmish in property rights war in Depression South (Taylor - 268).

SPECIAL FRIENDS: School-aged girl and elderly neighbor woman share many intimate moments of mutual pleasure and benefit (Berger - 17a).

SPECIAL TRADE, A: Care and devotion come full circle as girl ministers to incapacitated old neighbor who nurtured her as a baby (Wittman - 132a).

STAR MOTHER'S YOUNGEST CHILD: Star child brings gift of artless love and wonder to disenfranchised old woman in Christmas fantasy (Moeri - 87).

STOLEN TELESM, THE: With aid of winged horse and stone talisman, British children vanquish forces of evil convoked by vile old witch (Baxter - 150).

STONE OF TERROR: Boy and grandfather suspensefully seek to abolish the hysteria of witchcraft in superstitious Cromwellian era (Greaves - 308).

STONES, THE: Malicious mischief causes anguish for hapless old man suspected by unruly boys of being a Nazi spy (Hickman - 214).

STOPPING PLACE, THE: Philosophical elderly woman helps city girl adjust to life in the hinterlands (Dahlstedt - 191).

STORIES MY GRANDFATHER SHOULD HAVE TOLD ME: Stories culled from famous authors running the gamut of Jewish family life from Europe to America to Israel (Brodie - 165).

STORY GRANDMOTHER TOLD, THE: Black girl and grandmother share tale of two cats (Alexander - 9).

STRANGER AT GREEN KNOWE, A: Two uprooted individuals, beast and boy, take refuge at gracious elderly English woman's venerable estate (Boston - 158).

STREGA NONA: Disobedient oaf lets "Grandma Witch's" magical pasta pot run amok in Italian version of The Little Pot That Would Not Stop Boiling (dePaola - 37).

SUMMER LIGHTNING: Indigent old swamp man teaches restless, truant boy a curriculum of survival, simplicity, and devotion (Richards - 323).

SUMMER OF THE STALLION: Her beloved grandfather's brutal treatment of a wild stallion causes girl to reassess her idolatry (Hanson - 211a).

SURPRISE ISLAND: Boxcar Children explore vacation island and reunite grandfather with another lost relative (Warner - 278).

SWALLOW'S SONG, THE: While caring for senile grandmother, teen becomes involved with degenerate and hedonistic boy (Johnston - 310).

TAILOR OF GLOUCESTER, THE: Old tailor's benevolence to mice bears fruit in sartorial equivalent of The Elves and the Shoemaker (Potter - 94).

TAKE TARTS AS TARTS IS PASSING: A literal young man and his imaginative brother interpret differently advice given them by old woman (Clymer - 33).

TALES OF A CHINESE GRANDMOTHER: Traditional, patrician Chinese grandmother holds court for extended family and tells of ancient lore (Carpenter - 175).

TELL ME A MITZI: Two of these three urban family stories involve pair of preschoolers and grandmother (Segal - 107).

THANK YOU, JACKIE ROBINSON: Elderly black shares lonely boy's enthusiasm for baseball but suffers fatal heart attack (Cohen - 185).

THANKSGIVING TREASURE, THE: Determined girl makes friends with mulish misanthrope and is rewarded in his will (Rock - 250).

THAT JUD!: Taciturn but compassionate old guardian never loses faith in the probity of his infrequently feckless boy (Bragdon - 161).

THEN AGAIN, MAYBE I WON'T: Adolescent's anxieties include his own sexuality and his surgically mute grandmother's disfranchisement (Blume - 292).

THEY WERE STRONG AND GOOD: True account of author/illustrator's proud and spirited forebears (Lawson - 73).

THIS IS A RECORDING: Standoffish young teen proves her mettle and makes friends with her stately grandmother (Corcoran - 300).

THOUSAND PAILS OF WATER, A: Oriental boy and grandfather try to save beached whale but find that it takes more than four hands (Roy - 100).

THREE BUCKETS OF DAYLIGHT: Superstition seasons boy's existence at grandparents' home in the hills and "hollers" (Branscum - 163).

THREE STALKS OF CORN: Grandmother shares with granddaughter the reverence for corn in their Mexican-American culture (Politi - 93).

THROUGH GRANDPA'S EYES: Blind grandfather trains preschool boy to appreciate his "handicapable" world by the use of his other senses (MacLachlan - 80a).

THROWING SHADOWS: Bored boy and elderly Hungarian refugee woman pair up to make oral history of nursing home residents' reminiscences (Konigsburg - 220a).

TIMOTHY AND GRAMPS: Diffident English schoolboy gains acceptance of classmates by sharing with them his grandfather's adventures (Brooks - 23a).

TIT FOR TAT: Poor but altruistic old woman and wealthy old skinflint are repaid in kind (Van Woerkom - 128).

TOBY, GRANNY AND GEORGE: Enterprising mountain girl solves murder mystery and learns self-reliance from granny (Branscum - 164).

TOLIVER'S SECRET: Timid Revolutionary girl gains courage crossing enemy lines as emissary for her grandfather (Brady - 160).

TOM FOBBLE'S DAY: Blacksmith grandfather bequeathes to British boy a sled of his own craftsmanship and the symbols of family tradition (Garner - 202b).

TOUGH CHAUNCEY: Broken home and brutal, hypocritical grandparents exacerbate boy's delinquency (Smith - 326).

TOUGH TIFFANY: Heir to her thrifty grandmother's iron will tempered by compassion, poor black girl becomes a seasoned survivor (Hurmence - 215a).

TRANSPORT 7-41-R: A bizarre promise to an old man leads to healing of German refugee girl's emotional scars (Degens - 304).

TRAVELING WITH OMA: Dashing and original German granny embarks on vacation lark with adoring grandchildren (Kleberger - 219).

TREAD SOFTLY: This girl's grandparents might have said, "O, what a tangled web we weave, when first we practise to deceive" (Gerson - 202d).

TREASURE OF ALPHEUS WINTERBORN, THE: Teen and aging librarian pursue elusive treasure and become quarries of unscrupled heir (Bellairs - 153).

TREASURE OF GREEN KNOWE: Straitened British gentlewoman's tales of historic estate and bygone skulduggery lead great-grandson to long-lost treasure (Boston - 157).

TROUBLE ON TREAT STREET: Black boy's grandmother/guardian and Chicano boy's mother jeopardize their tenuous friendship through unfounded suspicions (Alexander - 138).

TWO HUNDRED RABBITS: To aid ambitious feudal boy, benign crone conjures a covey of comical conies to become minions of the king (Anderson - 11).

TWO OF THEM, THE: Simple and moving narrative of deep and abiding love between girl and grandfather; an anthem of birth, life and death (Aliki - 9a).

TWO PIANO TUNERS: Girl tries to convince grandfather that she is a tone off the old chord in emulation of him (Goffstein - 204).

TWO THAT WERE TOUGH: Two tough old birds grow old together in unfettered freedom until the human one's wings are clipped (Burch - 167).

TWO UNCLES OF PABLO, THE: Mexican boy changes lives of his two aging uncles, one wealthy but morose, the other gay but indolent (Behn - 152).

ULTRA-VIOLET CATASTROPHE!: Imaginative girl and adventurous great-uncle have much in common that is abhorrent to
some adults (Mahy - 81).

UNEXPECTED GRANDCHILDREN, THE: Fastidious retirees are
astonishingly disappointed when "unexpected grandchildren"
fail to appear (Flory - 48).

UNLEAVING: Teen ponders life, death, and love, reaching the same
conclusion as her warm, responsive, recently deceased grandmother (Walsh - 330).

UP A ROAD SLOWLY: Girl is initially resentful of living with exacting aging aunt and dilettante uncle at her mother's death
(Hunt - 215).

VIOLIN, THE: Battered violin forges friendship between accomplished elderly man and musically aspiring boy (Allen - 140).

WALKING AWAY: Adolescent experiences remorse when her loyalty
is divided between beloved rustic grandfather, who dies, and
lofty urban chum (Winthrop - 285).

WALKS FAR WOMAN: Indomitable Amerind feminist and survivor
tells of tribal justice and white man's injustice in her long,
turbulent life (Stuart - 329).

WATCH OUT FOR THE CHICKEN FEET IN YOUR SOUP: Grandma's
Italian cooking wins boy's friend's heart (dePaola - 38).

WHEN GRANDFATHER JOURNEYS INTO WINTER: Indian grandfather's legacy to boy includes appreciation of valor, self-
reliance, endeavor and the gift of life (Strete - 265a).

WHEN GRANDPA WORE KNICKERS: Nostalgic, amusing, thought-
provoking evocation of dress, home, leisure, travel and
classroom life of 1930's (Brown - 24).

WHERE'S GOMER?: Alas! Noah's favorite grandson misses the
boat (Farber - 44).

WHISTLING WHIRLIGIG, THE: A ghost and a salubrious aging
teacher help boy adjust to broken home and boarding school
(Shecter - 259).

WHY DID HE DIE?: Mother and son probe, in gentle verse, death
of a playmate's grandfather (Harris - 58).

WILD CATS OF ROME, THE: Brain-damaged old artisan provides
salvation and becomes hero to thirsty Italian felines (Cooper -
186).

WILDERNESS HAS EARS, THE: White girl learns the pride and power of matriarchal African diviner and of ancient Angolan traditions (Wellman - 331).

WILLIAM'S DOLL: Sage grandmother understands and endorses boy's need for a doll to father (Zolotow - 137).

WINDS OF TIME, THE: Runaway girl is sequestered from evil uncle in faded opulence by cultured elderly recluses (Corcoran - 301).

WISE OLD MAN OF THE MOUNTAIN, THE: Old guru teaches poor farmer and family humility and acceptance of their overcrowded condition (Dillon - 39).

WITCH HERSELF, THE: Girl's mother, in thrall of evil old witch, nearly perishes in conflagration that exorcises the hag (Naylor - 236).

WITCH OF THE CUMBERLANDS: Gentle, enigmatic but indomitable old herbalist is impelling force of suspenseful Appalachian mystery (Stephens - 328).

WITCH WATER: Terrified girls cannot convince parents of their vulnerability to demoniacal witch and her bestial consorts (Naylor - 235).

WITCH'S DAUGHTER, THE: Elderly relative rears girl in unnatural seclusion imposed by her dishonest employer (Bawden - 149).

WITCH'S SISTER: Suggestible, imaginative girls suspect one's sister of being in league with fiendish old witch (Naylor - 234).

WIZARD IN THE TREE, THE: Impotent old wizard and intrepid orphan girl are intended victims of the corruption they quixotically oppose (Alexander - 139).

WONDERFUL TREE, THE: Boy's grandfather explains the seasons and mysteries of nature, exemplified by pear tree and apple seed (Holl - 61).

YELLOW HOUSE MYSTERY, THE: Boxcar Children locate and rehabilitate elderly recluse in Maine wilderness (Warner - 279).

YELLOW POM-POM HAT, THE: Hated hat that grandmother knitted won't stay lost till girl's father finds a better use for it (Kaye - 69).

AUTHOR/SUBJECT INDEX
TO BIBLIOGRAPHY

II. MULTIMEDIA SECTION FOR
CHILDREN AND YOUNG ADULTS*

*Production or publication dates are given when available, but few
pre-date 1970. Annotations are also provided when available and
suggested age levels when determinable. All audiovisual materials
are distributed by the producer unless otherwise noted.

FILMSTRIPS AND SLIDES*

Aging--Always an Agony. Learning and Information, 1973. 1 SFS,
     color. Intermediate-Adult.

     Asks if aging in America and elsewhere must be accompanied
by the suffering of so many old people. Points out that aging is
part of a natural process and is not in itself an illness. Discusses
the problems of the aging brought on by an attempt to deny acceptance
of the fact that we will all grow old. (From the series The Ways of
Our World--Programs on Six Contemporary Problems.)

Aging Families. Butterick Fashion Marketing Co. , 1976. 2 SFS,
     color. Jr. High-High school.

     Explores the special problems of the aged in our society.
Reviews the changes family life has undergone and the reasons for
these changes. Examines contemporary trends in family life. From
A Family Life, Part 3--The Family in Transition.

America's Aged: The Forgotten Many. Current Affairs. 1 SFS,
     color. High school.

     In modern American society, old age has more and more
often come to mean segregation, neglect, and even exploitation.
This filmstrip examines how and why that has been the case--and
whether it will continue to be. Attention is given to social attitudes,
health and money problems of the aged, what the old have to offer
society, and their changing outlook.

Annie and the Old One. Miller-Brody. 2 SFS, color. Intermediate.

     Sensitive Navaho girl tries to forestall her wise and beloved
grandmother's inevitable passing in this poignant story set against
traditional and contemporary Indian life.

Care of the Aged and Coping with Death. Coronet, 1976. 2 SFS,
     color. Intermediate-High school.

---

*Sound filmstrips are accompanied by cassette tapes unless other-
wise noted.

Crisis strikes. What then? These two case studies of problems in family living from the Families in Crisis Series offer alternatives and open up questions. Documentary-style interviews with real life families probe the effects of crisis on careers and family relationships, as well as the institutions and societal attitudes involved.

Change and Loss--The Challenges of Aging. Trainex, 1976. 1 SFS, color. High school.

Presents the psychological effects of aging and defines normal reactions to change in work role, loss of occupational identity, change in kinship role, loss of social contacts, change in environment and loss of familiar surroundings. Explains how these changes and losses affect the individual's ability to fill basic human needs for emotional warmth, belonging, independence, dignity and self-esteem.

The Changes of Old Age. Eye Gate House, 1975. 1 SFS, color. Jr. High-High school.

From the Aging Series of four filmstrips which discuss the changes a person experiences from childhood through old age.

Coping with Death. (See Care of the Aged and Coping with Death.)

Death: A Natural Part of Living. Marshfilm. 1 SFS, teacher's guide. Intermediate-Jr. High.

An interesting and factual look at death as a natural part of the life cycle of all living organisms, from man to the smallest single-celled animal.

Death: A Part of Life. Guidance Associates. 2 SFS, discussion guide. Intermediate.

Describes ways in which children and adults behave when a loved one dies; considers the many attitudes and emotions death may stimulate; reviews aspects of the traditional funeral, cremation, mourning practices and their purpose.

Don't Count Your Chicks. Weston Woods. 1 SFS, color. Primary.

Foolish old woman dreams prematurely of fame and fortune on her way to market with a basket of eggs balanced precariously on her head.

The Eight Stages of Human Life: Adolescence to Old Age. Parts
     VII and VIII. Human Relations Media. 2 SFS or sound
     slides. High school.

     Part VII--The Mature Adult scrutinizes the physical changes
that men and women confront during their middle years and how
they cope with them. Describes the mid-life crisis, the empty nest
syndrome, menopause, the self-concept and the heightened creativity
and productiveness of middle age. Part VIII--Old Age explodes the
myths and stereotypes of old age and shows how many old people
lead rich, productive lives. Reviews the evidence of physical decline and the nature of the aging process. Looks at many of the
concerns of the old, such as fears about illness, dependency, coping
with loss of loved ones, dealing with physical and mental disabilities,
desire to leave a legacy, and attitudes toward death. Describes the
ingredients of successful aging.

The Elderly: A Forgotten Minority. Teleketics. Dist. by Social
     Studies School Service. 2 SFS, color. Jr. High-Adult.

     This set of filmstrips (available separately from the producer--
see entries under individual titles) focuses upon the plight of the
elderly in American society from two different vantage points. Walter and Sally shows the lifestyle of an elderly couple living in a
large city on their Social Security income. It reflects their financial
problems as well as their enduring love for one another and the way
in which they care for each other. The Gray Panthers: Wrinkled
Radicals shows the elderly as activists, challenging the role they
are expected to play in society. A teacher's guide suggests ways
in which the filmstrips can be used as discussion starters.

The Ending. Social Studies School Service. 1 SFS, color. High
     school.

     A dramatic portrayal of a teenager's encounter with age and
the certainty of death. Visuals show not only the incident described
by the narration, but also examples of what happens to the aged and
dying in our society. The narration reflects the apprehensions and
misunderstandings of young people about the elderly. Teacher's
guide offers ideas for the use of the filmstrip, complete script, and
discussion suggestions.

Families in Crisis--Care of the Aged. Coronet, 1976. 1 SFS,
     color. Intermediate-Jr. High.

     Presents a story which exemplifies the kinds of generational
and cultural conflicts which are possible for family members who
must care for elderly parents.

The Family.   Educational Dimension Corp.   2 SFS, color.   Primary.

In Part 2 we see how a family is made up of many generations from ancestor to newborn.

The Family under the Bridge.   Miller-Brody.   2 SFS, color.   Intermediate.

When Suzy, Paul and Evelyne are evicted from their home, their mother sets up house under a bridge in Paris, much to the chagrin of the old recluse, Armand, who thought he had claim to the site.   Despite the shaky beginning, Armand and the children grow to love each other, and their adventures around Paris make a warm and thoroughly enjoyable story.

Folks Don't Kiss Old People Anymore.   Teleketics.   1 SFS or sound slides.   Jr. High-Adult.

A series of three brief experiences that can be used together as a meditation that is not a scientific study of aging or even of alienation but rather a media opportunity to reflect on our own internal attitudes and feelings about growing old.

Fourteen Rats and a Rat-Catcher.   Weston Woods, 1980.   1 SFS, color.   Primary.

Once there was a little old lady, a nice little old lady, who lived above some nasty rats.   Or was it the rats who were nice and the lady nasty?   It all depends on one's point of view.

The Funny Little Woman.   Weston Woods.   1 SFS, color.   Primary.

Old woman of ancient Japan encounters subterranean adventures with gods and wicked monsters when she follows a rice dumpling through a crack in the earth.

A Garden for Everyone.   McGraw-Hill Films, 1968.   1 captioned filmstrip, color.   Primary-Intermediate.

Tells the story of an elderly widow who appears to dislike children and three little girls who learn that the woman's temperament is only a mask, concealing her empty existence.   From the Skyline Series.

Gramp: A Man Ages and Dies.   Sunburst Communications.   1 SFS. High school.

One day Frank Tugend, aged 81 and of dubiously sound mind--
but certainly of sound body--removed his false teeth and announced
that he was no longer going to eat or drink.   Three weeks later, he
died.   His death finished a three-year ordeal of deterioration through
which his family decided to care for him at home--even though he
was senile.   A realistic and touching filmstrip based upon photographs of a loved grandfather, narrated by his grandson.

Grandparents Are to Love.   Parent's Magazine Films, 1970.   Dist.
        by Learning Corporation of America.   1 SFS, color.   Primary-
        Intermediate.

        Uses the two stories Grandfathers Are to Love and Grand-
mothers Are to Love, by Lois Wyse, to explore the joys and conflicts of family life.   From the Family Feelings Series.

Gray Panthers.   Teleketics.   1 SFS, record only.   Jr. High-Adult.

        Aging and elderly people do not have to be confined to rockers
or rest homes simply because they are old.   We learn about some
options that have been found to make growing old a time of libera-
tion through Maggie Kuhn's narration.

Grieving.   Walt Disney Educational Media, 1980.   1 SFS, color.
        Primary-Intermediate.

        Deals primarily with death of a parent.   Helps children come
to grips with anger at the deceased for deserting them, fear of their
own mortality or of being left alone, and guilt for not showing more
appreciation of the loved one before his death.   Emphasizes the
need to demonstrate grief and the many acceptable avenues for doing
so.   Part of the series, Family Problems: Dealing with Crisis.

Growing Old American.   Aids of Cape Cod, 1976.   4 SFS.   Jr.
        High-High school.

        Examines the process of aging.   Reviews the aspects of
growing old, including health, income, social outlook, senior citizen homes and nursing homes.

How Would You Like to Be Old?   Guidance Associates, 1973.   2
        SFS, color.   Jr. High-High school.

        Interviews underscore the loneliness experienced by many
older people in our youth-worshipping culture.   The effects of forced
retirement are demonstrated, including the inadequacies of the Social
Security system, medical assistance plans and private pensions.   A
series of personal anecdotes reveals the special understanding to be

found between young and old.   Age integration is suggested as a community planning goal, making old age a useful, productive and fulfilling stage of life.

The Hundred Penny Box.   Miller-Brody.   2 SFS.   Intermediate.

Young Michael's progressive, unsentimental mother has no patience with Great-aunt Dewbet's ungainly box of the mementos of her life and black heritage.   Sympathetic boy and centenarian conspire to try to thwart the omnipotent adult who controls both their lives and save the box along with Aunt Dew's dignity.

I'll Miss Gram a Lot.   Society for Visual Education.   1 SFS, color.
    Intermediate-Jr. High.

Part of the set, Death: Facing a Loss, depicting children dealing with the deaths of loved ones.   It is designed to impart to students understanding of death and grieving.

John Brown, Rose and the Midnight Cat.   Weston Woods, 1980.   1
    SFS, color.   Primary.

Rose, a plump widow, and her dog, John Brown, are inseparable until a black cat intrudes upon their comfortable lives.

Living with Dying.   Sunburst Communications.   2 SFS or sound
    slides.   High school.

The young often fear death partly because the dying are often separated from the living in our society.   This program makes students aware of the dying process by describing it as a natural part of the life cycle.   It probes the basis of the human fear of death and examines the various ways man attempts to deny death and achieve immortality.   Students learn about the five mental stages in a terminal illness, the aging process, extended life expectancies, and the problems of the aged.

Looking at Death.   Walt Disney Educational Media, 1980.   1 SFS,
    color.   Primary-Intermediate.

Compares life and death to a good book with beginning, ending, and many chapters in between, with lingering memories of the best parts.   Emphasizes that death is a natural part of the life cycle in both the plant and animal world.   Examines feelings of grief and different types of funeral customs for formal leave-taking.   Encourages keeping mementos of the loved one to evoke memories that live on beyond death.

Mike Mulligan and His Steam Shovel.   Weston Woods.   1 SFS, color.
   Primary.

   Mike, an aging but energetic and optimistic steam shovel
operator, and his outmoded but intrepid machine, Mary Ann, meet
the challenge of digging the basement for Popperville's new town
hall in just one day but fail to provide themselves egress.   They
solve their predicament by retiring as caretaker and furnace, respectively, of the new building.

Millions of Cats.   Weston Woods.   1 SFS, color.   Primary.

   In quest of a pet kitten, a lonely old couple discover more
felines than they can manage, but the bellicose cats themselves
simplify the decision of which one to keep.

OK to Be Old: Approaches to Aging.   Sunburst Communications.   3
   SFS.   High school.

   Prepared in conjunction with the American Health Care Association, this program corrects the many prevalent misconceptions
about elderly people, reveals the profound problems this growing
population segment faces and explores various lifestyle options for
the elderly.   Interviews highlight the diversity of this age group.

Old People's Home--A Poetic Essay on Aging.   Concept Media, 1973.
   1 SFS, b&w.   High school-Adult.

   Uses photographs to help illustrate the ideas of W. H. Auden's
poem "Old People's Home." Questions the contemporary practice of
isolating the elderly in homes so that they are unseen and forgotten.
From the Perspectives on Aging Series.

Old Ramon.   Miller-Brody.   2 SFS, color.   Intermediate.

   Moving story of a young boy who, under the tutelage of a
wise old shepherd, learns about animals, how to overcome fear,
face death and responsibility, and the difference between living alone
and being lonely.

Onion John.   Miller-Brody.   2 SFS, color.   Intermediate-Jr. High.

   Imaginative Andy and superstitious, eccentric immigrant
Onion John, town character, are boon companions in adventure until
Andy's well meaning but overbearing father tries to modernize John's
Old World lifestyle and simple dignity.

Our Elders--A Generation Neglected. Scott Education Division, Pren-
    tice-Hall Media, 1972. 2 SFS, color. Jr. High-High school.

Discusses the reasons why the elderly are shunned and their
problems ignored, the psychological damage caused by this treatment, and the grim conditions in some nursing homes. Includes the
problem of poverty among the aged and the shortcomings of the Social Security and Medicare programs.

Perspectives on Death. Sunburst Communications. 2 SFS or sound
    slides, color. High school.

Students examine philosophical and religious attitudes toward
death and explore such pressing social issues as euthanasia, the
legal definition of death and the right to die. The program fosters
acceptance of dying as part of life. Question breaks allow students
to voice their own feelings.

The Pigman. Miller-Brody. 2 SFS, color. Jr. High-High school.

Based on Paul Zindel's book in which rebellious, alienated teens
play a practical joke on a lonely New York widower who disarms them
with kindness. Their friendship ends when the lively old man is hospitalized with a heart attack and the teens betray his trust. The shock
of the betrayal kills Mr. Pignati and sobers the teens into contrition.

Productive Retirement. Multimedia Instructional Material. 1 SFS.
    High school-Adult.

Actively retired senior citizens in the community are an un-
tapped resource. Many are ready and willing to put to use their
available skills in productive ways. This is the story of Experience
Incorporated (of Hemet, California), how it came into being, what
it does, how it does it, and how similar groups can be established.

"Pulling the Plug"--Mercy or Murder? Teaching Resources, 1976.
    Dist. by Social Studies School Service. 1 SFS. High school-Adult.

A filmstrip which investigates the dilemmas surrounding the
issue of the "right to die": what is meant by the "right to die, "
who can decide when extraordinary measures should no longer be
used, what is the proper relationship between medical possibilities
and human values, and what is death legally and medically.

The Right to Die. The Perfection Form Co. 1 SFS. High school-Adult.

Should a terminally ill cancer patient and a comatose woman
kept alive only by medical technology with no chance of recovery be
allowed to "die with dignity" or should life be sustained as long as
possible at all costs? This filmstrip discusses the moral, legal and
practical implications of this issue--for medicine and for our society
as a whole.

Strega Nonna. Weston Woods. 1 SFS, color. Primary.

Big Anthony gets into big trouble when he pays no heed to "Grandma Witch" in this Calabrian equivalent of the pot that would not stop boiling.

To Hell with Grandma. Audio Visual Narrative Arts, 1976. 4 SFS.
Intermediate-Adult.

An incisive and deeply moving account of what it's like to grow old in America today. Part 1 examines the aging process, discusses forced retirement and looks at how modern medicine has affected life expectancy. Part 2 investigates the financial and human aspects of nursing homes. Part 3 studies the various government programs and the benefits provided by Social Security, Medicare and Medicaid. Part 4 invites students to consider the various ways in which government and private citizens can make growing old easier.

Walter and Sally. Teleketics. 1 SFS, record only. Jr. High-
Adult.

A documentary about the enduring mutual love and care between an elderly couple. Together they struggle economically to eat and live, but manage to transform a seemingly dull existence into a life full of joy, humor, beauty and each other.

We Are Not Alone. Teleketics. 1 SFS, record only. Jr. High-
Adult.

A documentary on indefatigable Sister Ignatius Musgens, 85, whose work among the elderly offers them multiple options for enrichment and development to replace loneliness, fear, isolation and anxiety.

Your Family. Educational Record Sales. 4 SFS, color. Primary-
Intermediate.

Demonstrates the fascinating progression from baby to teenager to single person living alone to marriage to parent to grandparent and old age.

GAME OR SIMULATION

Dealing with Death. Greenhaven Press. Dist. by Social Studies
School Service. High School.

A Future Planning Game printed on both sides of one 17 x 22

sheet, containing five activities. Students simulate roles in decision-making concerning a proposed abortion for a pregnant teenager, the removal of respirators from a terminally ill family member, funeral arrangements for an aged grandfather, and which crimes, if any, merit the death penalty. Students also discuss controversial statements on death-related issues.

MAGAZINE ARTICLES*

American Girl

"Crying for Gran, " by R. M. Healey. American Girl, 61:30-31+, June 1978.
"I Remember--Grandpa, " by L. Malinsky. American Girl, 56:12+, April 1973.
"Old Age Homes, " by K. Fry. American Girl, 56:14, April 1973.
"Sugar Cookies, " by E. A. Kolton. American Girl, 55:14-15, May 1972.
"Tribute to an Old Woman, " by L. Alison. American Girl, 59:44-45, August 1976.

American Red Cross Journal

"Aging and Environment: Challenges for the Seventies, " by R. G. Bennett. American Red Cross Journal, 47:4-6, February 1971.
"Help Wanted for a New Age, " by J. B. Martin. American Red Cross Journal, 47:7-9, February 1971.
"A Need for Concern, " American Red Cross Journal, 47:3, February 1971.

American Red Cross Youth News

"Please Don't Push Us Aside, " American Red Cross Youth News, 53:24-25, May 1972.
"Ticket to Yesterday, " by L. Betker. American Red Cross Youth News, 53:3-6, May 1972.

Boys' Life

"Aaron's Gift, " by M. Levoy. Boys' Life, 62:40-43+, April 1972.

Canadian Children's Magazine

"My Grandparents, " Canadian Children's Magazine, 1:7, Spring 1978.

*Arranged alphabetically by title of magazine.

Children's Digest

"Hannah and the Whistling Teakettle, " by M. W. Skolsky.   Children's
     Digest, 28:74-88, July 1978.
"How Do You Grow Old?" Children's Digest, 23:5-7, February 1973.
"My Grandson Lew, " (poem) by C. Zolotow.   Children's Digest, 25:
     31-47, July 1975.
"The Night of the Leonids, " (excerpt from Altogether, One at a Time
     by E. L. Konigsburg).   Children's Digest 23:53-65, April
     1973.

Co-ed

"The Moon Cookies, " by B. Girion.   Co-ed, 24:53-56, January 1979.

Cricket

"Aunt Roberta, " (poem) by E. Greenfield.   Cricket, 3:66, August
     1976.
"Benjie on His Own, " by J. M. Lexau.   Cricket, 1:65-76, January
     1974.
"Grandma's Secret, " by J. D. Stahl.   Cricket, 3:67-73, August
     1976.
"Listen to the Angels Laughing, " by T. Aguallo.   Cricket, 5:11-15,
     September 1977.
"Mandy's Grandmother, " by L. M. Skorpen.   Cricket, 3:15-22,
     September 1975.
"A Mitzvah Is Something Special, " by P. R. Eisenberg.   Cricket,
     7:20-25, November 1979.
"My Island Grandma, " by K. Lasky.   Cricket, 6:9-16, August 1979.

Current Events

"Age in Our Lives, Part 1, " by S. Bank.   Current Events, 78:12,
     January 17, 1979.   "Part 2, " Current Events, 78:14, January
     31, 1979.   "Part 3, " Current Events, 78:15, February 14,
     1979.
"Lands of Long Life, " Current Events, 77:14-15, November 16,
     1977.

Daisy

"Lend a Hand, " Daisy, 6:16, January 1980.

Ebony Jr.

"Grandma's Getting Married!" by C. M. Brink.   Ebony Jr., 8:21-
     23, August/September 1980.

Golden Magazine

"Ghost Town Intruder, " by A. Adam. Golden Magazine, 8:8-12,
May 1971.

Highlights

"The Grandmother Mystery, " by M. Priest. Highlights, 29:36-37,
November 1974.
"Tony's Surprise, " by H. Gothrup. Highlights, 32:20-21, May 1977.

Horn Book

"The Smile, " (poem) by J. Aiken. Horn Book, 51:487, October
1975.

Humpty Dumpty

"My Grannies, " (poem) by M. Dawson. Humpty Dumpty, 23:78-79,
July 1975.
"Something Special for Grandpa, " by S. W. Tate. Humpty Dumpty,
26:58-64, October 1978.
"When Grandparents Are the Greatest, " by S. Calmenson. Humpty
Dumpty, 28:42-48, April 1980.

Jack and Jill

"The Best Grandson in the World, " by D. Skov. Jack and Jill,
41:42-45, November 1979.

Junior Scholastic

"Escorts for the Elderly, " Junior Scholastic, 79:12, April 28, 1977.
"Growing Old in America, " Junior Scholastic, 80:2-4, February 23,
1978.
"It Depends on Where You Live, " Junior Scholastic, 80:5-7, February 23, 1978.
"Young and Old: Different Points of View, " Junior Scholastic, 80:
8-9, February 23, 1978.

My Weekly Reader Eye

"Bell Ringer, " My Weekly Reader Eye, 54:11, March 3, 1976.
"Cane Raised over Kids, " (retirement communities). My Weekly
Reader Eye, 54:6, April 7, 1976.
"Getting Old in America, " My Weekly Reader Eye, 55:2-4, January
26, 1977.

"Grandparents: You Need Them, " by S. Bank.   My Weekly Reader
      Eye, 57:7, January 24, 1979.
"Hard Work + Good Food = Long Life, " My Weekly Reader Eye,
      56:6, May 10, 1978.
"Never Too Old to Learn, " My Weekly Reader Eye, 54:13, January
      14, 1976.
"Understanding Your Grandparents, " by S. Bank.   My Weekly Read-
      er Eye, 57:7, January 3, 1979.
"Work for Grandfolks, " My Weekly Reader Eye, 54:3, March 31, 1976.

National Geographic Magazine

"A Scientist Visits Some of the World's Oldest People, " by A. Leaf.
      National Geographic Magazine, 143:92-119, January 1973.

News Explorer

"Eldest American, " News Explorer, 31:2, December 11, 1972.
"Meals on Wheels, " News Explorer, 27:3, December 14, 1970.
"White House Conference on the Aging, " News Explorer, 29:2, No-
      vember 1, 1971.

News Trails

"Feeling Young, " News Trails, 31:7, October 14, 1975.
"Understanding Older People, " News Trails, 26:3, February 12,
      1973.

Parade

"Ali Helps Senior Citizens, " Parade, 57:2, February 18, 1976.
"Good Neighbor: Polly Urquhart, " Parade, 61:2, April 2, 1980.
"He's the Oldest, " Parade, 59:2, April 19, 1978.

Pictorial Education

"People in Society: Helping the Old, " Pictorial Education, 46:3+,
      May 1972.

Science World

"The Clock of Aging--Can We Turn It Back?" by J. Schuman. Sci-
      ence World, 34:9-11, April 20, 1978.

Scholastic News Citizen

"Building a Friendship, " (play) by S. Robbins.   Scholastic News

Citizen, 47:4-5, November 16, 1978.
"Hamilton School Hosts Older People, " Scholastic News Citizen, 46:
7, May 4, 1978.
"Super Champ and the Senior Citizens, " Scholastic News Citizen,
44:3, February 24, 1976.
"We're Not So Old, " Scholastic News Citizen, 48:4-5, April 10, 1980.
"Who's Too Old?" Scholastic News Citizen, 46:7, January 26, 1978.

Scholastic Newstime

"Gray Matters, " Scholastic Newstime, 50:2-3, March 9, 1978.
"Growing Older, " Scholastic Newstime, 51:2-3, March 22, 1979.
"Nader's New Concern, " Scholastic Newstime, 40:2, April 17, 1972.
"A New Look at the Old, " Scholastic Newstime, 40:6-7, April 24,
1972.
"Teen-aid for the Aging, " Scholastic Newstime, 42:7, April 2, 1973.

Search

"Growing Old in Other Countries, " Search, 5:12, November 21, 1974.
"Growing Old in the Land of the Young, " Search, 5:6-11, November
21, 1974.

Senior Scholastic

"The Gift of Life, " Senior Scholastic, 109:24, May 5, 1977.
"Image of the Aged, " Senior Scholastic, 100:16-19, April 24, 1972.
"Man of Odessa, " by J. Koth. Senior Scholastic, 109:18, May 19,
1977.
"A Student Writer Visits 'Home', " (nursing homes) by C. Belcher.
Senior Scholastic, 108:38-39, February 24, 1976.
"Why Call Them Golden Years?" Senior Scholastic, 101:13, October
9, 1972.

Senior Weekly Reader

"Live the Life of an 80-year-old, " Senior Weekly Reader, 31:7-
10, April 13, 1977.

Wee Wisdom

"About Grandmothers, " (poem) by G. T. Smith. Wee Wisdom, 77:
15, May 1971.
"The Best Show-and-Tell, " by R. Cross. Wee Wisdom, 86:16-19,
May 1980.
"Jill and the Chipmunks, " by P. Nielsen. Wee Wisdom, 84:4-7,
June/July 1978.
"Never Too Old, " by D. Lillegard. Wee Wisdom, 84:8-11, Febru-
ary 1978.

"New Friend, Old Friend, " by M. Katz.   Wee Wisdom, 85:10-13,
        April 1979.
"The Rummage Sale Treasure, " by J. Quimby.   Wee Wisdom, 86:
        16-19, December 1979.
"When My Granny Came to Visit, " by J. Garcia.   Wee Wisdom, 85:
        10-12, June/July 1979.

Weewish Tree

"Grandfather, " (poem) by S. Yazzie.   Weewish Tree, 7:32, Sep-
        tember 1979.
"Grandmother, " by D. Garcia.   Weewish Tree, 2:3, October 1973.

Young Citizen

"Old People Meet, " Young Citizen, 36:1-2, January 24, 1972.
"A Time for Growing Old... , " Young Citizen, 33:2-3, November 2,
        1970.

Young Horizons

"Teenagers and the Elderly, " by L. Page.   Young Horizons, 1:7-8,
        May 1976.

Young Miss

"Get to Know the Elderly, " Young Miss, 24:77, September 1977.
"Grandmothers Are the Greatest--or Are They?" by R. Saunders.
        Young Miss 19:50-54, January 1972.   Repeated in Young Miss,
        24:40-44, December 1977.
"A Hundred Handkerchiefs, " by C. Miskovits.   Young Miss, 20:38-
        45, February 1973.
"The Orphan, " by F. Downey.   Young Miss, 20:50-58, March 1973.
"To Know Why, " by J. Adams.   Young Miss, 27:8-14, May 1980.

Young World

"All Yours, " Young World, 14:2, November 1977.

                    MOTION PICTURES AND VIDEOTAPES

The Aged. WNET-TV, 1973. Dist. by Carousel Films.   16mm,
        color, 17 min. High school-Adult.

        Views a young man who returns from the Vietnam War to
find his parents incapable of caring for themselves. Follows his

weary struggle through agencies and private nursing homes and his
eventual impoverishment due to the problem.   From the Bitter
Vintage Series.

Aging.   CRM Educational Films, 1973.   16mm, color, 22 min.
          College-Adult.

        Examines some popular, although often mistaken, attitudes
toward the aged and their places in life.   Discusses two major
theories--the activity theory of Leisure World with Dr. Vern Bengt-
son of USC and the disengagement theory.   From the Developmental
Psychology Today Film Series.

Aging.   National Educational TV, 1963.   Dist. by Indiana University
          Audiovisual Center.   16mm, b&w, 30 min.   High school-
          Adult.

        Shows two elderly Jewish gentlemen playing cards, revealing
their attitudes about life, loneliness and the younger generation.
Asserts that the greatest evil to the elderly is the notion that an
old person is functionless.   Advocates re-establishing natural roles
of grandfather and grandmother in family life.   From the About People Series.

Aging.   Video Recording Corp. of America.   Video cassette, color.
          College.

        Approaches aging from a very practical standpoint, presenting
the philosophical need for an individual to start at an early age to
develop an awareness of one's self and to acquire a bank of inner
resources that can be drawn upon in later years when social communication becomes less and loneliness becomes greater.

Annie and the Old One.   BFA Educational Media.   16mm, color,
          $14\frac{1}{2}$ min.   Primary-Jr. High.

        Annie loves to hear the many stories her grandmother tells,
but one day the Old One reveals a sad truth--when the new rug on
the loom is finished she will go to Mother Earth.   Sadness comes
to Annie because she cannot imagine life without her and plots to
keep the rug from completion.   The Old One discovers Annie's distress and helps her to understand the cycle of life.

Best Boy.   Entertainment Marketing Corp.   16mm, color, 111 min.
          High school-Adult.

        After a life of total dependency on his nurturing but aging
parents, 52-year-old mentally retarded Philly must be weaned into

a home for retarded adults, while his mother suffers the dual pains of separation from her son and the hospitalization and death of her husband.

Cemetery of the Elephants. Films Incorporated, 1975. 16mm, color, 17 min. High school.

Presents an allegory about a young writer leaving home with his manuscript, Los Cemeterios de los Elefantes, and returning home as an old man after years of struggle, not having conquered the world.

Coping with Change. Association Films. (Free) 16mm, color, 28 min. High school-Adult.

Takes a look at people who have discovered that change is a part of growing, not just growing older. It focuses on members of the older generation who have successfully addressed the issue of aging and are experiencing the "Prime Time" of their lives. It shows that how you cope with change determines the rest of your life no matter how old you are.

The Day Grandpa Died. BFA Educational Media, 1970. 16mm, color, $11\frac{1}{2}$ min. Intermediate.

"Grandpa went to sleep last night, David--and he didn't wake up. " In this vignette of a boy's first experience with the death of a loved one, we watch David's struggle with the reality, from outright denial of the fact to gradual acceptance, of death as a part of life.

Death: How Can You Live with It? Walt Disney Educational Media. 16mm, 19 min. Intermediate-Jr. High.

A boy learns that his grandfather, whom he loves dearly, is dying. This poignant film encourages discussion on how one learns to accept death as a part of life, and the discovery that people who have touched us live on in treasured memories--to give us strength and direction.

Death of a Gandy Dancer. Learning Corp. of America. 16mm, color, 26 min. Jr. High-Adult.

A terminal cancer patient and his grandson are not informed by the boy's parents of the old man's impending death, and the boy is therefore unprepared for the emotional trauma of his loss.

The Detour.   Barbara Bryant and Caroline Morris, 1977.   Dist. by
          Phoenix Films.   16mm, color, 14 min.   Jr. High-High
          school.

     Focuses on the plight of dying patients in hospitals.   Shows
how modern medicine is keeping an elderly woman alive while she
struggles to die in peace with dignity.

Dew Drop.   Serious Business Co.   16mm, color, 16 min.   High
          school-Adult.

     Incorporates home movies, photos, and experimental effects
into a mesmerizing elegy that recounts the life, dying and death of
the producer's father.

The Dignity of Death.   ABC Learning Resources.   16mm or video-
          tape, color, 24 min.   High school-Adult.

     Probes life in a medical facility for terminally ill patients
with intimate views of patients, families and physicians confronting
the ultimate problems of life and death.

Dolly.   Jennifer Mead, 1976.   Dist. by Phoenix Films.   16mm,
          color, 10 min.   High school.

     Tells the story of an elderly woman who, confined to a wheel-
chair, pours out her life story in conscious and unconscious memories.

Don't Stop the Music.   U. S. Dept. of HEW, 1974.   (Free)   Dist. by
          Modern Talking Picture Service.   16mm, color, 18 min.
          High school-Adult.

     Depicts older Americans speaking for themselves.   Dispels
some commonly held myths about the elderly and demonstrates their
capacity for enjoyment, productivity, and an active life.   They do
have problems, though, and the film examines the ways communities
can help.

Dreamspeaker.   Filmakers Library.   16mm, color, 75 min.   Jr.
          High-High school.

     Old Indian shaman has healing effect upon emotionally dis-
turbed runaway boy.

The Elderly.   Film Dynamics.   Dist. by Treiberg Films and Film-
          strips.   16mm.   Intermediate-Adult.

This film describes some of the feelings, thoughts, anxieties and joys of today's elderly population. It traces their activities, reveals their attitudes toward society's treatment of them, and portrays their dreams and hopes for tomorrow. Their active contributions to society are numerous and cover many areas. The film offers a rich, revealing study of a serious problem in today's world, and possible attitudes and activities that may help resolve some of them.

Elderly Poor. Teleketics. 16mm, 60 sec. Jr. High-Adult.

A documentary in which one woman speaks eloquently of the problems, worries, concerns, and loneliness of the elderly poor.

Enverounen. British Council and Arts Council of Great Britain, 1976. Dist. by Films Incorporated. 16mm, color, 15 min. High school.

Shows an old man whose surroundings from the past evoke a flow of subconscious associations that form a labyrinth of memories.

The Faces of "A" Wing. WPSX-TV, 1974. Dist. by Pennsylvania State University. 16mm, b&w, 58 min. High school.

Presents an observational documentary, using minimal narration, designed to allow the viewer to experience life in one nursing home through a series of vignettes that focus on different people, including staff, residents and relatives. Examines how they relate on a personal and institutional level. From the To Age Is Human Series.

Family Portrait Sittings. Alfred Guzzetti. 16mm, b&w/color, 103 min. Jr. High-Adult.

Four generations of an Italian-American family in cinema verite, focusing on the producer's parents and great uncle.

The Final, Proud Days of Elsie Wurster. WPSX-TV, 1975. Dist. by Pennsylvania State University. 16mm, b&w, 58 min. High school.

Documents the final 30 days of Elsie Wurster's life before her death on Christmas Day in a Pennsylvania nursing home. Observes her with visitors and friends, taking therapy and treatment, and talking about her feelings, fears and memories. From the To Age Is Human Series.

For Gentlemen Only. National Film Board of Canada, 1977. Dist.
     by Wombat Productions. 16mm, color, 28 min. Jr. High-
     High school.

     Presents the story of two old men whose comfortable world
is threatened when their hotel, formerly for gentlemen only, decides
to admit women.

Four Women over Eighty. MTI Teleprograms. 16mm, color, 10
     min. Jr. High-Adult.

     Ordinary octogenarians and nonagenarians with an extraordinary
zest for life.

A Garden for Everyone. McGraw-Hill Films, 1968. 16mm, color,
     12 min. Primary.

     Tells the story of an elderly widow who appears to dislike
children and three little girls who learn that the woman's temperament is only a mask, concealing her empty existence. From the
Skyline Series.

Generations. Phoenix Films, 1980. 16mm, 11 min. Jr. High-
     High school.

     A gentle film about a brief encounter between youth and old
age.

Grandma Lives in Our House. King Screen Productions, 1970 (OP).
     16mm, b&w, 10 min.

     Depicts the lifestyle of a Japanese-American family living in
a household of three generations as told by the youngest daughter.
From The Family--As the Child Sees It Series.

Grandmother and Leslie. Perennial Education. 16mm, color, $28\frac{1}{2}$
     min. Primary-Intermediate.

     Part of the Look at Me Series of five films depicting such
family situations as a word game for a long car ride, sorting the
groceries, imaginative shadow play between father and son, home
math experiences, infant/sibling/grandmother interrelationships,
language development through story telling and puppetry.

Grandpa. Films Incorporated. 16mm, b&w, 29 min. High school.

     Impoverished but tenacious Jewish immigrant narrates his
struggle to succeed in business while clashing with his grandson
over value systems.

Grandpa. Iowa State University Film Production Unit, 1962. 16mm,
        b&w, 12 min. Jr. High-College.

Uses a dramatized incident about a young boy who hikes along
a railroad track with his grandfather to point out the responsibility
of the young for the old and the responsibility of the old for the
young.

The Gray Panthers. ABC-TV. Dist. by National Council of
        Churches. 16mm, color, 30 min. High school-Adult.

Describes the work of the Gray Panthers, a coalition of
elder activists centered in Princeton, N. J. Discusses the difficulties older people have in getting loans and establishing credit on
small, fixed incomes.

Hattie. Australian Dept. of Social Security, 1975. Dist. by Aus-
        tralian Information Service. 16mm, b&w, 9 min. Jr. High-
        High school.

Tells about a 76-year-old woman whose life is lonely and
empty. Tells how, after an active life, she has little to occupy her
time and wonders why society does not take advantage of the experience and knowledge accumulated by many older people.

"Hello in There. " Teleketics, 1979. 16mm, color, 21 min. Jr.
        High-Adult.

To relieve the boredom and sterility of her humdrum retirement home life, Mary blatantly shoplifts to attract attention. A
sympathetic public relations trainee from the shoplifted store befriends her, and older woman and younger woman help one another.

Henry. Paramount-Oxford Films, 1970. 16mm, b&w, 10 min.
        Intermediate-College.

Raises many questions of social significance, including what
place in life can one find that is uniquely one's own, how secure is
that place, especially if one is old, and what do the changing times
offer to an old man.

Home to Stay. Time-Life Multimedia. 16mm, color, 47 min. In-
        termediate-High school.

Staunchly loyal and loving granddaughter hatches a quixotic
scheme to spare her incipiently senile grandfather from institutionalization by his son, her uncle. Based on the novel Grandpa and
Frank.

<u>Hospice.</u>   Billy Budd Films.   16mm or videotape, color, 26 min.
          High school-Adult.

This film documents a growing movement to care for the
terminally ill at home or in home-like surroundings, allowing the
dying a chance to live fully with family and friends until their time
of death.

<u>The Hundred Penny Box.</u>   Churchill Films, 1979.   16mm, color,
          18 min.   Intermediate.

Young Michael's progressive, unsentimental mother has no
patience with Great-aunt Dewbet's ungainly box of the mementos of
her life and black heritage.   Sympathetic boy and centenarian conspire to try to thwart the omnipotent adult who controls both their
lives and save the box along with Aunt Dew's dignity.

<u>I Hate Elevators.</u>   Teleketics.   16mm, 60 sec.   Jr. High-Adult.

A young mother-to-be, alone and frightened, arouses fear
and hostility on a crowded elevator.   Only one older woman reaches
out with compassion and understanding and brings the young woman
reassurance and a moment of love.

<u>Journey Together.</u>   Films Incorporated, 1979.   16mm or videotape,
          color, 22 min.   Jr. High-High school.

Docudrama challenging youth to become involved in their communities.   A rudderless adolescent befriends a proud, irritable,
lonely and impoverished aging black woman and helps her file for
a senior citizen rebate on her fuel bill.   The teen herself benefits
psychologically from their relationship.

<u>Knock at the Door.</u>   Teleketics.   16mm, 30 sec.   Jr. High-Adult.

An old woman waits, the moment measured by the ticking of
a clock, until the knock of a visitor wakens her cat and canary,
breaks the lonely pattern of existence, and brings a moment of love
and awareness into her life.

<u>The Last Winters.</u>   Perspective Films.   16mm, color, 23 min.
          High school-Adult.

An 84-year-old lover imagines the worst when his 70-year-
old sweetheart appears to be missing.

<u>Learning to Enjoy.</u>   Association Films.   (Free) 16mm, color, 28
          min.   High school-Adult.

Gives the viewer a chance to meet some folks who have found that the later years can be a most satisfying time of life if you make your own choices, let go, take a risk, and allow yourself to pursue the things that bring enjoyment.

The Lost Phoebe.   Perspective Films.   16mm, color, 30 min.
        High school-Adult.

This film, based on the story by Theodore Dreiser, follows a grief-stricken widower on a poignant search for his dead wife, culminating in their reunion in death.

Love It like a Fool.   New Day Films.   16mm, color, 28 min.
        High school-Adult.

Malvina Reynolds, 76-year-old songwriter, folk singer, and activist, not only performs but also notes her feelings about aging, death, sex, and feminism. In jeans and caftans she fits none of the stereotypes often connected with old age.

Love Song of the Coocoo Birds.   Paulist Productions, 1972.   16mm, b&w, 27 min.   High school-Adult.

Shows how an elderly couple, reduced to loneliness and poverty, manage to retain their dignity because their love for one another gives meaning to their lives.   From the Insight Series.

Love Waits.   Teleketics.   16mm, 60 sec.   Jr. High-Adult.

The telephone rings in the lonely room of an elderly woman. Slowly and painstakingly she uses her walker to reach the phone before it stops ringing and is rewarded by a girl's voice saying, "Hello, Grandma?"

Maggie Kuhn: Wrinkled Radical.   Indiana University Audiovisual Center.   16mm, color, 27 min.   Jr. High-Adult.

Founder of the Gray Panthers discusses her fight for elderly rights.

Mandy's Grandmother.   Phoenix Films.   16mm, color, 30 min.
        Primary-Intermediate.

Unconventional, avant garde Mandy and her traditional, conservative grandmother clash on Grandmother's first visit in Mandy's home until they discover a common ground and begin to compromise and amend their expectations of one another.

A Matter of Indifference. Phoenix Films, 1974. 16mm, color, 50
          min. High school- Adult.

   This documentary presents a critique of society's ambivalence
toward the aged and includes an interview with aging activist Maggie
Kuhn on her struggle to gain recognition for "Gray Power. "

Max. Carousel Films. 16mm, color, 20 min. High school- College.

   A veteran Broadway stagehand gives some sound advice to a
young, inexperienced actress with uncertain talent.

Mike Mulligan and His Steam Shovel. Weston Woods. 16mm/
          Super 8/video cassette, color, 11 min. Primary.

   Mike, an aging but indefatigable steam shovel operator, and
his outmoded but valiant machine, Mary Ann, meet the challenge
of digging the basement for Popperville's new town hall in just one
day but fail to provide themselves egress. They solve their predicament by retiring as caretaker and furnace, respectively, of the new
building.

Millions of Cats. Weston Woods. 16mm or video cassette, b&w,
          10 min. Primary.

   In quest of a pet kitten, a lonely old couple discover more
felines than they can handle, but the bellicose cats themselves simplify the decision of which one to keep.

Miss Larsen--Rebel at 90. Henry Street Settlement, 1977. Dist.
          by Films Incorporated. 16mm, color, 16 min. High school.

   A lengthened version of the 1975 motion picture, Nobody Ever
Died of Old Age. Presents an adaptation of the book of the same
name by Sharon Curtin. Depicts the degradation of the human spirit
to which old people are subjected.

Murita Cycles. Direct Cinema. 16mm, color, 28 min. High
          school- College.

   Eccentric, junk- collecting widower rationalizes his unorthodox
lifestyle to his conventional film-maker son.

Nana, Mom and Me. New Day Films. 16mm, 47 min. High
          school- Adult.

   Amalie Rothschild's feminist examination of herself, her
mother and grandmother.

Nell and Fred.   National Film Board of Canada, 1971.   Dist. by
        McGraw-Hill Films.   16mm, b&w, 28 min.   High school-
        College.

        Relates the difficulty of elderly people in remaining independent
by focusing on a couple who must decide whether to move into a residence for senior citizens or to maintain their own familiar home.

New Deal.   WNET-TV, 1973.   Dist. by Carousel Films.   16mm,
        color, 5 min.   High school-Adult.

        Presents a non-narrative vignette of old folks eating alone in
cafeterias and coffee shops.   From the Bitter Vintage Series.

A New Life for Rose.   Edward Feil Productions, 1976.   16mm,
        color, 25 min.   High school-Adult.

        Presents the planning program of a senior housing project.

The Occupant of the Single Room.   National Educational TV, 1976.
        Dist. by Indiana University Audiovisual Center.   Video cas-
        sette, color, 20 min.   High school.

        Takes a look at the plight of elderly Americans living on fixed
incomes below the poverty level.   Shows how they are attempting to
cope with below standard conditions in New York City's single-room
occupancy hotels.

Old Age.   Time-Life Films, 1970.   16mm, 45 min.   High school-
        Adult.

        Examines the way in which people in various countries cope
with old age.   From the Family of Man Series.

Old Age: Do Not Go Gentle.   ABC Learning Resources.   16mm or
        videotape, color, 52 min.   High school-Adult.

        Documentary exposing the social and economic problems of
U. S. elderly and contrasting the dearth of solutions in the U. S. to
successful programs in Europe.

Old Age: Out of Sight, Out of Mind.   Indiana University Audiovisual
        Center, 1968.   16mm, 60 min.   High school-Adult.

        Provides a documentary on the institutions and rehabilitation
programs for the aged.   Includes U. S. Senate subcommittee investigations of nursing homes.   Shows Goldwater and Middletown hospitals

in New York and an "old folks" farm in Kentucky.   From The
Americas Crises Series.

Old Age: The Wasted Years.   Indiana University Audiovisual Center,
          1966.   16mm, 60 min.   High school-Adult.

Discusses the problem of reduced income for the aged caused
by retirement or unemployment.   Contrasts living in the slums with
that of luxury retirement.   Provides interviews with senior citizens,
government officials and social workers.   From The Americas
Crises Series.

Old, Black and Alive: Some Contrasts in Aging.   New Film Co.,
          1974.   16mm, color, 28 min.   Jr. High-Adult.

Uses a variety of interviews with aging blacks in order to
show the different ways in which blacks adapt to the aging process.

Old-Fashioned Woman.   Films Incorporated.   16mm, color, 40 min.
          Jr. High-Adult.

A Yankee grandmother stars in "roots" style documentary.

The Old Man and the Devil.   Ferguson Films, 1971.   16mm, color,
          17 min.   Intermediate-Adult.

Views the dilemma of the aged, using dramatization about
an old man and his encounter with the Devil while staying at a county
hospital.

The Old Woman.   ACI Productions, 1973.   16mm, color, 2 min.
          Jr. High-Adult.

Presents a confrontation between an old woman and Death in
the form of a skeleton.   Shows in animated style how the unwelcome
visitor leaves when he sees how much work the woman still has to
do.

One Old Man.   Churchill Films, 1975.   16mm, color, 10 min.   Jr.
          High-Adult.

Depicts daily events in the life of an 89-year-old man.

Shows his good humor and stoicism in the face of adversity.

Parks, Pleasant Occasions and Happiness.   Marvin Albert Films,
          1977. 16mm, color, 17 min. Primary-Adult.

     Dramatizes, without narrations, occasions of pleasure and
happiness that city parks provide throughout the seasonal calendar.
Depicts the companionship that an elderly man finds with an elderly
woman in the course of visiting a city's various parks in different
seasons over a two-year period.   Emphasizes the importance of
public parks for leisure and recreation.

Peege.   Phoenix Films.   16mm, color, 28 min.   Jr. High-
          Adult.

     Already a classic, this film shows how a young man
reaches out to his paternal grandmother, now isolated by old
age and failing mental capacities.   Companion film to Portrait
of Grandpa Doc.

Portrait of Grandpa Doc.   Phoenix Films.   16mm, color, 28 min.
          Jr. High-Adult.

     Haunting and sensitive flashbacks evoke young artist's special
relationship with his maternal grandfather who encouraged the boy's
precocious talent and instilled an open-minded view of life.

Problem--To Think of Dying.   KTCA-TV, 1977.   Dist. by Indiana
          University Audiovisual Center. 16mm, color, 59 min.   High
          school-Adult.

     Presents an open discussion with a moderator, widow Lynn
Caine, and terminal cancer patient Orville Kelly who express their
personal experiences and feelings relating to death from cancer.
Includes discussion about the emotional phases encountered, mistakes
they believe they made, and how they are coping with the question of
death.

The Rest of Your Life.   Gilbert Altschul Productions, 1967.   Dist.
          by Journal Films. 16mm, color, 28 min.   High school-
          Adult.

     Identifies and examines some of the problems related to re-
tirement.   Raises pertinent questions and explains the need for planning for retirement.

Rocking Horse Cowboy. Altus Films, 1976. Dist. by EBE Corporation. 16mm, color, 24 min. Jr. High-High school.

 Presents a character study recording the true story of a
modern day cowboy facing the problems of old age. Tells the story
in the man's own words and voice, revealing the life of a person
who followed his romantic dreams, only to find the life of a real
cowboy is bittersweet. From the American Character Series.

Rose Argoff. WNET-TV, 1973. Dist. by Carousel Films. 16mm,
 color, 9 min. High school-Adult.

 Presents a courageous old lady who tells about her life in
America after emigrating to this country from Russia. From the
Bitter Vintage Series.

Sallie, 1893-1974. Oregon State System of Higher Education, 1974.
 16mm, color, 54 min. High school-Adult.

 Records a funeral as it is occurring. Suggests that the
ceremony is really a celebration of the life of Sallie McGinnis, who
died at age 81.

Science--New Frontiers: Extending Life. BFA Educational Media.
 16mm, color, 15 min. Jr. High-High school.

 Until recent years, we have tried to extend the human life
span through control of diseases, the improvement of sanitary conditions, and better diet, increasing the probability that one would
live a full life. But recent efforts to improve this probability have
raised questions about the nature of man and the meaning of life.
Transplantation, the replacement of body parts with foreign materials, becomes more sophisticated daily. The questions to be an-
swered are difficult: When do we have the right to extend life?
When to let the natural cycle of life and death take its course?
Who will determine who should be saved? How do we manage the
problems of increasing population that arise from our efforts to
prolong life?

SRO (Single Room Occupancy). WNET-TV, 1973. Dist. by Carousel Films. 16mm, color, 13 min. High school-Adult.

 Presents the occupants of a welfare hotel as they comment
on the hopelessness and poverty of their lives. From the Bitter
Vintage Series.

Social Security--How Secure. NBC-TV, 1976. Dist. by Films Incorporated. 16mm, color, 52 min. High school-Adult.

Examines America's vast and little-understood Social Security Service with respect to its philosophy, purpose, fairness, financial soundness and the degree of security it offers to today's and future recipients.

A Special Trade.   Barr Films, 1980.   16mm, color, 17 min.
        Primary-Intermediate.

Youthful-spirited retiree becomes surrogate grandfather to a neighbor tot, teaching her to toddle, then roller skate, as she grows.   Gradually their relationship reverses as she becomes more dexterous and he requires more assistance.   When he is eventually confined to a wheelchair after a fall, the girl becomes the nurturer.

Stalking Immortality.   ABC Learning Resources.   16mm or video-
        tape, color, 58 min.   High school-Adult.

A hopeful look at alternatives to aging in which scientists reveal that the aging process may not be inevitable or irreversible.

Strega Nonna.   Weston Woods.   16mm or video cassette, color, 9
        min.   Primary.

Big Anthony gets into big trouble when he pays no heed to "Grandma Witch" in this Calabrian equivalent of the pot that would not stop boiling.

Sunday Dinner.   J. J. Linsalata, 1976.   Dist. by Phoenix Films.
        16mm, color, 12 min.   Jr. High-High school.

Tells the story of how an elderly lady and a local junkman collect food, wine, and other necessities to make their Sunday dinner cozy and homelike.

Talk to Me--A Visit with Mr. Carpenter.   Alfonso R. Tatano, 1974.
        Dist. by Art-Co Productions.   16mm, color, 8 min.   Jr.
        High-High school.

Presents a statement on growing old, featuring present and past experiences of Arthur H. Carpenter, an 85-year-old man who was a singer, an architect, and an artist, including his concern for the future.

Time Exposure.   Parish of the Air, 1969.   16mm, color, 27 min.
        High school-Adult.

Narrated by Ralph Bellamy, this film deals with the different stages involved in the process of aging.   From the One Reach One Series.

To a Good, Long Life.   BFA Educational Media.   16mm, color,
          20 min.   Jr. High-Adult.

This documentary film focuses on three old people who are leading vigorous, interesting lives.   The message is that age doesn't have to slow people down, and it doesn't have to keep old people from interacting with other people.

To Age Is Human Series.   (See The Faces of "A" Wing and The
          Final, Proud Days of Elsie Wurster.)

Tomorrow Again.   Pyramid Films, 1972.   16mm, b&w, 16 min.
          Jr. High-Adult.

A fictional story, presented in the form of a documentary, about a sweet old lady who lives in a shabby hotel for senior citizens.   Pictures the psychological problems which develop because of her loneliness and isolation.

The Violin.   Learning Corp. of America, 1973.   16mm, color, 24
          min.   Jr. High-Adult.

Portrays a young boy and his encounter with an old wayfarer musician.   Shows the magic that can emerge when two lives touch. Presents a setting of snowy mountains and a warm cabin which deepens the friendship.

The Violin Lesson.   VPI Division of Electrographic Corp., 1970.
          Dist. by McGraw-Hill Films.   16mm, color, 10 min.   Jr.
          High-Adult.

Presents a poignant look at a day in the life of a proud old musician who has seen better days.   Shows a violin class in session with the musician as instructor.   Ends on an unusual note as the class resolves itself in a most surprising way.

When Parents Grow Old.   Learning Corp. of America, 1972.
          16mm, color, 15 min.   Jr. High-Adult.

Tells how a young man on the verge of marriage must decide where his responsibilities lie when he is faced with the problem of a suddenly widowed father whose health is failing.   From Searching for Values--a Film Anthology Series.

Who Cares. Sterling Educational Films, 1970. 16mm, color, 13
        min. Jr. High-Adult.

Shows the conflict of an aging grandfather in the home of a
family. Questions where the old man should look for comfort in his
old age when his own flesh and blood don't care. From Family Life
Education and Human Growth Series.

With Just a Little Trust. Teleketics. 16mm, color, 15 min.
        High school.

An elderly black woman, her feet swollen with arthritis,
marches with pride and determination through an urban ghetto on her
way to help her daughter, a widow with three children, with her
chores. In the warmth and realism of her daughter's little apartment, the mother, by her faith, determination, pride, and refusal
to give in to self-pity, bolsters her daughter's sagging courage in
the face of almost insurmountable obstacles. Gospel music accom-
paniment.

The Wrinkle Squad. Paulist Productions, 1971. 16mm, b&w, 28
        min. Jr. High-Adult.

A dramatization about three old men who run afoul of state
bureaucracy when they open a child-care center as a way of halting
the feeling of uselessness that accompanies old age. From the Insight Series.

You Don't Die Here. University of California Extension, 1972.
        16mm, color, 19 min. High school-Adult.

Presents an impressionistic, open-ended documentary showing
death valley, in a fabric of images, as a cruel and sublime land-
scape in which a few old people live out their lives near nuclear
test sites and in the path of military aircraft.

You'll Get Yours When You're 65. CBS News, 1973. 16mm, color,
        40 min. Primary-College.

Depicts America's treatment of its senior citizens. Contrasts
this treatment and that of other countries, such as West Germany.
Dispels some of the misconceptions about the American health and
retirement systems. From the CBS News Special Report for Young
People Series.

PICTURES AND TRANSPARENCIES

Aging.   Lansford Publishing Co. , 1971.   14 transparencies, 9 x 11,
    color.   High school- Adult.

    Shows the extent of the problems of the aged, including
growth of the older population, life expectancy, population pyramid,
relative concentrations of older people by state, Social Security and
the aged, health care and illness.

Gramp--- A True Story of Living with Dying.   Social Studies School
    Service.   24 photo-aids, 11 x 14.   High school.

    A series of vivid photo-aids showing the actual process of
aging and dying, from photos taken during the final days of a beloved grandfather.   Avoiding the depersonalization of a nursing home
and the mechanization of a hospital death, Gramp dies at home, and
grandchildren and great-grandchildren appear throughout the picture
series and convey a sense of love and caring.

Grandfather and Grandmother Arrive for a Visit.   GAF, 1968.   Dist.
    by Western Publishing Co.   1 transparency, 8 x 10, color.
    Primary.

    Enables young children to verbalize their feelings and reac-
tions to a familiar situation.   From the Language Development
Series, Unit 2-- The Family.

Living with Aging.   Social Studies School Service.   28 photo-aids,
    11 x 14.   Intermediate- Adult.

    American society idolizes youth and forces its aged into non-
productive lives.   These photo-aids portray nursing and retirement
homes, the isolation of the elderly, the youth cult, education of the
elderly, and the activists of the aged, the Gray Panthers.

Living with Dying.   Social Studies School Service.   24 photo-aids,
    11 x 14.   High school.

    These photo-aids emphasize medical technology, the segrega-
tion of the dying, dying with dignity, funeral practices, grief, suicide, and death anxieties revealed by the American accent on youth.
Included is one copy of A Manual of Death Education and Simple
Burial.

RECORDS/CASSETTES/AUDIOTAPES

Aging in the Modern World. National Educational TV. Dist. by
     Indiana University Audiovisual Center. 1 10-in. disc, 33-1/3.

    Discusses the problems of aging, from man's adjustment at
various occupational levels to influence toward a healthier, longer
life with more leisure.

The Declining Years--Are They Golden. Center for Cassette Studies,
    1977. 1 cassette, 45 min. High school.

    Deals with the problems of the aged and their struggle to
maintain dignity and independence.

Grandpa and My Sister Bee. Children's Press, 1976. 1 cassette/
    book kit. Primary.

    A 3-year-old tot offers to ease Grandpa's aching back by
helping him plant wall flowers--or is she really helping?

Grandparents Have Rights Too. University of Oklahoma, 1961.
    1 3-3/4 IPS 1-track audiotape, 14 min. High school-College.

    Explains that although all families have some grandparent
problems, the relationship should be a rewarding one for all.
From the Family Life Radio Forum Series.

Simon's Extra Gran. Children's Press, 1976. 1 cassette/book kit.
    Primary.

    Because his own grandmothers live far away and his mother
is too busy with the baby, Simon needs an extra Gran to read him a
story. The pleasant old lady moving in next door fills the bill superbly.

What You Don't Know May Hurt You. American Physical Fitness
    Research Institute. (Free) 1 reel-to-reel audiotape, 30 min.
    High school-Adult.

    Program No. 3 (5 min.)--Researchers Probe the Aging Pro-
cess--poses some intriguing questions on gerontology. Do we have
to age with the natural passage of time? Must we deteriorate like
a broken down machine? Some answers may lie in eating better to
live longer and healthier.

RESOURCE MATERIALS

DeSalvo, Louise A., "Literature and the Process of Aging," Media and Methods, 16:22-23+, February 1980.

Di Perna, Paula. Compulsory Retirement: Pros and Cons. (Pamphlet) Dist. by Social Studies School Service.

This Public Affairs Pamphlet (available as a set of ten) summarizes the main arguments for and against compulsory retirement. It discusses the origins of the notion of compulsory retirement, recent legislation, and the changing realities of retirement for workers over 65.

Don't Count the Candles. CBS TV, 1968. (16mm film, 60 min.)

Presents an essay by Lord Snowden on the problems of old age and loneliness.

Firman, James P. and Anita M. Stowell, "Intergenerational School Projects: Examples and Guidelines," Media and Methods, 16:19+, Feb. 1980.

Laube, Clifford, "Up from Ageism," Media and Methods, 16:16-18+, Feb. 1980.

Mills, Gretchen C. et al. Discussing Death: A Guide to Death Education. ETC Publications, 1976. Dist. by Social Studies School Service. 140pp, paper.

Based on the theory that the more exposure children have to the subject of death, the more comfortable they will be with it, this book offers an interdisciplinary curriculum guide to death education in the classroom. The guide is divided into four age levels and stresses creative expression, sensitivity to social values, gaining knowledge, literary understanding, and study skills. Over eighty lesson suggestions deal with such topics as death in the life cycle, grief expression, immortality, and facing terminal illness.

Prolongation of Life. CBS-TV, 1968. (16mm film, 60 min.)

Shows that despite twentieth century wonders of medicine, man still looks forward to living no more than the Biblical allotment of three score years and ten. Presents the major elimination of killers and the manner in which old age will be made more enjoyable in the twenty-first century.

Smith, Gary R.   Teaching about Aging.   Center for Teaching International Relations, 1978.   Dist. by Social Studies School Service.

This activity booklet gives students the opportunity to examine
their perceptions about older people and explores the concept of aging
cross-culturally.   At the end of the unit, the students are required
to redefine their own aging process.   Each activity includes objec-
tives, an introduction, reproducible handouts, procedures, debriefing,
and suggested lesson material for activities entitled "Act Your Age, "
"We Are Now 70, " "161 Years Old, " and "Youth for Sale. "

Talking about Old People.   Education Development Center, 1971.
(16mm film, b&w, 19 min.)

Shows a classroom situation in which the students have read
The Kigtak Story and are discussing the problem that the Netsilik
Eskimos have in taking care of their old people.   From The Class-
room as a Learning Community Series.

Trojan, Judith.   Aging: A Filmography.   Educational Film Library
Assn. , 1972.

Annotated list of some 130 films about and for the aging.

Trojan, Judith.   American Family Life Films.   Scarecrow Press, 1980.

An annotated filmography of 2,103 items, 96 of which are
classified under "Aging" or "Grandparents. "

Trojan, Judith, "Film Portraits of Aging Men, " Media and Methods,
16:20+, February 1980.

Walker, Maxine, "Last Rites for Young Readers, " Children's Literature in Education, 9:188-197, 1978.

An examination of the changing attitudes toward death in
children's books.

TEXTBOOKS AND NON-FICTION BOOKS

Ancona, George.   Growing Older.   New York: Dutton, 1978.   Illus.
by the author.   Unpaged.   Primary-Intermediate.

This is a collection of memorabilia and anecdotes of a bygone era expressed by a baker's dozen of elders and recorded by the
author/photographer in many locations throughout the country.   The

interviewees represent many nationalities, races, and walks of life, and include the author's Mexican grandmother.   Four have never retired.   Preserved are pithy proverbs, optimistic outlooks, proud traditions, adversity overcome, opportunities snatched, moments savored, and only one regret about growing old: "My great grief now is that it never occurred to me that I would come to a point where I was alive and couldn't read" (on losing eyesight to cataracts). In prefacing this rich and colorful tapestry of age and experience, the author encourages young people to record for posterity the stories of their own grandparents and to adopt or borrow grandparents if they have none nearby of their own.

Bales, Carol Ann.   Tales of the Elders.   Chicago: Follett, 1977.
          Photos by the author.   158pp.   Bibliography.   Grades 4-8.

          Subtitled "A Memory Book of Men and Women Who Came to America as Immigrants, 1900-1930," this is a montage of thumbnail sketches and charming first person accounts, elicited in interviews and accompanied by photographs, of twelve elderly people from all walks of life who came to the U.S. during the Great Migration, from Russia, Mexico, Holland, Italy, Japan, Scotland, Greece, Sweden, Ireland and Poland.   To the youth of today who have never known true deprivation, prejudice or global conflict, they tell their experiences of war, starvation and discrimination plus much that is uplifting, heartwarming and amusing.

Bernstein, Joanne E. and Stephen V. Gullo.   When People Die.
          New York: Dutton, 1977.   Photos by Rosemarie Hausherr.
          Unpaged.   Grades 2-4.

          From the viewpoint of many nationalities, this book shows that there is a time to be born, a time to live, and a time to die in the great chain of life.   Over the course of a lifetime the body gradually wears out, the heart and brain eventually stop working. Life after death is discussed, and burial and cremation are explained euphemistically: "In cremation, heat is used to reduce the body to ashes."   Customs and beliefs of different cultures are mentioned.   The phases and feelings of grief are explored in the circle of family and friends.

Butler, Robert N.   Why Survive?   Being Old in America.   Harper
          and Row, 1975.   Dist. by Social Studies School Service.
          496pp, paper.   College.

          A Pulitzer Prize-winning indictment of America's treatment of its elderly, this book describes the realities of retirement, poverty, housing, nursing homes, pensions, medical care, employment, and senility.   The author urges radical reforms both in the way agencies treat the elderly and the attitudes Americans hold toward aging.

Curtin, Sharon R. Nobody Ever Died of Old Age: In Praise of Old
    People, In Outrage at Their Loneliness. Little, Brown,
    1972. Dist. by Social Studies School Service. 228pp, paper.
    High school-Adult.

    An indictment of what American society does with and to its
elderly, written by a nurse who has direct knowledge of nursing
homes, hospitals, and the world of the retired. The approach is
personal, giving the reader insight into the lives of the elderly
through detailed case studies.

Farber, Norma. How Does It Feel To Be Old? New York: Dutton,
    1979. Illus. by Trina Schart Hyman. Unpaged. Grades 2-4.

    A young-at-heart grandmother with an unabashedly lived-in
body responds unequivocatingly in verse to her granddaughter's query,
"How does it feel to be old?" She feels "very nice" not to have to
listen to parental advice, "quite brave, quite bold" to be outspoken
on issues (while unobtrusively wearing a NOW button), "free, free,
free" to eat what and when she pleases, "agreeable" not to have to
scold about broken dishes or windows, "clever--if clumsy" at games
and amusements. Under the wrinkles she notes her resemblance to
the young girl. Her photo album reveals her as a baby, a bride,
a mother of four, a brand-new grandmother. A discarded watch re-
minds her of a time when children and chores demanded her attention. She succumbs to the temptation to lie abed late of a morning,
dreaming of the best of bygone days as though they were never over.
She is mindful of the need to move slowly so as not to "disgrace"
herself by falling, but equally mindful of having to rush to complete
all that she wants to do in the remaining years. Finally, she prepares her granddaughter for her eventual death: "I'll be coming at
last to an end--/or a start--I'm not quite clear, " opening a door
for discussion of afterlife. 'Have you noticed, I'm shorter, almost,
than you?/I'm shrinking, you're stretching. What else is new?"
The life cycle turns inexorably on. A life that was once in as-
cendancy is now in descension, with no regrets. Superimposed
images of past and present supply poignancy and immediacy to the
sum of experience and memory that is old age, and to the companionable and loving relationship between youth and age.

Forrai, Maria S. A Look at Old Age. Minneapolis: Lerner, 1976.
    Text by Rebecca Anders. Illus. by the author. Unpaged.
    Primary.

    Eloquent photographs--of gnarled hands, exercise classes, re-
tirees doing volunteer work, pursuing hobbies, beginning vital new
careers, imparting skilled craftsmanship, sitting lonely on city
streets, living apart in retirement homes, eating institutional meals,
being useful to grown children and grandchildren, demonstrating
bread-making to a granddaughter, hiking companionably with a grandson, visiting the graves of friends, finding strength in religious de-

votion, and enjoying the fellowship of others--show small children
the diversities, joys and sorrows of old age.

Huyck, Margaret Hellie. <u>Growing Older.</u> Spectrum, 1974. Dist.
    by Social Studies School Service. 179pp, paper. High school-
    Adult.

A collection of articles on the problems of aging, including
mental and physical changes, sexuality, work, leisure, marriage,
living arrangements, self-concept, and relationships with children.
Stressing that the images of old age are socially determined, the
authors suggest ways that society and individuals can adapt and
change.

Klein, Leonore. <u>How Old Is Old?</u> New York: Harvey House, 1967.
    Illus. by Leonard Kessler. 45pp. Grades K-3.

This Science Parade Book demonstrates that age is relative.
A Mayfly has a life expectancy of a few days, while a giant tortoise
may live to be 150 years old.   Michael's grandma who is 60 says,
"You're as young as you feel. " She feels young and she also feels
like dancing.   When Michael, 8, is sick with measles, he feels
older than his grandma! His great-grandma at 80 is really old but
still takes an interest in painting.   Paradoxically, Klein says, "Old
people want to be young again.   Young people want to grow older
fast. "

Kubler-Ross, Elisabeth.   <u>On Death and Dying.</u>   Macmillan, 1969.
    Dist. by Social Studies School Service.   289pp, paper.   High
    school-Adult.

A report on the psychology of the dying, developed from interviews with terminally ill patients.   Outlines the five stages of reaction to terminal illness, how the patient's family can react, and
how our entire society can profit from a greater awareness of the
reality of death.

Moss, Gordon and Walter Moss.   <u>Growing Old.</u> Senate Committee
    on Long-Term Care of the <u>Aging, 1975.</u> Dist. by Social
    Studies School Service. 253pp, paper. High school.

Americans tend to ignore the fact that all people grow old.
This collection of readings directed at the teenager shows the problems of the elderly in American society, examines the institutions
which presently deal with them, and suggests ways in which our
treatment of the old can be improved.   Contributors include John
Demos and John O'Hara.

Paull, Irene. Everybody's Studying Us: The Ironies of Aging in
     the Pepsi Generation. Glide, 1976. Dist. by Social Studies
     School Service. Cartoons by Bulbul. 79pp, paper. Jr.
     High- Adult.

     Written from a senior citizen's view, this book explores the
problems of growing old in a youth-oriented "throwaway" society
which, the authors maintain, renders people as well as products
obsolescent after a given age. Utilizing an effective combination
of text and cartoons, the authors dispute many common stereotypes
of the aged in a breezy, satirical style which is funny even while
portraying social tragedy.

Raynor, Dorka. Grandparents around the World. Chicago: Whit-
     man, 1977. Illus. by the author. Unpaged. Primary-
     Intermediate.

     In 46 full-page black and white photos from 25 different coun-
tries, the author/photographer captures both the diversity of cultures
around the globe and the universal bond between grandparents and
grandchildren everywhere. The pictures speak eloquently and candidly of simple people engaged in mundane activities and require no
interpretive text beyond identification of locale.

Shanks, Ann Zane. Old Is What You Get. Dialogues on Aging by
     the Old and the Young. New York: Viking, 1976. 110pp.
     Bibliography, portfolio. Grades 4-12.

     A photographic essay on aging with a variety of recorded
attitudes on heterogeneous topics by an assortment of oldsters and
youngsters from all walks of life. Scenes do not glorify age but are
honest and realistic in presenting both positive and negative aspects.
The seventeen seniors between the ages of 66 and 96 and the nine
youths from 11 to 21 are candid about fears, health, death, friends,
loneliness, marriage, widowhood, sex, work, retirement, money,
nursing homes, and political and social action. Some stereotypes
are struck down and others upheld, but the object is to treat aging
as a part of life and to bring the subject out of the closet of taboos.

Silverstein, Alvin, Virginia Silverstein, and Glenn Silverstein.
     Aging. New York: Watts, 1979. 86pp. Bibliography. In-
     termediate.

     Illustrated with photographs, this comprehensive book begins
by analogizing human life spans with those of automobiles. Some
face an early demise through accident or disease; others lead long,
serviceable lives. Dozens of dynamic and renowned individuals are
cited who remained creative and vigorous in old age. The relationship of continued growth and relative size of organisms to longevity
are explored, and the "biological clocks" or genetic programming
that determine life spans are examined. The manifold physiological

changes that occur with aging are described, and the authors explain the history, theories and fads in the perennial search for eternal youth, followed by pioneering gerontological research toward retarding the aging process through glandular and chemical immunology. The treatment concludes with a look at changes in family patterns, retirement benefits, and living arrangements for the aging over the past generation.

Sobol, Harriet Langsam. Grandpa: A Young Man Grown Old. New York: Coward, McCann and Geoghegan, 1980. Illus. by Patricia Agre. 39pp. Intermediate-Jr. High.

Copiously illustrated with photographs, this is a penetrating and engaging double soliloquy focused upon Morris Kaye, 79, by the subject himself and his 17-year-old granddaughter Karen. Mr. Kaye relates the events that have molded his life from his birth as an Eastern European Jew to his recent widowhood, and amplifies his present raison d'etre in remaining active in business and adult education long past conventional retirement age. He describes his warm reciprocal relationship with his children and grandchildren, corroborated by Karen, but laments the loss of his contemporaries. In spite of wearing a pacemaker and contact lenses for post surgical cataract treatment, he remains philosophical about old age: "The dreams are gone, but there are memories instead." A photo album completes the book devoted to Mr. Kaye as a young man and to his dynamic current life.

Stevens, Margaret. When Grandpa Died. Chicago: Childrens Press, 1979. Illus. by Kenneth Ualand. 31pp. Primary.

Sensitive photographs show a girl and her bearded grandfather enjoying many activities together, especially gardening. One day they find a dead bird on the lawn, and Grandpa gravely explains the naturalness of growth, death and change. Together they bury the bird and plant a flower over its body. Inevitably the grandfather becomes ill and is hospitalized, never to return. When told of his death by her father, the girl first experiences anger at his desertion before she is able to shed cathartic tears. Her father encourages her to cry and reassures her about the purpose of funerals. She and her parents visit the funeral home and cemetery, and the girl contemplates telling her little sister about Grandpa's death when she is old enough to understand.

VanTassel, David D. Aging, Death, and the Completion of Being. Philadelphia: University of Pennsylvania Press, 1979. Bibliography. High School.

Considering the humanistic perspective on aging, twelve scholars from various humanistic disciplines trace the origin of our current attitudes regarding aging and identify the recurring models and myths of old age in our society.

DIRECTORY OF PRODUCERS AND DISTRIBUTORS

ABC Learning Resources
Dept. MM 129
1330 Avenue of the Americas
New York, N. Y.   10019

ACI Productions
35 West 45th St., 11th floor
New York, N. Y.   10036

Aids of Cape Cod
110 Old Town House Rd.
South Yarmouth, Mass.   02646

Alfred Guzzetti
41 Magnolia Ave.
Cambridge, Mass.   02138

American Physical Fitness Re-
    search Institute
824 Moraga Dr., P. O. Box 90024
Los Angeles, Calif.   90049

Art-Co Productions
P. O. Box 865
Cupertino, Calif.   95014

Association Films
Executive Offices
866 Third Ave.
New York, N. Y.   10022

Audio Visual Narrative Arts
P. O. Box 9
Pleasantville, N. Y.   10570

Australian Information Service
636 Fifth Ave.
New York, N. Y.   10020

BFA Educational Media
2211 Michigan Ave.
P. O. Box 1795
Santa Monica, Calif.   90406

Barr Films
P. O. Box 5667
Pasadena, Calif.   91107

Billy Budd Films
235 East 57th St.
New York, N. Y.   10022

Butterick Fashion Marketing Co.
161 Sixth Ave.
New York, N. Y.   10013

CBS News
51 West 52nd St.
New York, N. Y.   10019

CRM Educational Films
1011 Camino de Mar
Del Mar, Calif.   92104

Carousel Films
1501 Broadway
New York, N. Y.   10036

Center for Cassette Studies
8110 Webb Ave.
North Hollywood, Calif.   91605

Children's Press
1224 West Van Buren St.
Chicago, Ill.   60607

Churchill Films
662 North Robertson Blvd.
Los Angeles, Calif.   90069

Columbia Broadcasting System
383 Madison Ave.
New York, N. Y.   10017

Concept Media
1500 Adams
Costa Mesa, Calif.   92626

Coronet
65 East South Water St.
Chicago, Ill.   60601

Current Affairs
P. O. Box 398
24 Danbury Rd.
Wilton, Conn.   06897

Direct Cinema
P. O. Box 315
Franklin Lakes, N. J.   07417

EBE Corporation
425 North Michigan Ave.
Chicago, Ill.   60611

Education Development Center
15 Mifflin Place
Cambridge, Mass.   02138

Educational Dimension Corp.
P. O. Box 126
Stamford, Conn.   06904

Educational Film Library Assn.
43 West 61st St.
New York, N. Y.   10023

Edward Feil Productions
4614 Prospect Ave.
Cleveland, Ohio   44103

Entertainment Marketing Corp.
159 West 53rd St.
New York, N. Y.   10019

Eye Gate House
146-01 Archer Ave.
Jamaica, N. Y.   11435

Ferguson Films
1425 Brooklyn Ave.
Ann Arbor, Mich.   48104

Filmakers Library
133 East 58th St. , Suite 703A
New York, N. Y.   10022

Films Incorporated
733 Green Bay Rd.
Wilmette, Ill.   60091

Guidance Associates
757 Third Ave.
New York, N. Y.   10017

Human Relations Media
175 Tompkins Ave.
Pleasantville, N. Y.   10570

Indiana University Audiovisual
   Center
Bloomington, Ind.   47401

Iowa State University Film Pro-
   duction Unit
Alice Norton House
Ames, Iowa   50010

Journal Films
930 Pitner
Evanston, Ill.   60202

Lansford Publishing Co.
P. O. Box 8711
1088 Lincoln Ave.
San Jose, Calif.   95155

Learning and Information
315 Central Park West
New York, N. Y.   10025

Learning Corporation of America
1250 Avenue of the Americas
New York, N. Y.   10019

MTI Teleprograms
4825 North Scott St. , Suite 23
Schiller Park, Ill.   60176

McGraw-Hill Films
1221 Avenue of the Americas
New York, N. Y.   10020

Marshfilm Enterprises
P. O. Box 8082
Shawnee Mission, Kan.   66208

Marvin Albert Films
1003 Lenora Ave.
Seattle, Wash.   98121

Miller-Brody Productions
342 Madison Ave.
New York, N. Y.   10017

Modern Talking Picture Service
5000 Park St.
North St. Petersburg, Fla.   33709

Multimedia Instructional Material
Multi Media Office
Mount San Jacinto College
21400 Highway 79
San Jacinto, Calif.   92383

National Council of Churches
Broadcasting and Film Commis-
    sion
457 Riverside Dr.
New York, N. Y. 10027

New Day Films
P. O. Box 315
Franklin Lakes, N. J.   07417

New Film Co.
331 Newbury St.
Boston, Mass.   02115

Oregon State System of Higher
    Education
Film Library
1633 South West Park Ave.
P. O. Box 1491
Portland, Or.   97207

Paramount-Oxford Films
5451 Marathon St.
Los Angeles, Calif.   90038

Parish of the Air
(no address available)

Paulist Productions
P. O. Box 1057
Pacific Palisades, Calif.   90272

Pennsylvania State University
Audiovisual Aids Library
17 Willard Bldg.
University Park, Pa.   16802

Perennial Education
P. O. Box 236
1825 Willow Rd.
Northfield, Ill.   60093

The Perfection Form Co.
1000 North Second Ave.
Logan, Iowa   51546

Perspective Films
369 West Erie St.
Chicago, Ill.   60610

Phoenix Films
470 Park Ave. South
New York, N. Y.   10016

Pyramid Films
P. O. Box 1048
Santa Monica, Calif.   90406

Scott Education Division
Prentice-Hall Media
150 White Plains Rd.
Tarrytown, N. Y.   10591

Serious Business Co.
1145 Mandana Blvd.
Oakland, Calif.   94610

Social Studies School Service
10, 000 Culver Blvd.
P. O. Box 802
Culver City, Calif.   90230

Society for Visual Education
1345 Diversey Parkway
Chicago, Ill.   60614

Sterling Educational Films
241 East 34th St.
New York, N. Y.   10016

Sunburst Communications
Suite 91
41 Washington Ave.
Pleasantville, N. Y.   10570

Teleketics Films
Franciscan Communications
    Center
1229 South Santee St.
Los Angeles, Calif.   90015

Time-Life Films
43 West 16th St.
New York, N. Y.   10011

Time-Life Multimedia
Time and Life Bldg.
1271 Avenue of the Americas
New York, N. Y.   10020

Trainex
P. O. Box 116
12601 Industry St.
Garden Grove, Calif.   92642

Treiberg Films and Filmstrips
P. O. Box 802
Ventura, Calif.   93001

University of California Exten-
    sion
Media Center
2223 Fulton St.
Berkeley, Calif.   94720

University of Oklahoma
Audiovisual Services
650 Parrinton Oval 109
Norman, Okla.   73069

Video Recording Corporation of
    America
180 East State St.
Westport, Conn.   06880

Walt Disney Educational Media
500 South Buena Vista St.
Burbank, Calif.   91521

Western Publishing Co.
220 Mound Ave.
Racine, Wisc.   53404

Weston Woods
Weston, Conn.   06883

Wombat Productions
Glendale Rd.
P. O. Box 70
Ossining, N. Y.   10020

SUBJECT INDEX TO MULTIMEDIA MATERIALS